新时代商务英语专业本科系列教材
New Era Business English Series

总主编 / 翁凤翔　郭桂杭

Consumer
Behavior

消费者行为学

主　编 / 周肖儿

编　者 / （姓名拼音排序）

陈相云　龚梦颖

李志坚　庾　丹

重庆大学出版社

图书在版编目（CIP）数据

消费者行为学: 英文 / 周肖儿主编. --重庆: 重庆大学出版社, 2022.6

新时代商务英语专业本科系列教材
ISBN 978-7-5689-3309-4

I. ①消… II. ①周… III. ①消费者行为论—高等学校—教材—英语 IV. ①F713.55

中国版本图书馆CIP数据核字 (2022) 第086130号

消费者行为学

主编 周肖儿

责任编辑: 牟 妮　　版式设计: 牟 妮
责任校对: 刘志刚　　责任印制: 赵 晟

*

重庆大学出版社出版发行
出版人: 饶帮华
社址:重庆市沙坪坝区大学城西路21号
邮编:401331
电话: （023）88617190　88617185（中小学）
传真: （023）88617186　88617166
网址: http://www.cqup.com.cn
邮箱: fxk@cqup.com.cn（营销中心）
全国新华书店经销
重庆新生代彩印技术有限公司

*

开本: 890mm×1240mm　1/16　印张: 16.5　字数: 577千
2022年8月第1版　　2022年8月第1次印刷
ISBN 978-7-5689-3309-4　定价: 59.00元

前言

"消费者行为学"作为一门独立的、系统的应用型学科，其理论基础源于西方的营销学、经济学、心理学和社会学等，是市场营销专业的一门基础学科，一直以来与"市场营销"课程相辅相成，构成较为完整的知识体系。近年来，随着商务英语专业的设立，不少高校都在课程体系中设置了"消费者行为"这门课程，作为本专业高年级的专业领域课。市面上关于本学科的教材主要是面向有一定经管知识和理论基础的学生，针对商务英语专业编写的经管类教材相对缺失。在"以国内大循环为主体、国内国际双循环相互促进的新发展格局"大背景下，应用型大学的人才培养面临全新的需求。其中，商务英语作为一个新兴专业，既具备人文学科的基础和气质，又具有实用型专业的特点和培养标准，而作为课程体系建设中的基础环节，编写出符合专业特点、体现专业特色的教材显得尤为重要。

2020 年 11 月 3 日，全国有关高校和专家共同发布的"新文科建设宣言"中指出，新时代新使命要求文科教育必须加快创新发展。作为新时代文科的教育者，我们的任务是"构建世界水平、中国特色的文科人才培养体系"。商务英语专业属于"新文科"发展下催生的"新学科"，这对我们的教学理念和教学实践提出了全新的要求，一方面决定了我们要面向国家战略和社会需求重新定位，突出中国特色，重新定义外语学科，充实内涵，创新学科体系；另一方面我们要以培养卓越和拔尖创新人才为目标，确立新的评价要求和标准，培养跨学科、复合型的高素质人才。基于上述要求，本教材专注于跨学科知识体系的构建与融合，跨文化交际和经管能力的培养，以及价值观的引领，旨在推动文科教育的创新发展，为提升综合国力、坚定文化自信、培养时代新人和建设高等教育强国添砖加瓦。本教材在内容上注重展示我国在全面建成小康社会过程中在经济建设方面取得的巨大成就，结合商务英语专业对复合型人才的培养特点，坚持以学生为中心、以产出为导向，使其在学习过程中逐渐掌握相关的知识和技能，并逐步形成正确的价值观，从而具备符合新时代要求的职业素养。

教育部高等学校教学指导委员会于 2018 年 3 月出版的《普通高等学校本科专业类教学质量国家标准》中明确提出对于商务英语专业人才的培养目标，该类学生应该成为"具有扎实的英语语言基本功和相关商务专业知识，拥有良好的人文素养、中国情怀与国际视野，熟悉文学、经济学、管理学和法学等相关理论知识，掌握国际商务的基础理论与实务，具备较强的跨文化能力、商务沟通能力与创新创业能力，能适应国家与地方经济社会发展、对外交流与合作需要，能熟练使用英语从事国际商务、国际贸易、国际会计、国际金融、跨境电子商务等涉外领域工作的国际化复合型人才"。根据上述要求，本教材的编写把握了以下几个原则，同时也体现了本教材的创新特色：

第一，贯彻课程思政的整体思路，以价值观的塑造为引领。商务英语专业的"消费者行为"课程一般面向大四学生开设，为全英讲授，学生外语功底扎实，具备较强的跨文化交际能力，拥有基本的经管知识和能力。在这个即将步入社会、进入职场的关键节点，学生十分需要正确的价值观引导，树立必要的职业素养，全面融合思政理念能对其未来的职业生涯发挥有效的指引作用，使其成为拥有爱国情怀，具备国际视野的"外语＋"复合型人才。本书以心理学、营销学和实际应用为支撑点，让学生通过运用相关的心理学理论对自己的情感和态度进行分析解构，从感性认识上升到理性认识的层面。教学设计上思路完整，层层递进。经过"思维激发—回忆反思—理性分析—情感内化"的过程，学生始终发挥自主性，在教师的指导下既能达到知识和技能目标，也能实现潜移默化的思政育人目标。本书的主编周肖儿所讲授的"消费者行为"课程中"消费者的态度"一课被广东省教育厅认定为 2020 年度省级课程思政建设改革示范课堂，本门课程也被广州城市理工学院认定为首批校级课程思政示范课程。

第二，该教材由拥有丰富一线教学经验的教师编写，充分切合商务英语专业学生的学习需求。 商务英语是一门典型的新文科专业，体现了英语学科和商务学科的交叉与复合，隶属于外国语言文学，是外语类专业，与经济类或管理类专业有着显著的区别。因此，本专业学生的学科基础、学习特点和学习需求与经管专业学生都有较大差异。目前市面上的经管教材主要由国外引进，或者由经管专业的老师运用中文编写。前者在内容上与我国国情和意识形态上都有较大差异，参考性略为欠缺；而后者则无法满足外语类专业学生在语言上进一步提升的需求，影响到跨学科人才培养的效果。因此，本书基本采用英语编写，对一些关键的概念配备中文标注；同时在内容上注重采用在建设有中国特色社会主义的过程中，我国企业在对消费者研究方面较为前沿、并指导其在激烈的市场竞争中占据优势的典型案例，帮助学生对中华民族伟大复兴拥有更具象的认识，并能对外输出。

第三，练习的设计贯彻 OBE(Outcome-Based Education) 原则，即以学生的学习产出为核心，抛弃死记硬背，注重实际应用。 每一章的练习设计不再局限于对某一些基本概念或理论的掌握，要求学生将学习前置，带着问题来上课。通过全程布置学生用英语对视频和案例进行点评讨论、自身经历分享剖析、线上布置任务＋线下小组演示等教学活动，学生能运用专业优势，用英语讲好中国故事，并且能够完成外语＋经管的知识和能力体系的构建。

本书在编写的过程中，得到广州城市理工学院外国语学院领导的大力支持，在此深表感谢。当然，由于经验和资源的相对欠缺，本书仍存在一定的不足，希望能得到专家的批评和指正。

编者

2022 年 3 月

《消费者行为学》导读

杨德锋

（暨南大学管理学院市场学系主任、教授、博士生导师、博士，
主要研究方向：市场营销与品牌管理）

消费者研究一直是企业营销策划前的必要步骤，其结果为商业决策提供主要依据和有力支撑。从宏观经济层面来说，对消费者行为进行深入研究，使得企业能将有限的资源投入到最能满足人民群众需求的地方，有利于社会资源合理分配，对于当前优化产业结构、节能减碳有着重要意义。国家"十四五"规划中就提到，在畅通国内大循环的过程中，我们应"依托强大国内市场，贯通生产、分配、流通、消费各环节，形成需求牵引供给、供给创造需求的更高水平动态平衡，促进国民经济良性循环。"这充分说明，深入了解消费者需求，从而制定和调整企业发展战略，能够有助于国民经济的健康发展。

2021 年我国全年社会消费品零售总额为 440 823 亿元，消费对于整体经济的发展持续发挥了主要拉动作用。尤其是在当前世界疫情仍然严重、世界经济发展存在诸多不确定因素的大背景下，深入实施扩大内需的战略尤为必要，在全面促进消费的过程中，企业应"顺应居民消费升级趋势，把扩大消费同改善人民生活品质结合起来，促进消费向绿色、健康、安全发展，稳步提高居民消费水平。"由此可见，对于消费者的调研应该持续进行，不断积累经验，因为其消费习惯、偏好和需求会随着社会发展和生活水平提升而呈现个性化、差异化、品质化的趋势。近年来，时常听到企业说"生意不好做"，一些零售产业状况萧条，但新经济发展蓬勃，各种数据不断刷新。这当中体现的是对于市场动态是否能精准把握的差异。在当前消费升级转型的大环境下，获得有价值的消费者洞察关系到企业生死存亡，使其能预判未来的市场走势，调整经营方针，抢得发展先机。

企业发展的另一要素是人才，而高等院校一直是人才培养和输送的主力军。其中，应用型大学与企业用人需求联系更为紧密。这意味着高校在学科设置方面应该更有针对性，使学生经过四年的大学学习后，能够在走向社会、走进职场的时候具备用人单位需要的知识、技能和职业素养。长期以来，商科教育对于营销学课程的重视程度远远高于消费者行为，这本无可厚非，但事实上两者是一个硬币的两面，其相互补充，缺一不可。从学术研究的层面来说，对于消费者的研究层出不穷，呈现多样化的态势，前景无限；而从就业应用的层面来说，掌握基本的消费者研究理念和方法，结合营销学的基础，更有利于学生构建完善的知识网和技能库。因此，"消费者行为学"作为一门专业领域课对于商务类专业学生的整体素养提高可以发挥更多的作用。

在当前"一带一路"建设的大背景下，复合型人才的培养是大势所趋。一方面，学生需要具备扎实的专业知识、较强的实践能力和创新的思维；另一方面，高效的跨文化沟通能力也必不可少。因此，"商务＋英语"的复合型人才应运而生。而在此过程中，针对这种独特的教学需求、符合对应层次高校办学特点的全英教材担当了较为重要的角色。基于构建多元高等教育体系的指导思想，本书立足于为应用型大学培养复合型人才的教育理念进行编写。作为主要面向商务英语专业学生编写的教材，本书的知识体

系和理论结构较为完整，覆盖本门学科的主要知识点，其编写具备如下特点：

第一，注重理论与实践相结合。每一章的开头以相关的案例导入，课后练习也设置了案例分析使学生对本章的知识和理论进行深化和综合运用。习题的编写立足于应用，强调实际运用能力和团体协作，使学生能做到自主学习、主动实践。

第二，注重本课程的跨学科性，编者背景的复合性助力培养复合型人才。《消费者行为学》是一门涵盖心理学、营销学、社会学等的一门综合性学科，其起源于西方国家，大部分概念和理论的出处都是英语。编写团队主要为大学英语教师，对概念和理论的理解和阐述较为准确且到位，同时也与学生的商务英语专业知识背景相吻合。本书主编从事英语专业的本科教学超过十二年，在此过程中，其一直亲身参与到各项跨国商业研究当中，积累了丰富的消费者调研经验。书中内容呈现出编者对外语教学和商务项目两者的经验融合，有助于复合型人才的培养。

第三，平衡学术科研性和实际应用性。除了包含主要的经典理论，本书同时也收集了一些较新的研究结果，学生在阅读过程中能够获得学术研究的启发，为其以后从事科研提供指引。另外，主编曾任职于全球领先的市场研究集团、中国最大的市场研究公司，书中的多样材料均来自于其在进行消费者调研的过程中真实采用的资料，能使读者接触到商务项目中原本的内容，更有利于将来与其职业发展接轨。

第四，注重编写内容的本土化和爱国情怀。目前市面上本门学科的教材主要为国内学者编写的中文课本，以及翻译自外国原版教材的读本，前者主要用中文介绍我国品牌和企业，以及中国的消费者行为，而后者则主要侧重于国外的情况。本书的特色在于运用英语对外介绍我国的情况，选用的案例涵盖面广、有代表性。结合商务英语专业学生将来的就业特点，能使学生具备"讲好中国故事"的能力，对外展示我国在全面建成小康社会中在经济发展方面取得的巨大成就。

第五，注重案例年轻化和趣味性。当前在校大学生主要为"00后"，很快主流将是"05后"，活化课本内容，使其产生兴趣、激发学习动力十分重要。本书对案例的选取注重贴近年轻人，每一章开头的导入案例都与大学生的生活高度相关，这些熟悉的事物能产生趣味性，更能引发思考，从而使学生对每章的学习内容更加投入。

总的来说，本书较为适合商务英语专业的高年级学生作为教材学习使用，同时也可以作为商科学生快速了解本门学科的梗概、掌握用英语介绍我国在相关领域发展情况的有益读本。

CONTENTS

CHAPTER ONE

Introduction

(Basic concepts and Research methods)

Learning objectives

After learning this chapter, you will be able to:

- understand the reasons for studying consumer behavior and the scope of this field;
- comprehend the relationship between consumer research and other related disciplines;
- master the effective ways of consumer research;
- acquire the ability to decide appropriate methods according to specific research needs.

Lead-in Case

China's Shifting Retail Landscape Signals The Permanence of Change Post-Covid-19

China's rebound from COVID-19 has been unique. It came faster, with more demonstrable economic tailwinds for the economy than other markets. But it has also been a bellwether that has helped point to consumer behaviors elsewhere that have inevitably followed China's lead. An example is the rebalancing of retail playing out around the world.

Pandemic-led shifts to further online adoption and an increased focus on neighborhood and small-format stores have become an ongoing normal. Historically, China has demonstrated a mature omnichannel shopping base, with consumers that are already years ahead of the majority of other markets in online shopping. In the third quarter of 2020, online sales in China grew by 27% for the year to date, while physical store sales declined by 4%. The declines at physical stores were largely due to COVID-19-related closures, and there has been some recovery in the remainder of the year. China has four main city tiers, based on inputs such as population size, growth levels, location and infrastructure. Key cities (including Shanghai, Beijing and Guangzhou) and A cities (including Chongqing, Tianjin and Dalian) saw the highest closure rates, while B cities and C cities were less impacted. "Due to market resilience and robust foundations, by August, around 80% of stores has reopened, signaling both a rebound in physical and some fascinating new developments in the e-commerce space."

Online retail has continued on its growth trajectory. In addition to sales growth, online shopping in China saw huge category expansion among shoppers during the onset of COVID-19. While e-commerce growth in China prior to the pandemic was primarily led by personal care categories, consumers began purchasing other categories like dairy, staple foods, beverage and liquor. For example, online growth in dairy has surged from 34% to 55% for the year to date October 2020, versus the same time a year ago, and staple foods jumped from 30% to 48% growth for the same period.

An adjacent trend that rapidly accelerated in China during COVID-19 was online to offline (O2O) shopping. Offering the best of both worlds, consumers purchase items online and have their items selected, (often by third parties) and delivered within a short delivery time of one to two hours. During the initial days of the epidemic, consumers valued the convenience and safety of these services, and the O2O growth rate jumped up to 20% from January to March. Between March and June, although COVID-19 was under control and consumers could return to normal, the O2O growth continued at a rate of 6%.

Retailers and brands that have resisted adapting to COVID-19-shifted spending, perhaps hoping for a return to old habits, now find themselves lagging behind faster-moving competitors that adjusted for the ongoing change. Those that have embraced the change in shopping preferences and pivoted their offerings to suit new consumer needs are already gaining traction. Areas they have addressed include distribution efficiency, sales force optimization, innovation planning, assortment and pricing.

Introduction

As it's self-evident to any marketer, the macro environment has always been changing, which pose constant challenges to all businesses struggling to survive and trying to gain an upper hand amongst the fierce competition. A thorough and insightful understanding of target consumers is essential to the success of all marketing plans. Therefore, the study of consumer behavior is closely related to the formulation of marketing strategies.

In practice, the four key factors (product, price, promotion and place) composing a marketing plan all move around target consumers. Without a meticulous understanding of them, marketing strategies are doomed to fail. To be more specific, target consumers are in the center of every aspect of marketing planning.

Product: the product benefit(s) should satisfy the unmet needs of target consumers;

Price: the "sweet spot" that matches target consumers' value perception;

Promotion: the appropriate ways to deliver marketing messages, thus driving and triggering consumption behaviors;

Place: the selected channel(s) that should be accessible, preferable and most effective to target consumers.

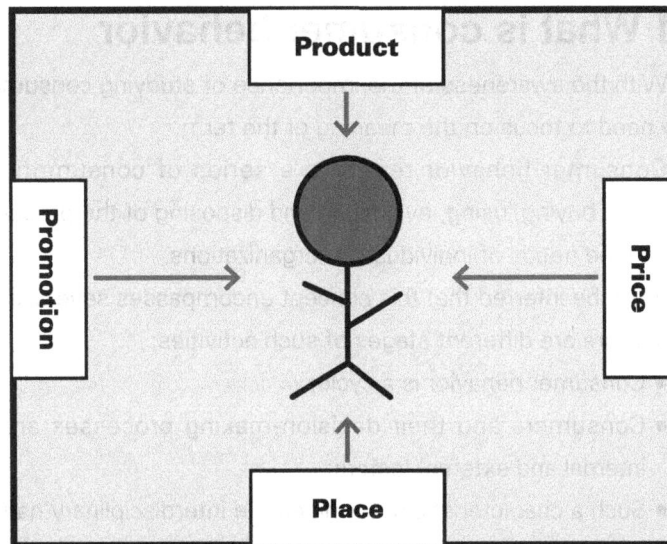

Figure 1-1 Illustrates the relationship between the 4Ps of marketing
mix and their target consumers

In other words, marketing and the study of consumer behavior are the two sides of the same coin: consumers are the main body of the market, any marketing strategies need to answer questions like: What are consumers' needs? How and what would they choose to satisfy these needs? When and where would they purchase? How would they evaluate the experience with the chosen products and services? What would they do to dispose the used products? Without definite answers to these questions, effective marketing strategies would not be possible.

Furthermore, the market is ever changing, so the study of consumer behavior is a constantly on-going process. Just like the lead-in case, COVID-19 pandemic has completely changed most people's lives. For most businesses, the market landscape can never be the same. In the category of retail groceries, consumers' lifestyle is one of the key variables to their consumption behavior. This new normal has prompted retailers to react quickly and adapt to consumers' new purchasing preferences and habits. Otherwise, sales slumps or even bankruptcies might be unavoidable.

To obtain an overall understanding of this subject, this chapter tries to find answers to the following questions, which constitute its key structure:

(1) *What* is consumer behavior? The key definition of this field.

(2) *Who* are we going to study? The necessity to divide consumers into different groups and the methods to do it.

(3) *Why* do consumers make their purchase decision the way they are? The internal and external factors that have an impact on consumer behavior.

(4) *How* consumer research is conducted? The basic methodology and measures used to collect information from consumers.

消费者行为：指的是个体或组织为满足需求而进行的一系列挑选、购买、使用、评价和处置的消费活动。

1.1 What is consumer behavior

With the awareness of the importance of studying consumer behavior, we now need to focus on the meaning of the term.

Consumer behavior refers to a series of consumption activities of choosing, buying, using, evaluating and disposing of the products and services to fulfill the needs of individuals or organizations.

It can be inferred that this concept encompasses several aspects:

- There are different stages of such activities;
- Consumer behavior is a cycle;
- Consumers and their decision-making processes are influenced by internal and external factors;
- Such a characteristic determines the interdisciplinary nature of the study of this field.

1) Three stages lie in the consumption process

Every one of us is a consumer, engaging in various consumption activities in our daily lives. So think of yourself and reflect on the way you buy things, ranging from a soft drink you pick in a convenient store, your favorite shirt or dress flattering your silhouette, to the laptop you use to accomplish different tasks... The process can be divided into three stages.

Pre-purchase stage: Consumers are immersed in an environment full of marketing messages, some of which they are more or less aware of. For different types of purchases, they either merely have a vague idea about what they need or/and go a step further to get to know more and thus shortlist several options.

Purchase: Consumers concentrate on selecting the suitable products or services to meet their demands. The time and effort devoted to the decision-making depend on the different levels of involvement of the purchase.

Post-purchase stage: Consumers start to use and experience the chosen products/services, judging with their own criteria whether purposes have been served. This step has the biggest impact on the future: whether there'll be repeat purchases, whether consumers are satisfied or not and the corresponding reactions like complaining or recommending.

2) Consumer behavior is a cycle

To consume in its literal sense means to buy and use over a period of time. This process would happen again after a certain interval. The three stages in the consumption process go on over and over as long as we live. The end of the last stage signifies the beginning of the first stage, maybe not immediately, but eventually. It is its repetitive characteristic that makes consumer behavior researchable and predictable.

Most of our daily necessities, such as clothes, food, beverages, shoes, etc., share this same feature. For example, when shampoo is used up, a new bottle is to be bought because the need of washing hair still exists. Therefore, the study in this field has a lot to deal with the consumption patterns of Consumer Goods.

The experience of the last purchase affects how decisions are made in the next round.

So it's the marketers and the manufacturers' responsibility to optimize and maximize consumers' favorable feelings during the whole process, otherwise they'll lose customers.

3) Consumer behavior is influenced by internal and external factors

Almost all human beings living in the modern society need to exchange resources for survival and gratification. Consumers are, in the first place, human beings. What goes on in the consumers' mind determines their actions. How they perceive the world, what different motivations consumers have, how and why consumers of different personalities have various purchase habits, what marketing message they'd pay attention to and remember, how they interpret such information, why some messages work while others don't... These are the key questions that are essential to the psychological aspects of consumer behavior. Namely, consumers' sensation and perception, learning and memory, motivation, personality, emotions and attitudes are the internal factors that play a critical role in the consumers' decision-making process.

On the other hand, human beings are not isolated. The environment consumers live in shapes their self-concept and lifestyle, which are the two determinants on how they behave in terms of consumption activities. The external factors include: culture and subculture, demographics, social status, reference group and family. These sources have direct or/and indirect connections with consumers, and thus impose overt or covert influences on every aspect of their lives, including how consumers utilize all sorts of resources to maintain life and achieve different goals.

These subjective and objective aspects work collaboratively to dominate the doings of each individual. It is the combined actions of these influences that lead to the making of every purchase decision. As a result, these key influences constitute the main knowledge structure of this subject. The multi-disciplinary characteristic of the subject determines the research scope involve marketing, psychology, anthropology, sociology, economics, etc.

Throughout this course, we'll learn chapter by chapter the content of each influential factor to uncover the nature of consumer behavior. Chapter One introduces what the field of consumer behavior encompasses; Chapter Two showcases the social influences on consumers, specifically, the impacts of reference groups, brand community, key opinion leaders and family on their decision-making; Chapter Three talks about how cultures, subcultures and cultural values play a part in consumption behavior. Chapter Four to Chapter Eight have to do with the psychological aspects of consumers as individuals: Chapter Four gives details about consumers' sensation and perception, Chapter Five presents how consumers learn about and remember consumption-related information, Chapter Six concerns the motivating elements and mechanisms for consumers' behaviors and the ways to measure them, Chapter Seven involves the formation and transformation of consumers' attitudes; Chapter Eight demonstrates how consumers' personalities vary and the critical roles of lifestyles. With the understanding of the internal and external perspectives, Chapter Nine will take a closer look at how consumers make their purchase decisions. Finally in Chapter Ten, the effects of marketing activities and the commercial environment on consumers will be explained and summarized.

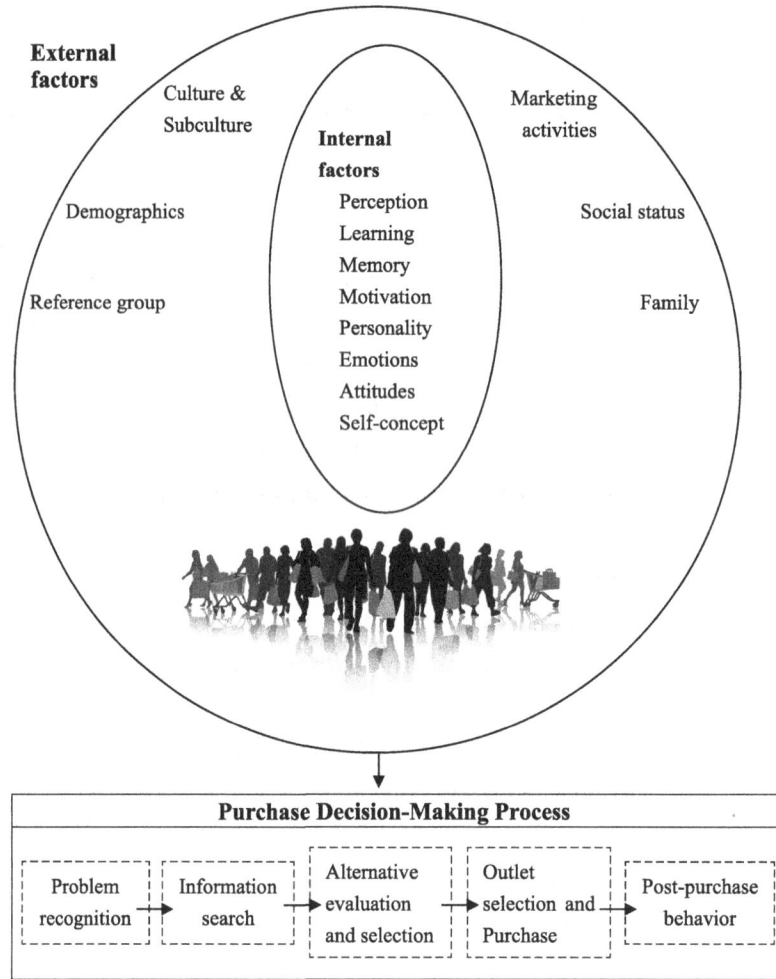

Figure 1-2 The internal and external influences on consumer behavior

1.2 Who are we going to study? The necessity to divide consumers into different groups and the methods to do it

There are various kinds of consumers, whose thinking and doings can vary tremendously. It is strategic for businesses to select a certain group of consumers to be the target, and come up with a set of relevant strategies aiming at them. **Market segmentation** is the practice to divide the market into groups of consumers possessing common needs or features. The picture below demonstrates how consumers of cold medicine can be classified as four different types based on two dimensions: horizontally their *attitudes* towards cold, some are proactive in treating the cold, and some tend not to react until the cold gets to them; vertically their *requirements* for the effects of the cold medicine, some want the medicine to maintain performance even with a cold, and some others expect the treatment should not harm the body. This way of segmentation has created four segments: Balance, Performance,

市场细分：将消费者分成具备共同需求或特征的组别的行为。

Harmony and Reassurance. The descriptions of each segment are like a typical consumer's monologue when talking about what cold medicine they would like and how they expect the body to be treated. With a detailed understanding like this, corresponding ways of communications can be much more effective in driving sales.

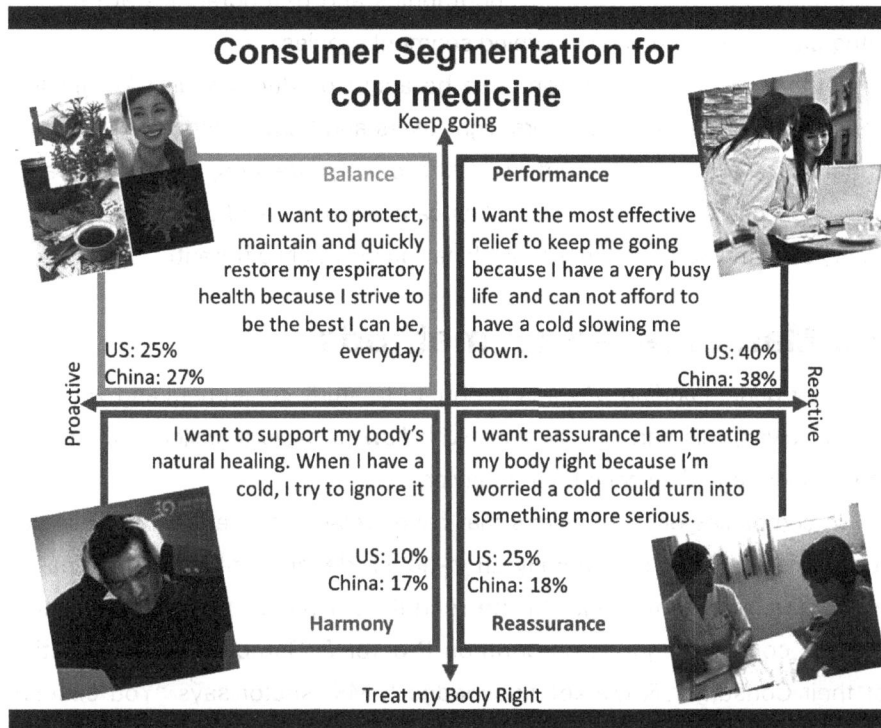

Consumer Segmentation for cold medicine

Keep going

Balance	Performance
I want to protect, maintain and quickly restore my respiratory health because I strive to be the best I can be, everyday.	I want the most effective relief to keep me going because I have a very busy life and can not afford to have a cold slowing me down.
US: 25% China: 27%	US: 40% China: 38%

Proactive / Reactive

I want to support my body's natural healing. When I have a cold, I try to ignore it	I want reassurance I am treating my body right because I'm worried a cold could turn into something more serious.
US: 10% China: 17%	US: 25% China: 18%

Harmony / Reassurance

Treat my Body Right

As you can see in the example above, segmentation is not just about simple divisions of consumers according to the most obvious features like age and gender. It's more about getting to know what consumers' temperament and mindsets are. Demographics and psychographics are the two major ways for segmentation. **Demographics** are the *measurable* and *descriptive* characteristics of a population, including age, gender, income, educational level, etc. It can serve as the foundation for any segmentation because: (1) demographics are the easiest and most logical ways to divide consumers; (2) it is cost effective to reach and locate demographic segments; (3) changes in the population's age composition, income distribution and geographic features can yield business opportunities; (4) demographic characteristics are strongly linked to consumption behaviors, attitudes and media exposure.

人口统计特征：人口中可测量及可描述的特征，包括年龄、性别、收入和教育程度等。

Psychographics is the way to classify people according to their lifestyle, personality, and attitudes. It has to do with how the objective world gets into people's subjective experience. It's often the case consumers with the same demographic characteristics vary in a lot of ways like personality, interests, and opinions. With the use of psychological, sociological and anthropological factors, the market is segmented into groups according to their tendency to make a particular decision about a product, person, ideology, or otherwise

心理统计特征：根据消费者的生活方式、个性和态度将其分类的方法。

hold an attitude or use a medium. Just like the example of cold medicine segmentation shows, the four types of consumers, Balance, Performance, Harmony and Reassurance can have common demographical features, like they are probably at the same age range, with a similar income and educational background, but with very different mindsets in terms of choosing cold medicine. That's why psychographics and demographics are usually integrated in defining and describing segment profiles.

Other segmentation criteria can be about product usage (like dividing consumers into users, non-users, light users and heavy users, etc.), benefits sought (like anti-hair loss, anti-dandruff, color-protection, restoration, anti-split-ends, smoothness, etc. in the hair care category), and geography (like the lifestyles in the south and north of China can be vastly different).

1.3 Market research methods

After understanding *why* it is important to study consumers and *what* this field involves, this part mainly deals with *how* to explore, collect and analyze information regarding consumer behavior.

In companies or corporations that have well-established market research mechanisms, there is generally an in-house department or sector dealing with consumer knowledge. In the recruitment page of the world's most famous consumer goods corporation Proctor & Gamble, the introduction of their Consumer & Market Knowledge (CMK) sector says "You observe behavior and listen to consumers to uncover the objective truths that power our most critical business decisions. In every meeting, on every call, in every presentation to leadership, you represent the most important person in the room: the consumer." Such description manifests the significance of consumer research. These research operations are usually outsourced to

Figure 1-3 The consumer research process

independent research agencies. Both sides cooperate closely to accomplish shared goals. Therefore, it is critical for them to communicate adequately and develop common understanding, to avoid and eliminate future mistakes caused by misunderstanding. Figure 1-3 illustrates the necessary procedure of consumer research.

The following parts introduce what each step in the process is about.

1. Preparation

Once the company/corporation approaches the agencies to express their research needs, both sides would discuss and clarify the challenges the client is facing, what needs to be achieved and how things are done. It is the research agency's task to draw up a research proposal to describe the background information, key objectives, research design, deliverables (usually a report and related research records), timetable, and costs.

- *Background understanding*: Before actually contacting target consumers, it is important to have a preliminary understanding of the project. Most of the market research projects have specific and practical marketing questions to answer. Research background includes where the company stands in the market, how the brand is doing in the category, who its major competitors are, and consumers' basic attitude towards the brand. Experienced marketers and/or researchers would be able to identify the challenges and difficulties the company faces, and the usage habits and struggling points on the consumers' side. Without clear knowledge of what issues need to be addressed, it's impossible to conduct research properly or obtain desirable results.
- *Objective establishment*: After knowing the basic conditions of the project, particular research objectives should be summarized and articulated based on the situation. In this way, the marketing team and corresponding agency would have a consensus on what needs to achieve throughout the whole process. To allocate resources more efficiently, the research scope should not be too broad or too narrow.

In execution, the market research process is primarily project-based. In the spirit of obtaining firsthand information and economical allocation of resources, each project is tailor-made to cater to the specific marketing needs at the moment. Consumer research runs through the whole marketing process: before, during and after product launch. Table 1-1 shows some of the typical research focuses that can be developed into more detailed research objectives.

Stage	Research focus
Before product launch	• Review of the current product usage and habits, identification of struggling points and unmet needs • Ideation of the new product concept • Tests on the product concept, package, communication contents (including ad campaigns, ways of communications), types of sales promotion and pricing
During & After product launch	• Tracking of market share and the effectiveness of communication messages • Pro & Cons vs. competitors • Product modification and upgrade based on usage experience • Adjustments in terms of sales channels, and promotion contents and activities • Consumers' perception on product positioning and brand equity • Customer satisfaction

• *Research design*: To put it simply, consumer research is like a tool box for marketers to employ at any step of marketing planning to solve specific problems to move further. The two major research approaches, qualitative and quantitative, are the essential ways to explore, describe and present research results. The usage of either type or the combination of the two should be selected and designed to serve different purposes.

2. Qualitative research methods

Qualitative research is about getting insights from consumers. What matters is NOT how many respondents are for or against the idea, but rather the *reasons behind* their choices. For example, many consumers use fabric softener in their laundry process, but for different reasons: some wants their clothes straightened without ironing due to lack of time; some desire the anti-static feature of the product to avoid unpleasant feelings in winter. These insightful yields are obtained through detailed investigations into consumers' lives.

Qualitative research is conducted in a semi-structured fashion, with a lot of open-ended questions being asked, depending on the expertise of experienced researchers commonly known as moderators. The role of a qualitative researcher involves writing a discussion guide before the interviews, encouraging respondents to express their opinions, directing the discussion towards the designated goals and probing where necessary, and finally summarizing, analyzing and reporting the findings after fieldwork. A well-trained and skillful moderator should be able to create a relaxing atmosphere for discussion, induce the respondents to share their personal experience and express their true thoughts in a natural but efficient way, filter and extract insightful and valuable information and transform them into business opportunities.

Typically, qualitative research takes the form of focus groups, in-depth interviews, in-home visits, ethnographic immersions, and shop-along. Each method has its own characteristics and different functions. To obtain optimal results, sometimes multiple methods would be adopted.

- *Focus groups*: Typically consisting of 6–8 respondents with similar features and lasting for 2–2.5 hours, focus groups enjoy the benefit of getting the opinions of several people at one time. It is hosted by a moderator, who is a professional researcher with a thorough understanding of the project, the product and the client. The group dynamics can stimulate consumers' thoughts, and abundant learning can be drawn through the interaction between the moderator and respondents.

- *In-depth interviews*: It is also called one-on-one interviews, which is usually suitable for topics that to some extent require *privacy*. For instance, industry professionals (such as doctors or real estate traders) are usually recruited to provide insiders' knowledge and perspectives. Information like this is somewhat sensitive, which they won't talk freely if other people are around. In-depth interviews are also more effective for special products or special respondents, which either require privacy or special attention. Like the usage of condoms, interviews are likely to be done one by one. As for the elderly, in-depth interviews can help them concentrate and follow the interviewer's directions easily, so as to achieve desirable outcomes.

- *In-home visits & ethnographic immersions*: This research method is more or less like an in-depth interview, but it happens at the consumer's home. Researchers and the clients can actually immerse in the consumer's living environment to get to know how the product is actually used in an authentic setting, and how the consumer's lifestyle affects their decision-making. Instead of listening to the consumers talking about the products in a research facility, researchers have the opportunity to observe the consumer's life to get a fuller picture and notice some crucial details that otherwise might be neglected. For products like pet foods, in-home visits could be a suitable way to gain more and better results due to the special role division of the purchaser (the pet owner) and the user (the pet). An in-home visit usually lasts for 0.5–1.5 hours, while ethnographic immersions, which adopts an anthropological field study approach, might last for up to four hours.

- *Shop-along*: This form usually follows an in-home visit. By going to the store the consumer usually frequents to buy the product in question, researchers can see how purchase decisions are made in the store.

Discussion guide: Below is an example of what a discussion guide looks like for focus groups of skin care products. As it can be seen, the discussion would be divided into several sections, starting from how consumers perceive the product category, new trends in the market, and their purchase behavior; then the discussion is moved onto a brand-specific section, including users' impressions of the brand, their feedback on the TV commercials to be launched, and their comments on the products and prices.

Brand X Focus Group Discussion Guide (135 mins)

Warming up (5 min)

- Moderator explains roles, general purposes of the study, no right/wrong answers, etc.
- Respondent introduction — name, people in household, employment, hobbies.

(A) Overall skincare market (45 mins)

I. (a) Talk about the overall skincare market and your thoughts about that

- What's new about skincare in town (type, texture, packaging, style, smell, usage, etc.)? How do you know that?
- Did you notice any change/ trend in terms of skincare category? How is it relevant to you? Why?
- What's your favorite skincare brand now and 3 years ago? (Write on paper) Anything different? Why?

(b) Talk about your skincare shopping /buying/consuming behavior

- Where do you purchase skin care products? (Write the store name on paper)
- Usually where would you go to find your products in the store? (probe counter or planogram or promotion stack)
- When do you purchase? How often?
- How much do you spend per month? (Write the amount on paper)
- What product do you purchase most often? Which brand? Which series? (Write on paper) Why?
- How do you use them? Tell me the typical daily routine. What occasions? (morning/ night/ office/at home...)

II. Brand sorting exercise

- Show all brands (products) on table, ask them to have a short discussion on the sorting criteria; then start to categorize the brands according to their own criteria.
- Why do you categorize the brand in this way? Why is brand X placed here? (Probe if anything related to positioning and pricing)

(B) Brand X sessions (85 mins)

I. Tell me something about brand X

- What does the brand tell you? How do you feel about it?
- If brand X were a person, how would you describe him/her? Why? (age? gender? What does he/she wear? What is his/her nationality/occupation/personality/ shopping habit?)
  Are you interested in him/her? What's his/her relationship with you? Why?
- How did you come about knowing this brand?
- What are the key drivers for trial and purchase?
- Are you a frequent buyer? How often?
- Do you use it together with other brands? What are the other brands? Why?
- What do you like about this brand?

• What do you dislike about this brand?

II. Let's focus on communications of brand X

(Rotate TVC: group 1 TVC A & TVC B / group 2 TVC A & TVC C)

• [Unaided] Do you recall any brand X communications? If no, probe TVCs and print ads.
  – Can you describe it? What are the messages? Do you like it? Why or why not?
• [Aided] Show TVCs and print ads: Did you see these? (count)
  – What did you see? (let them talk freely)
  – What is the core message brand X wants to tell you?
  – Do you like them? Why or why not?
  – Do you think these are reliable? Why or why not?
  – Do you think these are relevant to you? Why or why not?
  – Do you think these are relevant to the brand? Why or why not?
• How do you get new things and stay updated on skincare products? What is the most credible / influential / frequent channel/media you use? Why?
• If brand X is planning to use a celebrity, who do you think would match the brand to enhance the brand image and your liking to the brand?
• If brand X used these celebrities (show them the board), who do you think would match the brand most? Why?

III. Then let's talk about brand X products

• Do you know how many product series brand X has?
• How many and which products out of the current portfolio are you using? Why or why not?
• Do you think it is effective?
• How do you use it? Tell me your typical daily routine. What occasions? (morning/ night/office/ at home)
• Any new product ideas for brand X? What is lacking in the product range?
• Here is our new product. Do you feel interested? Why or why not? (check the interest/involvement level)
  Please try a bit on your hand, how do you feel? Good or not? Why?

IV. Tell me what you think on prices?

• Do you know how much are the products of brand X? Are these reasonable?
• Are you aware of any price promotion on brand X? What are the prices?
• Did you see these bonus packs? Are these attractive? Why or why not?

(C) Thank and close

• See if any additional questions from the brand X team;
• If no, thank the respondents and end the discussion.

- The End -

Recruitment screener: Since qualitative research relies heavily on the expertise of the researchers and what the consumers say, it is essential to recruit authentic, qualified and articulate respondents. The clients and the research team would work collaboratively to set criteria for the recruitment to ensure valuable findings can be obtained. One of the necessary steps in the recruitment process is to draw up a screener to find the right people. Below is an example of a screener for the focus group discussions on beef and lamb consumption.

Q9	Which of the following statements best describes you, when it comes to deciding what food to buy for yourself or your child / children?		
	I decide completely by myself.	1	CONTINUE
	I decide most times; sometimes other members of my family decide.	2	
	Sometimes I decide; sometimes other members of my family decide.	3	CLOSE
	Most times, other members of my family decide.	4	
	Other members of my family always decide.	5	

Q12	How often have you purchased *the beef and/or lamb* in the past 2 months?	Beef	Lamb	
	At least once each week (weekly).	1	1	CONTINUE
	At least once every 2 weeks (fortnightly).	2	2	
	At least once every 3 weeks.	3	3	CLOSE
	At least once every 4 weeks (monthly).	4	4	
	At least once every 6 weeks.	5	5	
	At least once every 8 weeks.	6	6	
	Less often.	7	7	

Note: At least beef or lamb must be bought at least once every 2 weeks fortnightly. (check quotas)

Q13. Please share with us details about the premium protein meat you bought.

	Brand	Country of origin	Price	Size of product	Part of beef (Rib/Chuck/Sirloin)	Cuisine you made out of it
Beef #1						
Beef #2						
Lamb#1						
Lamb#2						

Note: SH recruit high end protein meat price >159 RMB/500g; CD >89 RMB/500g.

Q14	How often do you cook and prepare WESTERN CUISINE styles at home?		
	Every day or nearly every day.	1	CHECK QUOTA – GROUP 1&2
	4–5 times a week.	2	
	2–3 times a week.	3	
	Once a week.	4	
	Twice a month.	5	
	Once a month.		

Continued

	Cook and prepare mostly Chinese cuisine styles, at least Twice a month.	6	CHECK QUOTA–GROUP 3
	Hard to tell / do not cook at home.	7	CLOSE

Q15	Which of the following places do you regularly purchase premium protein meat (beef and/or lamb) from?		
	City Shops.	1	
	City's Super.	2	
	Ole.	3	Check quota–high end modern retail
	Sam's Club.	4	
	Metro.	5	
	Other high end retail stores (Please record specific name:____).	6	
	None of the above.	7	CLOSE

3. Quantitative research methods

Quantitative research focuses on *numbers and statistics*. In contrast with the semi-structured interviews with open-ended questions of qualitative researches (QUAL), quantitative approaches (QUAN) follow relatively fixed structures with procedures with strict guidelines. The essential steps like research design, sampling, data collection and execution can critically affect the results of a QUAN study. Observation, experimentation, survey are the three major forms of quantitative research.

Observation: One of the challenges in consumer studies is that consumers might not behave the same as what they claim. It is not uncommon that a new product receives positive responses in preliminary researches but fails in the market. Consumers might favor the idea of this new product in an interview but make different choices in the real setting, taking into consideration a lot of circumstantial factors. How do we know how consumers truly behave in the retail outlets? Observation can provide an objective perspective on consumer behavior.

Most observations are done in actual stores. Trained researchers would take notes about the consumer flows at different time during the day, the composition of these flows (age, gender, shopping units, etc.), the things they buy, and the things they pick up but haven't bought. *Inventory audit* can also be quite informative in figuring out merchandise sales. By counting what's left in stock, the products sold can be calculated. These statistics can be broken down by brand or/and by category, which can be used to evaluate the effectiveness of different sales and marketing plans. Electronic means like *Physiological observation* can use monitoring devices to track consumers' eye movement when they see or read an advertisement.

Experimentation: In contrast with the actual setting where observations take place, experimentation is conducted in a relatively *controlled* environment. This can be illustrated by the simulative supermarkets built by major retail giants to investigate how purchase decisions are made in a store. Target consumers are invited to shop in these places.

Surveillance devices like CCTV have been installed to record the whole process (consent and confidentiality agreement would be signed beforehand), mock-up shelves with products of major brands have been arranged to create an authentic atmosphere. Sales-related tests can be done: the stopping power of different package designs on shelves, the closing power of different sales promotion strategies, how shoppers compare and choose among various brands, etc.

P&G coined the term FMOT (First Moment of Truth) in 2005 to refer to the 3 to 5 seconds when a shopper notices an item in a retail environment (invariably due to the packaging interrupting the shoppers' attention to prompt brand recognition) and makes a decision as to whether or not they purchase the item. The model comprises of three points of contact that are key to maintaining that brand or product preference in that moment. The first contact point is a stimulus such as a TV commercial; a mention on a radio station; a magazine Lift-Out; an online video; an email; a banner ad, etc. The second involves the consumer visiting the store or searching the web to locate the product or service. The third is the moment the consumer locates the product either in the store or online. Regardless of whether there is only one brand or a range of brands, the consumer faces the FMOT. The buying decision that they make will be influenced by their in-store or online experience. Based on the research, consumers spend seven seconds in front of the shelf before they decide which brand to buy. Therefore, it's really important to gain the consumer's attention at this critical moment.

(A consumer is wearing eye movement tracking goggles connected to a monitoring device that can be observed and recorded by researchers.)

Survey: Probably considered as the most typical way of quantitative research, *surveys* are systematic ways to collect information from a large amount of people. Three aspects need to be determined when it comes to survey design: 1. sample size, sampling criteria and corresponding method; 2. the way to reach and interview respondents; 3. what and how questions should be asked (questionnaire formulation). There are four types of surveys: face-to-face, telephone, mail, and online, each one of which has its advantages and disadvantages.

Face-to-face surveys: Roadside or mall intercepts are typically the most effective ways for interviewers to reach designated respondents. The response rate is relatively higher than other approaches since it's hard to turn down a request proposed in person. This approach also enjoys the strengths of being able to ask open-ended questions and probe. The completion rates are higher as well. However, its weaknesses lie in the high costs of interviewers and incentives, the limited locations to reach dispersed targets, and the biased results caused when respondents feel obliged to provide polite or socially desirable answers.

Telephone surveys: This approach is more cost-efficient than in-person surveys, since interviewers can make phone calls randomly from a call center. Computer-aided telephone interviews (CATI) are a well-established way to conduct telephone surveys. The response rate is higher than mail surveys thanks to the personal contact. To some extent, probing and open-ended questions can be asked, but visual aids can't be used. The results obtained from telephone interviews might be relatively simple.

Online surveys: It's getting more and more popular and has become the mainstream of quantitative research due to its cost-effectiveness and ability to reach a wide range of dispersed respondents. With considerable incentives (cash or coupons) and the easy access to online questionnaires, consumers are more likely to click on and finish the survey. The downside is without the presence and assistance of interviewers, consumers are likely to get impatient if the questionnaire is too long or there are too many open-ended questions, or the answers they type in might not be up to standard, resulting in a higher percentage of waste. Hence, the design of the questionnaire is of vital importance.

Mail surveys: The use of mails is diminishing resulting from the widespread popularization of communication technology. Less and less people would respond to such surveys. They are further discouraged because the paper questionnaire needs to be mailed back to the sender, which is quite outdated.

4. Questionnaire design

The function of a questionnaire in quantitative research is quite different from that of a screener for qualitative research. The former is meant to draw out meaningful information from a sizable audience; whereas the latter serves to select the right kind of people to participate in discussion. As a result, a carefully drafted questionnaire is crucial to the quality of research data. When compiling questions, several principles should be followed: 1. No leading questions; 2. Don't ask two questions in one; 3. Ask clear questions; 4. Use consumers' language; 5. Respondents must be able and willing to answer the questions. A well-written questionnaire should have a reasonable structure with a logical flow.

The roles of QUAL and QUAN studies can be *complementary*: QUAL can dig out some useful insights or opinions but is somewhat subjective; QUAN is supposed to be objective, so it can support and verify these results with data. If a soft drinks company intends to launch a new flavor, with a few candidates at hand: watermelon, cherry, passionfruit, lemon, etc., a QUAL test can be done to identify and elaborate consumers' preference, followed by a QUAN test for them to "vote" for their favorite flavor. In this way, a holistic picture can be drawn to have a thorough understanding. Another usage of the mixed method is that a QUAL test should be conducted to revise the questions and determine the options in the questionnaire in a QUAN study. Without a QUAL test beforehand, the questionnaire might not be optimal, which will have an impact on the final results. It is important to keep in mind each one of the approaches serves their specific purposes, so either one of them will not stand alone in a comprehensive study.

5. Data analysis

The data collected in either QUAL or QUAN projects need to be analyzed after fieldwork, but in different ways. In a QUAL project, the data are collected in the forms of respondent profiles, diary, audio recordings, videos, transcripts and most importantly the researchers' notes. It relies on the researcher's professional skills and experience to analyze and summarize the research findings and propose recommendations. On the other hand, the QUAN data collected in a survey would go through the processing stage, including coding the responses and quantifying (e.g. converting respondents' answers into numerical scores), then tabulating and analyzing with the use of sophisticated analytical programs.

6. Report creation & presentation

Research reports are typically divided into four sections: 1. The introduction of basic information like the research background and research design (methodology, recruitment criteria, respondent profile); 2. Major conclusions: summaries should be outlined concisely and to-the-point, so that the clients are able to grasp the most important learning of the project at one glance; 3. Research findings: key findings are to be presented in a way that is condensed and pertinent, and then detailed findings would further display what has been obtained in the research; 4. Recommendations: the quality of this part depends on the researcher's familiarization of the category and the brand, their perceptions and understanding of target consumers and their ability to transform fieldwork learning into valuable commercial opportunities.

The creation of a research report routinely takes two weeks. After it has been crafted and submitted, there might be feedback from the clients' side, so back-and-forth revisions are to be expected. Once the report has been finalized and approved, some clients would request a presentation, which involves higher levels of executives to be informed about the latest market trends in consumer behavior. Researchers are supposed to walk them through the whole research process and deliver insightful results with business implications.

Summary

A thorough and insightful understanding of target consumers should be the foundation of the formulation of all marketing plans. The relationship between the study of consumer behavior and marketing is like the two sides of the same coin. The study of consumer behavior is a constantly on-going process due to changes in the macro environment.

Consumer behavior refers to a series of consumption activities of choosing, buying, using, evaluating and disposing of the products and services to fulfill the needs of individuals or organizations. Instead of simply focusing on the buying behavior, the whole consumption process involves at least three stages: pre-purchase, purchase and post-purchase stages. Consumers and their decision-making processes are influenced by internal and external factors, which determines the interdisciplinary nature of this course. Internal factors include: sensation and perception, learning and memory, motivation, attitude, personality and lifestyle; external factors include: social relationships like family, reference group and key opinion leaders, culture and subculture, as well as direct and indirect marketing influences.

It is strategic for businesses to select a certain group of consumers to be the target, and come up with a set of relevant strategies aiming at them. *Market segmentation* is the practice to divide the market into groups of consumers possessing common needs or features. The two major tools to segment consumers are demographics and psychographics.

Market research is the process of exploring, collecting and analyzing information regarding consumer behavior. Research agencies should communicate with the clients adequately, keep in mind the clear research objectives and the research background, So as to avoid and eliminate future mistakes caused by misunderstandings, there are three steps in the market research process: preparation (research design and recruitment), execution (ways of qualitative and/or quantitative researches), and later stages (analysis and reporting).

Qualitative research is about getting *insights* from consumers. The major ways are focus group discussions, in-depth interviews (one-on-one), in-home visits and ethnographic immersions, and shop-along. It's essential to construct an effective discussion guide and recruit the right respondents to elicit valuable answers. Analysis of qualitative research relies on the expertise and experience of the moderator.

Quantitative research focuses on *numbers and statistics*. The major forms are observation, experimentation and survey. It is critical to establish and follow a standardized structure for future execution.

The roles of QUAL and QUAN studies can be *complementary*. The decision of choosing which type of research methods should be based on the nature, background and the objectives of the research.

Exercises

(1) Consumers and the items they consume can take many forms. Give examples of three different types of consumers and examples of three different types of items they could consume, including products, services, and ideas.

(2) List the three stages in the consumption process. Describe the issues that you considered in each of these stages when you made a recent important purchase. Identify questions that might be asked from the consumer's perspective and from the marketer's perspective in the prepurchase and purchase stages of the consumption process.

(3) Based on the knowledge learned in this chapter about research methods, could you design a project to explore an area or an aspect of college students' online purchase and/or consumption habits, using both QUAL and QUAN approaches? Present your ideas in the form of a research proposal, including the research topic, research objectives, sample size, sample criteria, research methods and detailed research design.

(4) Questionnaires and screeners are quite similar: both are presented to the respondent as a set of questions designed to elicit information in the research process, but what are the differences between the two? Based on the research topic selected for Question 3, draft a questionnaire according to your research objectives.

Case Analysis

Read the following news report about the growing trend of camping in China. Conduct a survey among your fellow students about their views and needs for weekend outings, using the research methods introduced in this chapter. Present your results to the class.

Happy Campers Exercising "Tent-up" Demand

"Glamping", or glamor camping, now part of leisure lexicon as consumers return to nature while practicing social distancing

With consumption upgrades and the revival of the tourism industry in China, a new type of camping is gaining ground as a leisure business, attracting an increasing number of tourists. Different from traditional camping options, which often involve meticulous packing of tents, ropes, sleeping bags, binoculars, telescopes, foods and beverages, a new style of high-end camping provides complete facilities and offers a luggage-free experience.

"In addition to camping necessities, the camping base offers all things that you can possibly think of — earplugs, air mattresses, blankets, mosquito repellent, toiletries, meats, barbecue facilities, beer and ice buckets. It is just so convenient. I can just tell my friends: 'Let's go camping and head off with no preparation,' said Beijing's Meng Ke, who has experienced the new type of camping."

Xiaohongshu, a lifestyle platform, said that during Dragon Boat Festival that fell between June 12 and

Campers enjoy themselves at Dare Glamping's campsite in Daxing district, Beijing, in July.

June 14 this year, online searches for "camping" surged 400 percent year-on-year, and Beijing, Chengdu of Sichuan province, Shanghai, Chongqing and Hangzhou of Zhejiang province topped the list of camping search destinations. It is reported that camping in suburbs involves short driving times, satisfies people's desire to be close to nature and is thus gaining in popularity. "Many camping enterprises were at full capacity during the Festival. They said that it was hard to get a tent without a reservation," said an official from the app.

Data also showed that in 2020, camping-related posts increased 271 percent year-on-year, while views of such posts surged 170 percent year-on-year. Between Jan 1 and May 31 this year, camping searches were 428 percent higher than that in the same period of last year. With the popularity of camping, "camping gear" "campsite recommendations" and "camping photos" become hot topics online.

"Glamping" is a combination of glamor and camping—essentially luxury camping. According to Qichacha, a Suzhou, Jiangsu province-based company that tracks business registrations, in 2020, camping-related enterprises soared by 8,521, or 227 percent year-on-year. This year, by June 10, there were 7,854 newly registered camping-related enterprises.

Zhu Xian, founder of new-type camping Dare Glamping shared his story of establishing the company. At the beginning of 2020, when COVID-19 broke out worldwide, Zhu, then a senior executive at an outbound travel company, suddenly had no business. "As there was no work to do, I suggested that we just take a break. During six months of rest, starting from Beijing, I took my wife and son on a road trip. We went to the Ningxia Hui autonomous region, the Inner Mongolia autonomous region and the furthest place we traveled to was Hoh Xil, Qinghai province."

"We encountered a lot of beautiful scenery, including prairies, deserts and snow-capped mountains. However, we could only appreciate the scenery from our car. When we got out of the car, the sun was too hot and we had no place to sit." That was when Zhu began to purchase tents, folding tables and chairs, and pots for cooking. "When we bought those things, our sense of well-being increased a lot. I found that there was finally a place for us to hang out and enjoy the scenery, and my son could run a little bit and come back to the tent to fetch some food and drinks. With the happiness level increased,

I bought more things, and the things I bought became more expensive," One day, Zhu made a list of all of the camping-related things he bought. After calculations, there were over 230 items worth around 100,000 yuan ($15,460). "One thing I noticed was how many times should we camp to make these things worth the price; and every time we camp, it takes great time and effort to haul over 230 items to sites and back. That was when I thought of starting a camping company, which offers all camping-related items and hires professionals to organize the items and offer services. Customers need to take nothing. They just need to take their families to come here," Zhu said.

Zhu chose the first campsite for his firm in Sanya, Hainan province. They rent the land used for camping from village governments concerned. A consumer may have to fork out up to 800 yuan for the basic package per night. The cost includes all items related to camping, an afternoon tea, a barbecue dinner and a breakfast. Since Dec. 7, Dare Glamping kicked off its new-type camping services, it had been operating at full capacity. "We didn't take one day off. The steady stream of customers forced us to run the business around the clock. They shared their experiences online on social media platforms, and word-of-mouth generated even more customers," Zhu said. Within six months, Dare Glamping's campsites expanded to nearly 20.

To better develop new-type camping, Chao Chenglin, a marketing expert, suggested camping enterprises should pay attention to their services based on consumer safety and comfort levels, as well as special characteristics of scenic spots. "For consumers, safety, comfort levels and user experience are the three prerequisites for travel, which raise the bar for company operations and services," Chao added.

CHAPTER TWO

Social Influences on Consumer Behavior

Learning objectives

After learning this chapter, you will be able to:

- understand social influences from marketing or non-marketing sources that can be delivered personally or by mass or social media;
- identify different types of reference groups and their characteristics;
- demonstrate how each type of reference groups can affect consumer behavior;
- comprehend the roles family life plays in consumers' purchase decision-making process.

Lead-in Case

The Success of Xiaohongshu As a Social E-Commerce Platform

Established in 2013, Xiaohongshu, which translates to the "Little Red Book" or RED, began as an app for users to submit reviews and share overseas shopping tips with other users. It provides an all-in-one platform with both social media and e-commerce functions for its China users. This social E-commerce app now has over 200 million registered users as of 2019. If you're in the field of e-commerce, you should definitely learn how to master the platform created by this billion-dollar startup rapidly taking over China.

With a focus on beauty and fashion, it acts as a platform for people to post and share shopping tips, product reviews and lifestyle stories (in the form of pictures, videos and text).

The platform has developed into a trusted source for advice and recommendations from other users and like-minded people. It has successfully created a thriving community user interactions/engagement, careful curation, and authentic information sharing.

Noticing users' demand for buying foreign goods, RED launched its own cross-border e-commerce platform, the "RED store" in 2014. It connects Chinese consumers with global brands by enabling users to buy overseas products directly through the app. Since then, RED has formed strategic partnerships with many overseas brands including Lancôme, Swisse and Innisfree.

With the business model of a social e-commerce platform, RED achieved great success in recent years, especially in 2015, when it grew its GMV from approximately 1 million RMB to over 100 million in just 6 months. It's continuously growing and now has over 200 million registered users as of 2019. In 2018 its topline revenue was RMB 1.49 billion and it projects to earn nearly RMB 3 billion in 2019!

There are several factors attributing to the success of RED:

1) Young, high-purchasing power demographic

According to its official website, RED has reached 200 million registered users as of Jan. 2019, with those born in the post-90s and post-95s as the most active users. From statistics, over 50% of users were under 30 years old, while more than 80% of them are female. With young urban females who value quality as the main user demographic, RED serves as an effective platform for selling and advertising skincare, cosmetics and fashion products. Given that the app is extremely popular among China's Generation Z, RED is an ideal marketing platform for brands who would like to target a young and sophisticated demographic.

2) Thriving online community

RED has successfully created an online interactive community through having their users share informative content including product reviews, OOTDs, and make-up tips.

Apart from creating your own content, users can also "Save" posts, interact with others through "Likes"/"Comments", or even press "Follow" to subscribe to a particular user/brand that they like. RED also lets users share posts externally through Weibo/Wechat, which is rare given how some platforms in China punish users for linking to rival platforms.

To maintain high-quality content, RED doesn't allow self-advertisement or verbal abuse. With an emphasis on "authenticity", it further fosters trust and honest sharing among users by enforcing these policies. So much so that descriptions such as "No.1..." or "The best..." are strictly prohibited on all brand stores or advertising!

Apart from sharing and commenting, RED uses a recommendation algorithm to create a customized homepage based on users' browsing and search history. It also offers an "Explore" feature based on this same data. This function allows users to focus on topics they are interested in and sort out unwanted information. "Nearby" shows hot topics according to the user's location, while "Follow" shows latest posts from subscribed accounts.

Thanks to its engaging features, RED has successfully built a tight bond among its like-minded users, lovingly calling themselves "小红薯" (literally Little Sweet Potatoes in English). According to its official website, RED had 30 million monthly active users in 2018, three times more than the previous year.

3) Extensive word-of-mouth marketing

The app's user-generated content led to the emergence of several Key-Opinion Leaders (KOLs) becoming active on the platform. Similar to KOLs (Influencers) on Instagram, most of them share useful tips and interesting content about beauty and lifestyle. These KOLs work with brands to promote products to followers resulting in increased brand awareness, user engagement, and followers. Examples of RED influencers include Austin Li, nicknamed The Lipstick Master/Brother (口红哥), who tries on luxury brands' lipsticks such as Gucci and M.A.C. He has accumulated 3,169,800 followers and his comments are constantly shared by other lipstick lovers. Apart from those who became famous after joining RED, some celebrities such as Nana Ou-Yang, have also opened their own accounts on RED, which has helped to further boost the app's traffic and credibility.

So how do KOLs foster WOM marketing? In fact, a single share from a user on RED already brings online exposure to your product. Once your product is shared by a user, other users will be able to view details about its features, benefits and prices. If other users find it attractive, they may even further share it within their social circle, with the possibility of it going viral! It significantly raises brand awareness and helps to generate customer leads.

4) Direct link to an e-commerce store: closing the Loop

RED brought its app to the next level by launching an e-commerce platform, called the "RED store", which allows users to purchase the products directly from merchants after reading reviews. With the store, users no longer need to worry about the authenticity of the products (a huge concern in China's e-commerce industry). The feature greatly reduces consumers' search and time cost, and further encourages the "Read-Like-Buy" cycle within the app.

Introduction

It's natural to think consumers' mindsets are affected by the people around them, like their family members, friends, colleagues, relatives, etc. But is it possible that consumers' choices are influenced by total strangers? As the Lead-in Case shows, the social media platform RED (also known as Xiaohongshu) facilitates many young users to post their vivid experiences and persuasive reviews of using certain products or services, becoming an important reference for youngsters aspiring to a trendy life in China. What's worth noticing is that these users may not know each other personally. It is so popular because the contents are (to some extent) genuine and objective, interesting, aesthetically pleasing and more detailed than the information provided in mass media. Consumers can get a better sense of what's new and in trend, which will become a strong driving force for them to try out the things being introduced.

In fact, we are immersed in all kinds of information in our daily lives, some of which is more influential than others. The sources of information and the ways in which it's delivered largely determine its credibility. People are more likely to believe sources that are well-respected and highly thought of. For instance, beauty tips are often shared among girls. If your best friend tells you how effective the eye cream she's using is, including the product's benefit (like moisturizing, reducing puffiness, smoothing fine lines, etc.), texture and scent, along with the before and after comparison, you'd feel a strong urge to give it a go. Aside from the rational considerations supported by information, some decisions are made due to the social relations consumers are in, which are to some extent quite subjective and/or hard to explain. In this chapter, we'll take a close look at how consumers' purchase decisions are influenced by external factors like different types of information and social relations.

Throughout this chapter, we'll try to answer the following questions:

● What are the major types of information sources? How effective can each of them be?

● How do social relationships play a part in affecting consumers' purchase decision-making? How does it work?

● How do family members make collective decisions as a whole? Alternatively, how does family life influences each member's decision-making?

2.1 Sources of information

Living in the modern commercial world, we are bombarded with all kinds of information related to products and services: some are created intendedly by marketers to arouse and respond to consumers' unmet needs and establish a positive image in their minds, some are delivered personally by the staff representing the company, some are evaluated and diffused by independent organizations to provide a relatively objective perspective, and some are created by other consumers resulting from their actual experience. Each type of information sources has its own level of credibility and capacity of interactive communication. The chart below displays the four types of information sources and how credible and interactive each type is.

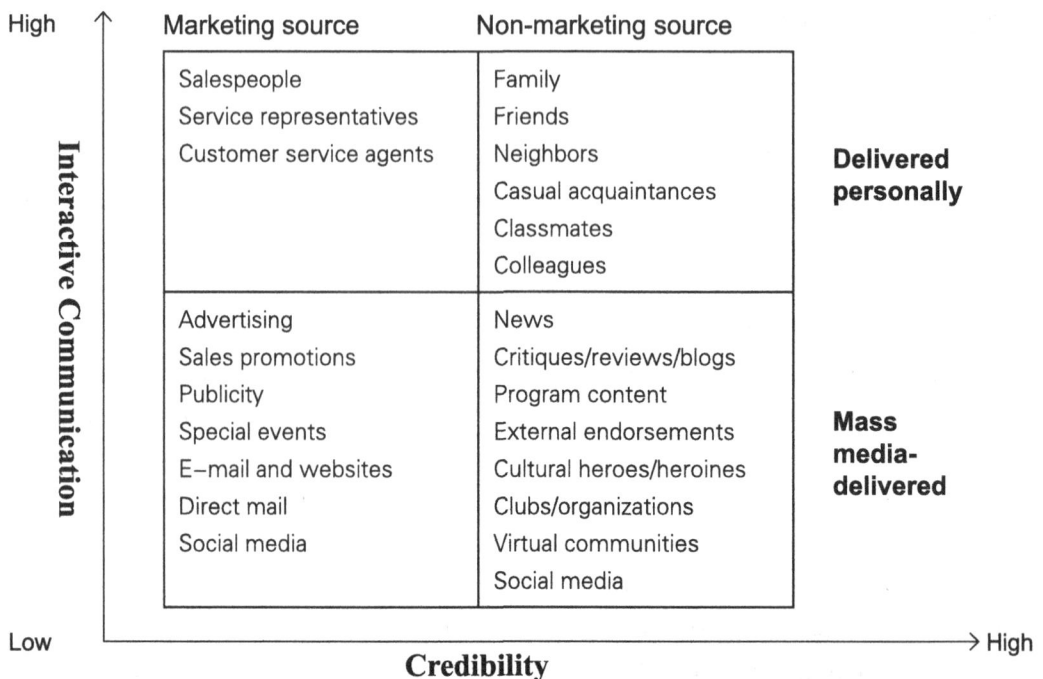

	Marketing source	Non-marketing source	
High ↑	Salespeople Service representatives Customer service agents	Family Friends Neighbors Casual acquaintances Classmates Colleagues	**Delivered personally**
Interactive Communication	Advertising Sales promotions Publicity Special events E–mail and websites Direct mail Social media	News Critiques/reviews/blogs Program content External endorsements Cultural heroes/heroines Clubs/organizations Virtual communities Social media	**Mass media-delivered**
Low		**Credibility** → High	

Figure 2-1 Levels of interactive communication and credibility of information sources

As we can see from this chart, information delivered personally is highly interactive, which enables further probing and more information to be elicited; whereas mass media-delivered information is usually a written piece with a complete structure, so its ability to facilitate interactive communication is relatively low. In terms of credibility, typically consumers perceive non-marketing sources are more reliable, allowing for negative (but objective) comments, while marketing sources seem less believable because they are designed to look good.

Imagine if you are going to buy a new car, you are intended to collect all kinds of information from the four types of channels mentioned above, like you will pay attention to some noticeable car ads of famous brands, even reading the small words in the ad; you will search for detailed reviews written by professionals on car-related websites or social media apps; you'll consult your friends who drive the cars of the same brands you are interested in; you'll also go to an authorized car dealer to talk to the salespeople in the hope of finding out some answers to your own questions as well as having a test drive. During this whole process, the friends' comments might exert the most influence on you because they are the people you trust, and they are also car users who can share with you their own driving experience. The limitation is that sometimes you don't happen to know someone who has used the product you want to buy. This is where professional reviews in independent media come along. It is considered to be the second most reliable source because the content is created by experienced industry insiders, while comparisons across several brands and/or models are possible. But the downside is that such posts might not facilitate two-way communications between the target consumers and the experts. That means if you have some particular questions, you might not be able to get desirable answers. When visiting a car dealer, a salesperson will be available to provide the information you seek for, tell you the sales promotion you might be interested in, rebut counterarguments, emphasize and explain important and/or complex information. Such interactive communication will help you better understand the brand and the product you aim at, assisting you to make an informed decision. But the negative aspect might be that you might be too engaged in this interpersonal situation that some disadvantages of the car might be neglected or too polite to turn the salesperson down. So to some extent, salespeople as a kind of marketing source delivered personally might not be highly credible.

2.1.1 Reference groups

Among all the social relationships, *reference groups* have a predominant impact on consumer behavior. Human beings are social animals, which means we live our lives taking reference from other people who are similar to us. A reference group is any individual or group in reality or imagination perceived as having significant relevance upon a person's evaluations, aspirations, or behavior. As you can see in this definition, a reference group might be a

参照群体是指在现实生活或虚构想象中，被认为对个体对事物的评价、志向或行为有显著关联的个体或群体。

social group we belong to, like the class we are assigned to in college; or any desirable individuals or groups we aspire to identify with, like a popular Internet celebrity specializing in matching clothes. There are different kinds of groups that exert varying degrees of influences, with which the individual has direct or indirect connections. Primary groups, such as family and friends, have strong ties and frequent interaction with us, the communication of which is informal and face to face. Secondary groups, such as professionals, clubs, and religious groups, involve weaker ties and less frequent interaction, the communication of which is relatively discontinuous and more formal.

> **群体规范**是指群体所确立的，每个成员必须遵守的行为准则。

Group norms refer to the code of conducts that is established among group members and followed by each one of them. Each type of group has its own norms, some are explicitly stated, and some are implicit and conventional. Individuals will receive affirmation or recognition as rewards if their attitudes and behavior live up to the norms; if an individual deviates from or violates the norms, the group would correct such behavior in various ways, including sanctions and punishment. Group members conform to norms voluntarily or coercively, which means they can actively imitate other people's behavior, or have to take actions under group pressure.

Consumers are influenced by reference groups in three ways:

(1) <u>Informational influence</u>: The individual seeks information about various brands from an association of professionals or independent groups of experts, or from those who work with the product as a profession, or brand-related knowledge and experience from those friends, neighbors, relatives or co-workers with reliable information about the brands.

(2) <u>Utilitarian influence</u>: The individual's preferences for a particular brand have a lot to do with the desire to satisfy the expectations of the people with whom he or she has social interaction.

(3) <u>Value-expressive influence</u>: The individual perceives that the choice and/or purchase of a certain brand will enhance his or her own image; or it would project what the individual would like to be; or that the people choosing, purchasing or using a certain brand possess the characteristics that this individual would like to have, like being admired or respected by others.

The levels of influences that reference groups have on an individual differ in terms of brands and product categories. This matter is looked at in two dimensions: whether the product is consumed in private or in public; whether it's necessary for our daily lives or whether it's a luxury item. Generally speaking, the less necessary the product is, or the more frequently the product is used in public, or the more visible the usage of the product or brand is, the bigger the strength of reference group influence. An easy example to be cited is designer handbags that ladies love. A new handbag is not a must since most working women have more than five of different sizes to match different outfits and occasions. But once it's being carried, other people (esp. other women) would take a look at the design and notice the brand. For ladies at middle class or above, it's a symbol of wealth, status and personal taste. So when shopping for a new item, comments and preferences of the primary group would be taken into consideration.

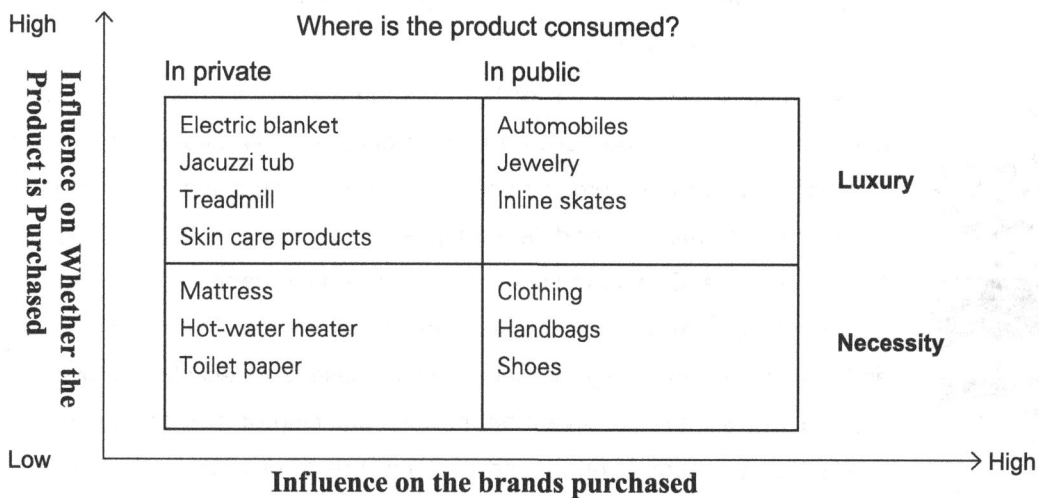

Figure 2-2 Influences of reference group on different types of products

As the diagram above shows, reference groups impose strong power on the brands an individual chooses for the products used in public like cars and clothing. For daily necessities consumed in private settings like toilet paper, the influence of groups on the brands chosen is minimal. So it's not surprising when you see in the homes of some consumers with a full set of premium beauty products on the dresser whereas their toilet paper is coarse and cheap.

2.1.2 Brand community

Brand community consists of a group of consumers whose social relationships are based on usage of or interest in a brand or a product. It is a kind of reference group in which the members don't personally know each other at first. What attracts them to form a community is the common usage of a particular brand or product, which usually belongs to the category of durable consumer goods like cars and cameras. Like the major brands Nikon and Canon in China, each has their own membership clubs with active members participating in the shooting activities. Since shooting with professional cameras takes skills and experience, consumers are more likely to engage in inquiries, discussions, works sharing and photography competitions

品牌社区由一群社会关系基于某品牌或产品的使用或兴趣的消费者组成。

on the forum. There are organized shooting tours in which members can travel to a scenic spot, listening to mini-lectures on how to use the cameras in a better way, receiving shooting tips from professionals, learning from each other, and enjoying the sense of creation and achievement. Very frequently, experienced amateur photographers would coach beginners how to shoot, meanwhile maximizing their enjoyment of the product, so that both sides can benefit from a network of satisfied members. The combination of online and offline activities can effectively increase product users' emotional involvement and thus enhance brand loyalty.

Spring outing organized voluntarily by Chery owners in 2021

Another typical example of brand community is car owners actively participating in the group driving tours organized at weekends or for long distance. Depending on product positioning, leisure tours and/or adventurous tours could be arranged for different types of cars, like a sedan, an SUV, or a four-wheel drive. Getting to know how to drive a car better is somehow like having a long-term relationship. One needs to know the features of the car and how to take advantage of them. Joining these tours enables car owners, especially new ones, to have a better understanding of how this car model works, enjoy natural scenery and the pleasure of driving during holidays, as well as build up connections with other consumers who have made similar purchase decisions as yours, who might most probably belong to the same social class as you. For the car manufacturer, such activities facilitate interactions among users and foster positive feelings for the brand, which might also vividly illustrate to potential customers what it would be like when owning and driving this car.

意见领袖是能够就某一特定的产品或服务提供建议与信息，并能在非正式的沟通传播中影响其他人的态度和行为的人。

2.1.3 Opinion leader

Other than groups, consumers are easily influenced by opinion leaders as well. An opinion leader is a person who gives advice and information regarding a certain product or service, and can frequently influence others' attitudes and behavior in informal communications. In a particular circle, opinion leaders are well-known as the "go-to person" for specific types of information. They actively prescreen, interpret, or provide product and brand-related information to the people around them and their followers.

Opinion leaders are very powerful in getting consumers' attention, altering consumers' attitudes and driving sales. Such social power can be broken down into the following five aspects:

01 Expert power	They are technically competent.
02 Social power	They are socially active and highly connected in their circle, wielding legitimate power by virtue of their social standing.
03 Knowledge power	They filtrate, evaluate and synthesize product information unbiasedly.
04 Referent power	They are typically similar to consumers in terms of values and beliefs.
05 Credibility/benchmark power	They often try out new products, absorbing much of the risk and reducing uncertainty. Contrary to company-sponsored communications which only show positive aspects, opinion leaders offer practical experience of the product, including positive and negative comments.

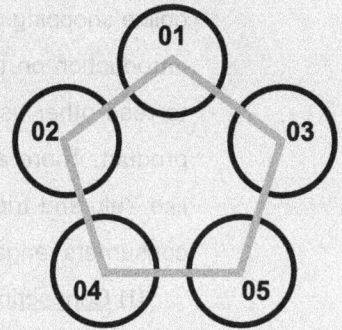

Online opinion leaders

Livestreams of key opinion leaders or KOLs and celebrities are becoming increasingly popular in China, as consumers tend to attach credibility to their recommendations. Some 56 percent of Nielsen survey respondents said they would prefer to buy products recommended by KOLs or celebrities, while 34 percent were indifferent. The city of Hangzhou even offered Li Jiaqi, one of China's top livestreamers, who is now a celebrity of sorts, residency status in June, 2020. That is recognition for the fact that he commands as many as 37.96 million fans on Taobao.

2.1.4 Word-of-mouth

Word-of-mouth (WOM) is information about products and services created and delivered by individuals to others. It has been proven to be powerful and influential to consumers because it is perceived to have been created based on actual usage experiences of the WOM giver, who receives no material gain from the manufacturer and/or marketers by sharing such information. What's more, unlike the purely favorable messages in marketing promotions, there are positive and negative WOM, which enhances the objectivity of the comments. In other words, the authenticity of such information and the neutral position of the WOM giver establish its credibility.

> 口碑是个体产生并向他人传播、关于产品或服务的信息。

We are all too familiar with the casual conversations we have with our friends, colleagues and/or acquaintances, when we introduce or share our pleasant experience with some products and services, from the special colors of a type of eyeshadow, to the delicious foods in a newly-open restaurant. WOM is commonplace not only in real life settings, but also across all major online shopping platforms. It has become the habitual practice after we browse the product introduction on the page of Taobao or JD, we would click on the product review section to read other users' comments and check out what it'll actually be like to be using the product. There are even digital platforms based basically on WOM generated by users, like Yelp and tripadvisor, etc. One study found out the three dimensions that determine consumers' engagement in digital WOM in online social networks:

(1) Connection strength—this means how intimate and how frequently the information seeker has with the source. The more contacts the two sides have, the stronger the connection strength, therefore higher engagement.

(2) Similarity in terms of demographics and lifestyles among group members. If the information seeker and the source share common characteristics like age, gender, educational background, income and social status, the former would be more involved in getting WOM from the latter. We can easily relate to the experience when shopping online for clothes, we'd focus on comments from the people who have similar body types with ours. In the case of baby care products like milk formula, diapers, and toys, similarities should be based on the age and gender of the baby, even though the decision maker is the mother.

(3) Source credibility—from the information seeker's perspective, this means how reliable the source's expertise is in the area of sought advice. For instance, if you ask for advice from a friend who's a teacher about which education institute is more suitable for your kid, your friend's opinions are considered to be quite trustable because you know he or she is an industry insider. On the other hand, this friend might not be able to give you valuable advice on which medicine is more effective in treating headaches.

Consumers are more likely to seek WOM in categories they are *not familiar* with. It works particularly well for objects that are of intangible nature, like services and intellectual properties. As we can see, tangible products enable us to associate with relevant experiences to have a general idea of its benefits and effects. However, it's sometimes not easy for consumers to perceive the experiences of getting a service, like what it's like to dine out in a new restaurant serving Mexican foods, the actual conditions of a family-run inn in a travelling destination you've never been to, how professional and/or creative an advertising agency can be, etc. A very typical example is when parents are choosing a training center for their kids to learn a hobby like playing a musical instrument, ballet or painting, other parents' comments are remarkably persuasive. The sales of educational institutes to a large extent rely on the positive feedback from parents. As for intellectual properties like books and movies, consumers would check out reviews before placing an order. For high-involvement purchases, accumulation of WOM for unfamiliar categories can manage consumers' expectations and eliminate the potential risks without financial costs.

For marketers, WOM serves as the reinforcement of advertising in this era of social media popularization. The collaborative model can work this way: traditional ways of promotions like advertising can arouse brand awareness and establish authority; WOM provides vivid, authentic and more comprehensive product data as a complementary and useful information source. User-generated content on social media is a kind of e-WOM. Digital platforms like Dianping, Xiaohongshu and Douban facilitate users to post their experiences of trying out a fancy restaurant, using an imported product that has not been massively launched on the local market, sharing opinions on a newly released movie, etc., with strong driving forces for sales. Chinese consumers have gotten used to resorting to these apps before making a purchase decision.

Due to its pervasive nature, WOM can be a double-edged sword for marketers when negative comments, esp. by KOLs, appear online. So it's of fundamental importance for marketers to keep track of the sources of negative WOM and adopt positive attitudes when dealing with the situation. Instead of ignoring complains or derogatory feedbacks, companies that value consumers' feelings, address the issues, and respond in a meaningful way will succeed in reducing negative WOM. In 2018, hidden camera footages emerged showing cleaners at more than a dozen five-star hotels in China using dirty towels to clean toilets, cups and showers, sparking outrage on social media. The blogger who posted the video, under the pseudonym Huazong, said he had spent more than 2,000 nights in 147 five-star hotels across several major Chinese cities. The clip has been shared for more than 80,000 times online and a topic section on Weibo dedicated to the video has been clicked on 99 million times. Major international hotel chains have been caught up in the scandal, including the Waldorf Astoria in Shanghai and the Park Hyatt in Beijing, which have both since apologised. China's Ministry of Culture and Tourism has ordered investigations into the apparent breaches of hygiene standards. As we can see in this case, negative e-WOM can be even more impactful since people are more likely to articulate unpleasant experiences. What differentiates the images of businesses in the minds of consumers depends on how well the matter is handled. Once there is a major crisis, businesses should take immediate steps to solve the problem, restore confidence, and begin recovering their reputation.

2.2 Family

Another type of social relationships that exerts potent influences on consumer behavior is family. It's called "social" simply because it is a contrast to the concept of individual. Family can be defined as a group of individuals living together who are related by marriage, blood, or adoption. A broader term might be **household**, which refers to one person living by himself/herself, or a group of individuals living together in a common dwelling, whether they are related or not. The impact a family has on the individual is quite special because every one of us has inseparable ties with our family, which inevitably shapes the way we think and the way we behave, including how

家庭: 因为婚姻、血缘或收养关系而共同居住的一群个体。

....

户: 单独居住的个人；或者一群在同一处所共同生活的人，不管其是否有亲属关系。

we purchase. On the other hand, a family can act as a unit to make collaborative decisions: different roles are taken on by different family members, like when purchasing children–related products, the parents are the deciders, whereas the kids are the users.

2.2.1 Family life cycle

As households transform from young singles to young married couples, then with children, expenditures rise progressively and remain high. At later stages of the family life cycle, spending plummets as couples are getting old, and children are growing up and living on their own. At different phases, consumers as family units have different buying preferences and consumption patterns. The implications for marketers are immense, so it is necessary to have a general understanding of the connections between features of each family life stage and corresponding purchase decision-making processes. For example, households going through a life cycle change tend to switch brand preferences and embrace marketing efforts.

All households go through different stages over time. In each stage, there are a number of problems that household decision makers must solve. How these problems are tackled relates closely to the selection and maintenance of lifestyle and, thus, to consumption. Each stage encompasses unique needs and wants along with financial conditions and experiences. Take young married couples for instance. At the early stage of a marriage without children, the major need of the couple is recreation. Some couples adopt an outdoorsy lifestyle, participating in lots of physical activities. Some others develop a more sophisticated urban lifestyle, like going to museums or cocktail parties. As one or more kids are born, their problems and needs have shifted to focuses on raising a child.

There are various types of household structures, the status of which has a lot to do with personal choices. This part is going to present the traditional family household structure.

1) Young singles

This group consists of young male and female individuals, the subgroups of which are people living with one or both parents, and the ones living alone or with other individuals. This stage is also called the bachelor stage.

Young singles living with parents are mostly still students or have recently graduated from university and are starting to their working careers. People like this have relatively lower incomes, with the income level of an entry-level employee. But they also need to pay less for fixed expenses, since part of which is undertaken by the parents. Members of this group are active in their social lives, going to bars, movies, theatres and concerts. A significant portion of their discretionary income would also be spent on sports equipment, gym club membership clothes, and personal care items.

Young individuals living by themselves are relatively older, with higher income as well as more to spend on living expenses. With a less financial burden, they are recreation-oriented, willing to pay for basic kitchen equipment, furniture, entertainment, vacations, and dating.

2) Newly-married couples (with no children)

Marriage or cohabitation brings about a new stage of the family life cycle. Two young singles acting as a whole greatly altered their lifestyles in the process of developing a shared living pattern. Joint decisions and shared roles in household responsibilities are fresh experiences in many cases. Being present and future-oriented, young married couples need to consider seriously about major issues like savings, household furnishings, major appliances, and more comprehensive insurance coverage.

Resulting from dual incomes, households of married young couples are relatively affluent. They are more likely to spend more on tickets of live performances, expensive clothes, luxury vacations, restaurant meals, and alcoholic beverages, with higher affordability in nice cars, stylish apartments, and high-quality home appliances.

3) Full nest

Full nest I: The term refers to the nuclear family consisting of a father, a mother and children under the age of six. The birth of the first kid to a family leads to many changes in lifestyle and consumption patterns. Needless to say, the category of baby care products is largely purchased, like baby clothes, diapers, furniture, food, and health care products. Due to the wife's withdrawal from the labor force fully or partially, for several months to several years, the household income more or less reduces. In order to offset the decline in the disposable income, adult expenditures like adult apparel, alcoholic beverages and education are reduced. At the same time, choices of vacations, restaurants, and automobiles have to make changes to accommodate young children.

Full nest II: The children in families at this stage are older than six and are more independent. These families have specific needs in education, like lessons of all types (musical instruments, dance, calligraphy, gymnastics, and so on). Other purchases include toys, dental care services, and a wide variety of snack foods. Larger homes and cars are desired due to greater demands for space. Therefore, a considerable financial burden is created, which is somewhat relieved by the likelihood of the wife to pursue her career again as the children enter school. Time spent by both parents in the full-time career during the week, as well as transporting children to multiple events at weekends entail tremendous time pressure. As a result, products and services providing convenience and efficiency would be an appeal to these families and an opportunity for marketers.

4) Empty nest

Independence of the children signifies the family entering the empty nest stage. At the beginning of this stage, both adults typically have jobs, with relatively senior positions in the corporate hierarchy, so they are satisfied with their income and beginning to consider retirement. Dining out, expensive vacations, second homes, and luxury cars can be easily afforded. Home ownership is at its peak at this stage, along with other properties, which is the reason why this segment is a prime market for financial services.

A few years later, either or both of the couple retired, with a considerable income cut. People at this stage are present-oriented, enjoying travel and recreation. Medical appliances and medical-care products are purchased to assist their health, sleep and digestion.

5) Solitary survivor

At this stage, one of the spouses has passed away. The status quo of being older, single and generally retired spawns many particular needs for housing, socialization, travel, and entertainment. They are to some extent worried about security and the economy due to a drastic income reduction.

6) Other types of households

Dual-career families: In China, a large proportion of families consist of couples who both have jobs. In terms of consumer behavior, there are several important implications. To begin with, these families have higher discretionary spending. They tend to spend more than other types of families in childcare, dining out, and services in general. What's more, switching between different roles of work and family doesn't allow much time for cooking, housekeeping, and other domestic activities. As a result, dual-career families particularly value offerings that are efficient and convenient. Maybe this is why ready-to-cook meals take up larger and larger space in the refrigerators in supermarkets. At McDonald's, more than 60 percent of sales come from drive-through customers. In these families, household responsibilities are taken on by many husbands. And in America, a small but growing number of men (as many as two million fathers) stay home to care for children.

Divorce and single-parenthood: The divorce rate in China is getting higher and higher. Even though policies like enforcing a "calm down" period of 30 days have been implemented, many divorces still occur every year. So it's time to face it and find out its implications for lifestyle and consumption pattern. During the transition period of splitting up, consumers go through critical steps like getting rid of old and/or sentimental possessions, forming a new household, and developing new habits of consumption. Remedy shopping and treatment services contribute to forming a new personal identity and relieve a mental burden during and after the divorce. For instance, a recently divorced consumer might purchase a brand new vehicle, furniture, or clothing, get a new hairstyle, or begin going to singles' events.

Divorce also affects the household structure. If the couple didn't have any children, the newly divorced usually adopt the types of single people's purchasing and consumption patterns previously discussed. The only difference is these new singles are perhaps a little bit more mature and have a larger amount of disposable income for accommodation, transportation and fashion. If, on the other hand, there are children involved, divorce would lead to single-parent families. The parent living with the kid(s) has to juggle between his or her career and child rearing, which means that convenience products—such as packaged foods—may become a daily life necessity. In comparison with married parents, there may be a tendency that single parents have lower incomes, spend less on most things, and tend to rent apartments rather than buying a permanent place. Moreover, divorced individuals with children form stepfamilies, which have unique consumption needs, such as duplicate supplies of clothing and other items that children need when spending time in two households.

2.2.2 Family decision-making

1) Household decision roles

Marketers should take into consideration household purchase situations and household decision roles altogether. Individuals are by default regarded as the decision maker and the consumer (user), but when it comes to families, there are additionally three types of possibilities: sometimes there is more than one decider, sometimes there is more than one consumer (user), and sometimes the decider and the consumer (user) are not the same person. The table below shows nine possible relations in family decision-making patterns:

Purchase decision-maker / Purchasing pattern / User	One member	Several members	All members
One member	Possibility #1	#2 badminton bat	Possibility #3
Several members	#4 breakfast	Possibility #5	Possibility #6
All members	Possibility #7	Possibility #8	#9 refrigerator

Based on the analysis of household purchasing roles, the following questions need to be well thought out before formulating marketing strategies aiming at families:

(1) Is the product used by one person or by all family members?

(2) Will one person or the whole family go to buy it?

(3) Is the product expensive? Would the purchase of it has an impact on buying other things?

(4) Are there differences regarding the value of this item? If so, how can the conflicts be reduced?

(5) Can the product to be purchased be used by multiple members in the family? If so, is it necessary to modify or improve the product to satisfy more people's needs?

(6) Which family members would have a direct influence on the purchasing decision of the product? What media or information should be used to convince them?

2) Types of family decision-making

As we know, one particular family member can play different parts in the household purchase decision-making. According to different types of purchases, in different families, the role of decision maker can be completed by different members of the family. Hence, there are four major types of family decision-making: *wife dominant, husband dominant, joint and separate*. The first two types are self-explanatory, while joint decision-making means the couple would discuss and decide together, like buying an apartment or a family car; separate decision-making means the husband or the wife acts as an individual consumer and only considers his or her personal needs, like buying female hygiene products or laptops. What's more, opinions of the kids should not be neglected, which have become increasingly influential as they grow older.

3) Factors determining purchasing roles

Family decision-making patterns don't always remain the same. Changes in some other factors would also influence family purchasing roles. They are:

(1) <u>Product feature</u>: This factor includes the product's price, importance and whether it could be used by other people. If the product's price is so high that it affects other family expenditures, most family members would take part in the decision-making one way or the other. Some unimportant products like toilet paper would not involve the whole family to decide.

Whether the product is sharable also plays a part in the decision-making pattern. For spending on a family sedan or vacation destination, the possibility of collective decision-making is quite high; but when the product is mostly used by a certain member, the decision is basically made by this individual.

(2) <u>Social class</u>: People belonging to different social classes would vary in terms of making decisions. Generally speaking, the style of high-end and low-end families (or established and grassroots families) tend to be independent, while that of middle class families tend to be equal or collective. But as the accumulation of wealth and elevation of the education level, such distinctions would gradually diminish or even disappear.

(3) <u>Family life cycle</u>: As it has been introduced earlier in this chapter, families at different stages have different decision-making patterns. Especially when the children participate more or have more say over the decisions, they have a further influence over the final decision.

(4) <u>Family role allocation</u>: There are particular roles assigned to members of the family, some of which undertake certain responsibilities. The more specific such a role is, the more likely this member makes independent decisions. For example, the wife has a special role in terms of feeding the baby, so she has more autonomy when purchasing infant clothes and foods. Likewise, the husband might be solely responsible for home maintenance, so he can choose whatever he wants when it comes to buying repairing tools.

(5) <u>Personal characteristics</u>: These features include relative power distribution, the level of involvement regarding different types of products, the level of education, etc. When one spouse has considerably more financial power than the other, he or she has bigger rights to make decisions. Alternatively, if one family member is more involved in the domain of certain products, there is a better chance for him or her to influence other members in the family.

Summary

Consumers' purchase decisions are influenced by external factors like different types of information and social relations.

Sources of information can be classified according to whether it's created by marketing activities, and the way it's delivered. The two aspects determine its levels of interactive communication and credibility.

Social relations that affect consumer behaviors are reference group, brand community and key opinion leaders. A reference group is any individual or group in reality or imagination perceived as having significant relevance upon a person's evaluations, aspirations, or behavior. There are primary groups and secondary groups, depending on whether the consumer has a direct personal relationship with them. Reference groups exert informational, utilitarian and value-expressive influences on its group members. Reference groups impose strong power on the brands an individual chooses for the products used in public like cars and clothing. For daily necessities consumed in private settings like toilet paper, the influence of groups on the brands chosen is minimal.

Brand community consists of a group of consumers whose social relationships are based on usage of or interest in a brand or a product. An Opinion Leader is a person who gives advice and information regarding a certain product or service, and can frequently influence others' attitudes and behavior in informal communications. The powers they have on their followers are expert power, knowledge power, credibility power, reference power and social power.

Word-of-mouth (WOM) is information about products and services created and delivered by individuals to others. The three dimensions that determine consumers' engagement in digital WOM in online social networks are connection strength, similarity, and source credibility. Consumers are more likely to seek WOM in categories they are not familiar with. For marketers, WOM serves as the reinforcement of advertising in this era of social media popularization. It's of fundamental importance for marketers to keep track of the sources of negative WOM and adopt positive attitudes when dealing with the situation.

Family can be defined as a group of individuals living together who are related by marriage, blood, or adoption. A broader term might be household, which refers to one person living by himself/herself, or a group of individuals living together in a common dwelling, whether they are related or not. At different phases of the family life cycle, consumers as family units have different buying preferences and consumption patterns. It is necessary for marketers to have a general understanding of the connections between features of each family life stage and corresponding purchase decision-making processes.

There are different situations when it comes to family decision-making process, resulting in various types of decision-making patterns. Marketers should take into consideration household purchase situations and household decision roles altogether. Since the husband and the wife are the major income sources and are both relatively strong and wise among all family members, there are four major types of family decision-making: wife dominant, husband dominant, joint, and separate. Factors determining purchasing roles include the product feature, the social class, the family life cycle, and the family role allocation.

Exercises

(1) Think about every one of your family members, friends, or acquaintances. Could you identify the people who act as opinion leaders, product innovators, and market mavens? Describe what each person does. Give a specific case when this person had some influence on other people's decision-making. Share you observations with the class.

(2) Think about some goods and services that you have purchased recently. Did word-of-mouth communication influence your purchases? To what extent?

(3) Students in groups are assigned with the task of forming or joining a brand community. Decide upon a brand that none of the group members would actually use. Then, search information of the brand widely and post positive comments of the brand among group members. It can be achieved on a message board (贴吧), an online chat room or a Wechat group. After having done this for a set period, group members can discuss how they feel about the brand. Have you purchased any product of the brand or not, do you feel more "loyal"? Have positive attitudes been developed among group members? Do they find themselves engaging in WOM outside the group? Present your findings to the class.

(4) Describe how opinion leaders can be formed and found on the Internet. Analyze and summarize the advantages and disadvantages of using opinion leaders on the Internet. How would this form of opinion leadership be different from any other form of opinion leadership (if at all)?

Case Analysis

Read the following news item. Incorporate your own experience of purchasing via livestream sales, and analyze how online influencers play a part in swaying consumers' decision-making, using the knowledge learned in this chapter.

Short Videos, Livestreaming Redefine Retail

Emotional e-connect overcomes short attention spans of many consumers

In traditional commerce, businesses keenly peddle their merchandise, highlighting features, functionalities and alluring price tags. In short, all eyes are on the products, and the relationship between customers and merchants is as simple as transactional. However, enriching media forms from short videos to livestreaming are rewriting the retail playbook in China. Merchants are elbowing their way to capture people's significantly shortened attention span, and that's when emotional connection kicks in.

"We are witnessing a shift from rack-based shopping to discovery-based shopping, and eventually to trust-based shopping," said Jason Yu, general manager of consultancy Kantar Worldpanel China. "I choose to buy something not necessarily because of the products per se, but because of the person selling it."

This retail "new normal" can be traced back to the early days of livestreaming, a real-time interaction between customers and store owners materialized by technological readiness, that is, smartphones and high-speed internet connections.

For long, livestreaming has remained an obscure practice, which found popularity only in the realm of online gaming. But when Taobao, China's top e-commerce site, introduced the function five years ago, it took off and turned into something of a must for businesses aspiring for a younger generation of consumers. It is believed that new media forms as such stand to offer sellers and influencers a more personal, straightforward way to engage with their audiences.

"I think it comes down to the available supply and the shopping habits of Chinese consumers today." said Zhao Lidong, who oversees product development and content commercialization at Taobao Live. "In China, people are used to consuming hours of content on their smartphones. They embrace innovative tools."

Today, the platform has groomed a handful of influencers, or better known as "hosts" in the online shopping lexicon. Many admit to buying for the sake of supporting, their beloved characters. "Since the height of the COVID-19, I've formed a habit of watching livestreaming session every night and see what I can buy," said Liu Min, a sophomore student in Shanghais, who has spent over 10,000 yuan ($1,553) through livestreaming since last year. "Of course, the deals are good. But the host is more like a big sister, taking care of our daily needs. I don't even bother to go to the supermarket."

The model is now embraced by a growing number of players, who adapt to, and make variations on this influencer-driven shopping in a bid to keep abreast of varying consumer interests.

As the livestreaming industry proliferates, brands can no longer solely rely on key opinion leaders — KOLs or Wang Hong — to market their projects, due to costs and quality control issues. Instead, they employ key opinion consumers — KOCs — who specialize in product reviews for a smaller patch of followers. "KOCs make eminent sense to retailers due to their higher perceived reliability and trustworthiness," said Jennifer Ye, partner and China consumer markets leader at consultancy PwC. "To appeal to younger consumers in China, it is critical for brands to find KOCs that embody the right brand values, and who can reliably connect with target audiences through user-generated content," said Ye, citing the example of Chanel partnering with a local media company to establish a network of micro-influencers.

Peng Jingxuan, 26, who is doing her second master's degree in France, unexpectedly developed a cult following after posting her videos playing guzheng, a traditional Chinese musical instrument, on Bilibili, China's top video portal and community for notably the Generation Z population. During her performance, she dressed up in traditional Chinese costumes and wore makeup in ancient Chinese style. With a fan base of 1.5 million and many of her videos played more than 1 million times each, brands spanning cosmetics to snacking utilize her services. "Because my videos are essentially promoting the rising China cultural tide, I'd favor brands whose brand-positioning aligns with my online persona, namely an advocate of Chinese culture," Peng said of her rationale in choosing merchants to collaborate with. For instance, high-flying snacking brand Three Squirrels and Synear Foods are among the labels that insert their commercials into Peng's videos.

"The key learning from the trend of Guo Chao, or the rising Chinese cultural tide, is that to be culturally relevant, brands need to understand and respond to their audience in a way they can relate to," said Ye.

CHAPTER THREE
Culture and Values

Learning objectives

After learning this chapter, you will be able to:

- understand the influence of culture on consumer behavior;
- explore the relationship between subculture and market segmentation;
- apply particular values to do effective marketing.

Lead-in Case

Yay or Nay? US Fast-Food Giants Now Offer Chinese Regional Food

KFC launched hot-and-dry noodles, also known as reganmian, at more than 100 restaurants in Wuhan, Hubei province, on January 18, 2021. From Chinese burgers to ice cream doused in chili oil, US fast-food giants are infusing their offerings with a Chinese flair. McDonald's and KFC have long localized their menus to appeal to the Chinese palate, but their latest takes on traditional dishes and ingredients seem to be causing quite a buzz, and not always the good kind.

Earlier this year, McDonald's China added roujiamo, a street-food staple from Shaanxi province, to its menu. Known as the "Chinese burger", it's meat sandwiched between two flat buns. The limited-edition special, which the company said was in celebration of the upcoming Lunar New Year, was met with frowns and confused looks. Many said that the roujiamo on offer looked nothing like the advertisement, while others said that the sandwich is a snack and has no place on any breakfast menu. There was also a bit of confusion about how much meat was hiding between the bread —some complained the filling was less-than-generous, and others had no issue with it. But the general consensus seemed that MacDonald's is more gifted at making classic burgers than their Chinese counterpart. "It does not taste good," one customer who introduced herself by her last name Zhang told CGTN. The amount of meat didn't bother her, but she said she prefers her roujiamo from a food stall than a fast food chain.

Undeterred by the negative roujiamo reviews, the Golden Arches on Monday served another dose of controversy. It debuted a "spicy chili oil sundae", which combines a vanilla-flavored soft serve covered in chili oil. The item is part of a new promotional activity whereby McDonald's offers once a month a new creation, first redeemable by members for free using a coupon and then available to the public for a limited period. The sweet-and-spicy dessert was due to be sold in select McDonald's stores, including in Shanghai and Shenzhen, from January 26 to 31. However, the company said Tuesday it is suspending the offer "due to the COVID-19 pandemic" in a statement published on Weibo, a Chinese Twitter-like platform.

The menu addition was predictably divisive. Some were optimistic about the flavor and called it "innovative", others, however, noted that the combination of spice, oil, and ice cream spells bad news for their digestive system.

KFC is also taking the same path as McDonald's. The fast food chain, known for its fried chicken, introduced hot-and-dry noodles to the menus of 100 stores in the dish's birthplace, Wuhan in central China's Hubei province. The noodles, called reganmian, can be ordered alone or as a set, with soy milk, deep-fried dough (or youtiao) and fried eggs. Reganmian is a common go-to breakfast choice for locals in Wuhan, and KFC's version is the result of a partnership between its parent company Yum China and the Hubei Provincial Government to support locally-produced ingredients. The team-up draws on previous efforts to support local farmers and food producers who have been hit by COVID-19, which in China was first recorded in Wuhan, and the subsequent 76-lockdown in early 2020. "Overall, the taste is good," one customer surnamed Bao told CGTN, adding "but a portion is still not enough for one person."

Analysts say that these new concoctions are a way for fast food chains to draw foot traffic following a tough year on the catering industry in 2020 because of the coronavirus pandemic, according to Chinese business outlet Sina Finance. With competition heating up in first- and second-tier cities, out-of-the-box offerings can also help foreign brands stand out in an increasingly crowded fast food space.

Introduction

Undeniably, the increasing globalization is bringing profits for enterprises. However, it also poses unprecedented challenges, for they now have to serve consumers from different cultural backgrounds. Enterprises have developed high cultural awareness and adopted different approaches to reach their target consumers. Sometimes, they succeed; sometimes, they fail. This uncertainty emphasizes the necessity to take culture into consideration in advertising and marketing. In this section, the influence of culture on consumer behavior will be examined first.

Within a national culture, there exist different cultural segments, which are formed based on distinct and homogenous characteristics. They are called *subcultures*. The importance of examining subcultures lies in the fact that they direct advertisers and marketers to the right market segments. There are different types of subcultures:

Gender subcultures: the cultural divisions based on gender roles

Age subcultures: the cultural divisions based on age differences

Geographic and regional subcultures: the cultural divisions based on regional differences

Values are beliefs that exist consistently in a society, widely accepted and hard to change. Values guide people to act properly in a culture and assess the significance of different actions. Consumers, in possession of various values, behave differently. In this section, we will identify a number of core values that carry significant consumption connotations in the Chinese market. They are harmony, filial piety, achievement and success, face, and health.

3.1 Culture and subculture

3.1.1 Culture

What is culture?

A definition of culture seems a prerequisite before we get involved in the discussions about culture and its correlation with advertising and marketing. However, culture is such a pervasive and elusive term that it is not easy to define in an all-inclusive fashion. The policy here is to approach it metaphorically, seeing it as a society's "personality" or the "lens" through which the people in a particular society think, feel and behave. Culture may refer to the tangible objects, such as the cars, clothing and artifacts a society produces. It may also mean intangible ideas and feelings, such as virtues, laws and preference. In terms of consumer behavior, we may see culture as the sum total of learned beliefs, values, and customs that serve to direct the consumer behavior of members of a particular society. (Schiffman, 366)

Beliefs refer to a feeling that something is good/bad, right/wrong, or valuable/valueless. It denotes a person's understanding and judgment of the things concerned. It is usually presented by the mental or verbal statement "I believe..." and leads people to behave correspondingly. For example, with the introduction of the reform and opening up policy, many Chinese people are keen on imported goods, which are perceived to be loaded with the quality secured by advanced technology and the good taste of foreign high fashion.

Those beliefs that exist consistently in a society, widely accepted and hard to change, are values. **Values** help people to determine what actions are best to do or what way is best to live, or to assess the significance of different actions. For instance, some Chinese advertisers are actually inviting consumers to buy home-made products when they put forward the slogan "爱用国货" (love to use domestic products), which echoes the patriotism held by people. In another case, the increasing awareness of environmental protection effectively prompts people to choose the products that bear environmental concerns in their advertising claims.

If beliefs and values are implicit and need much probing to appreciate, customs are quite overt because they are usually imbedded in people's behavior. Customs include everyday behavior and routine behavior. These

文化可以视作指引某一特定社会成员的消费者行为的习得的信念、价值观和风俗的总和。

价值观帮助人民决定什么行为是最好的，最好的生活方式是什么，或者对不同行为的意义进行评价。

behaviors have to correspond to specific situations. That is, a situation determines whether certain behaviors are acceptable or not. For example, according to the Chinese table manners, adults are supposed to pick up their food with chopsticks, as opposed to the Indians who grab their food by hand.

Although beliefs and values are different from customs in the degree of visibility, they all denote people's behaviors—beliefs and values as guides for behaviors, customs as usual and acceptable ways of behaving. More importantly, as the basic elements of culture, they show how the advertisers may get their target customers to buy their products if and when they can "play" culture well. Nowadays, the increasing exchanges between cultures make it difficult to study culture as it is becoming diffused. At the same time, it is becoming more important to study it because of its pervasive influence on consumer behavior. (Schiffman, 2017: 367)

The influence of culture on behavior is so powerful and natural that people take it for granted. It seems that they do not need to find any justification for doing a certain thing, because they consider it simply the right thing to do. This reveals the fact that people are inextricably immersed in their own culture and it is difficult for an individual to perceive his/her own culture from the perspective of an outsider. It is only when he/she encounters people with different cultural beliefs and practices that an individual begins to appreciate the influence of his/her own culture. People will not understand what they eat, wear and how they greet each other are a cultural phenomenon until they meet people from other cultures who may eat, wear and greet quite differently. For example, while pork is widely served in the families of Chinese Han ethnicity, people of Hui ethnicity avoid pork products. For advertisers, sensitivity to cultural issues plays an important role in the effectiveness of their advertising and marketing efforts, because culture stipulates the underlying dimensions that determine consumer behavior.

What is the function of culture?

Now, it is not difficult to grasp the importance of culture for those interested in consumer behavior. But why can culture assume such an important position? The answer naturally lies in the function of culture. To put it simply, culture is there to satisfy the needs of the people within a society. (Schiffman, 2017: 368) These needs may belong to different realms but can be roughly classified into two categories—personal needs and social needs. Culture, it is safe to say, provides reliable reference by which people behave properly and acceptably while striving to satisfy their needs in a particular situation. For instance, Chinese culture teaches us what to eat for the breakfast (preferably something providing various nutrients "早饭吃好"), the lunch (preferably something offering sufficient calories "午饭吃饱"), the dinner (preferably something easily digestible "晚饭吃少"); how to eat (with chopsticks and/or spoons); and where to eat (at home or a restaurant, not on a street). Besides, people eat different foods for different traditional festivals—Mooncakes for Mid-Autumn Festival, Zongzi for Dragon Boat Festival, to name just a few. Culture also provides standards concerning suitable dress for specific situations (such as what to wear around the house, in a wedding, at a funeral, at a graduation ceremony, or in a business negotiation). However, the dress code keeps changing. According to a BBC report, the last decade has witnessed the trend of casualization of fashion, even in the business world. Trainers, for instance, which used to be forbidden in office, are now enjoying unprecedented popularity in the workplace.

Apart from satisfying personal needs, culture also shapes the framework within which people interact with other members in a society. Primary school pupils in China have long been conducting the practice of standing up to salute their teachers who have just stepped into the classroom. This practice is positively perceived as a way to establish a healthy and beneficial teacher–student relationship. Other examples may include how to give/receive a business phone call, how to treat one's guests, and how to give a gift. Underlying the examples is the fact that culture is a crucial factor to clarify the identity of individuals and nurture their social connections with other members.

What needs to be pointed out is that culture is not static. Instead, it keeps evolving, leading to altered beliefs, values and customs. When they can satisfy the needs of people, they survive and flourish. In contrast, if they fail to yield the expected satisfaction, they will be modified or even replaced by those that are more responsive to the current needs and desires. For example, cosmetic surgery was once considered unacceptable in China because people perceived their body as naturally inherited from their parents. They should keep their body intact, not even leaving a scratch on their hair and skin. This was considered as the beginning of filial piety. "We inherit our body from our parents, including our hair and skin. Not hurting or damaging it is the beginning of filial piety." (身体发肤受之父母, 不敢毁伤,孝之始也) Nowadays, however, the increasing identification with western culture and the prevalent aesthetic assimilation promote more and more females (and males) to undergo major or minor plastic surgeries so as to possess the standard protruding forehead, double-edged eyelids, high nose bridge and pointed chin. As is realized across the country, cosmetic medicine is really a big business. Cosmetic products and services are draining Chinese consumers' purse. Therefore, while the influence of culture on consumer behavior is prominent, it should also be noted that consumers do not wait passively to be manipulated by culture. To some extent, they may actively opt for the beliefs, values and customs that positively and effectively respond to their needs.

In what ways does marketing influence consumer behavior?

By now, we have realized how culture may influence consumer behavior. For the sake of continuous growth in sales, marketers have to monitor the culture of their target market, because culture is the medium connecting products and their potential buyers or users. Only when they know how to use culture to communicate with consumers can they have their products or services purchased. Marketers can adopt two ways to communicate with consumers and thus swing their behavior.

On one hand, they share beliefs, values and customs with consumers. Cultural messages are included in the marketing claims, and then become internalized and popularized among consumers. When the marketing claims echo what has already been in consumers' mind, consumers readily identify themselves with the products or services. A good example is the success of Feihe Milk Powder (飞鹤奶粉), which has recently harvested a 60% sales increase from a stunning slogan "Feihe Milk Powder, 55 years specially developed for the Chinese, more suitable for the Chinese baby physique" (飞鹤奶粉，55年专为中国人研制，更适合中国宝宝体质). How can such a slogan induce mass buying? The secret lies in the fact that the slogan is in line with a common sense among Chinese people, that is, the unique features of a local environment always give special characteristics to its inhabitants (一方水土养一方人) . It is well known among Chinse new mothers that after giving birth, they have to undertake the traditional practice "sitting the month" (postpartum confinement). For a whole month, they have to follow a set of rules such as staying indoors, keeping warm (they are even advised not to take a shower to avoid catching a cold), and taking a warm, light and nutritious diet (this is considered a good way to produce breast milk of high quality). Their western counterparts, however, can enjoy ice cream or go to work as usual, never troubled with postpartum diseases. To most consumers, this contrast between the postpartum practices justifies their identification with the marketing claim that Chinese babies need home-made infant formula. Naturally, consumers are detached from their previous loyalty to the foreign brands like Meadjohnson, Frisocare and Wyeth.

On the other hand, marketers teach beliefs, values and customs to consumers. This strategy is applied frequently to those products or services that involve specialty such as high-tech products and medical consultation. Producers or marketers are usually at a superior position, knowing more and better than consumers. Thus, they automatically have the advantage to influence consumers. For example, over the past serval years, a new form of after-school training item called "child programming" is presented to Chinese parents. For most of them, programming is a very specialized and unfamiliar subject. However, this does not hinder them from spending heavily on it because they are convinced, as they have been promised by the marketing claims, that child programming will ensure a bright future for their children. How did the marketers make it? In a way, parents' superficial knowledge of child programming is taken advantage of. The marketing scheme of this kind usually begins by showing their target consumers the origin of child programming (in Britain and USA, two key developed countries) and its recent development in the west, and then cites some central or local policies concerning child programming to illustrate that children in China need to master this new skill. Let's look at how one of the earliest investors explains his initiation "What led us into the trade is the disciplinary trend in the future of child programming " (我们看重的是少儿编程未来的学科化趋势). It is obvious that the startups are very assertive and they believe they have captured the trend of education. In contrast, consumers' knowledge about it is quite limited. Marketers/Investors, in this case, are the source of information, distributing any message that parents need. To some extent, marketers have become the authority in this field. They will greatly influence consumer behavior. Besides, the prevalent anxiety about education on the part of Chinese parents transform this new trend to a national craze. Another typical example is in the field of telecommunication. Possibly, people can be impressed by what the wireless phone services often stress, such as the clarity of their connection, the nation-wide coverage of their service, or the free long-distance calling, as well as the flexibility of their pricing plans. However, it is not easy to say whether wireless phone subscribers genuinely desire these benefits from their wireless service providers or whether they have been taught by marketers to desire them. In a sense, although specific product advertising may reinforce the benefits that consumers want from the product; such advertising also teaches future generations of consumers to expect the same benefits from the product category. (Schiffman, 2017: 371)(5G)

Then, what is the mechanism that makes "teaching" happen? It is the unique way human beings approach the culture they are living in. While people get hold of innate characteristics like race, sex and skin color the moment they are born, they acquire culture by constant learning. At an early stage of life, they begin to learn beliefs, values and customs from parents, friends and teachers. There are various learning activities like playing toys with other children, going shopping with Mum, or attending a birthday party of a family member. These activities, according to anthropologists, can be categorized into three forms: formal learning in which adults or brothers and sisters teach a younger member to behave properly; informal learning in which a child learns by voluntarily imitating the behavior of others, like a parent, a classmate or even a virtual hero; technical learning in which teachers instruct the child about what should (not) be done, how it should be done, and why it should be done. (Schiffman, 2017: 370) Among them, a firm's advertising and marketing messages can best strengthen informal cultural learning by offering their audience a series of behavior to imitate. For instance, when superstars endorse a product or service, they tend to cause mass buying on the part of thousands of fans who choose to trust and follow their idols. The announcement by Jay Zhou that "Love it? Buy it!" (爱玛电动车，爱就马上行动) makes the Aima electric bicycle once one of the top brands in the market. Jiangzhong Hedgehog Fungus Biscuits even aspires to make people cultivate a new habit by presenting the adverting claim that (猴姑饼干，猴头菇制成，养胃；上午吃一点，下午吃一点。)Through extensive repetition, the desired beliefs, values and customs will be imparted to a much larger population.

How is culture expressed in symbols and rituals?

In order to acquire a common culture, the members in a society need to use a common language to communicate with each other. Marketers also need to communicate with their audience effectively with a language. However, the language they use is somewhat different from what we use in our daily life. They usually use symbols that help convey the desired product images or features. These symbols may be verbal, like the slogans or the print in newspapers or magazines. For instance, "Good Air-Conditioners are made by Gree (好空调，格力造)"; and "Ubiquitious communication facilitated by China Mobile (中国移动让沟通无处不在)." Here, the positive images of Gree and China Mobile are clearly conveyed to consumers by the words. Symbols may also be nonverbal, like texture, color, layout and figures. In the following picture, the feathers and clouds symbolize the soft texture of the pillow. Combined with the moon, stars and the dark blue sky, the picture suggests that owning this pillow will grant you a sound sleep. Besides, the price and channels of distribution symbolically say a lot about products and services. A famous saying "Cheap things are no good. (便宜没好货)" , a kind of common sense in China, for instance, has refrained people from buying goods at a low price. Items at a street fair usually incur people's disdain while those at luxury shops invite people's admiration.

Apart from the verbal or nonverbal symbols, advertisers can use ritualized experiences to communicate with their audience so as to influence their behavior. A ritual is a type of symbolic activity consisting of a series of steps (multiple behaviors) occurring in a fixed sequence and repeated over time. (Schiffman, 2017: 373) Rituals make their presence at every important stage of our life and involve a lot of events, like graduation ceremonies, interviews, and funerals. What matters most to advertisers is that rituals tend to be replete with ritual artifacts (products) that are associated with or somehow enhance the performance of the ritual. (Schiffman, 2017: 373) For example, couplets, fire crackers, family feasts, red pockets, and new clothes are linked to Chinese New Year. What's more, other events, like birthday parties, wedding anniversaries, signing ceremonies, propel the consumption of relevant products and services.

How is culture examined?

When it comes to examining culture, the same difficulty arises, since culture is such a sophisticated and ambiguous term. Depending on different theoretical preferences and standards, people may adopt different approaches to examine culture. A convenient way would be to take into account the common cultural characteristics shared by a particular population and position culture at different levels. First, when the common cultural characteristics are shared by a population from multiple nations, we examine culture at a supernational level. A typical example would be the case of Asian nations. While each Asian country displays features that distinguish it from its neighbors, there is no denying that Confucianism underlies the cultural temperament of many Asian nations like China, Korea, Japan, Singapore, Vietnam, and Mongolia. These nations embrace such core Confucian values as benevolence, righteousness and propriety. Advertisers who aim to influence Asian consumers need to attain a good understanding of Confucianism. Second, when the common cultural characteristics are shared by a population from a particular nation, we examine culture at a national level. We may, for instance, separately explore Chinese culture or American culture. Not surprisingly, a product that appeals to Chinese consumers must be loaded with the cultural expectations of Chinese people while the one that represents American spirit will win Americans' heart. Third, if the common cultural characteristics belong to a population that shares one demographic feature like race, religion, age, sex, occupation and geographic location, we examine culture at a group level. Correspondingly, people may target their advertising and marketing appeals to White/Black consumers, Christian/Buddhist believers, young/old people, male/female buyers and southerners/northerners. These groups may coexist inside a larger cultural community but possess beliefs, values and customs that set them apart from other members of the same society. A full understanding of the various groups enables advertisers to better approach their target customers.

3.1.2 Subculture

It is obvious that culture is responsible for the basic behavioral patterns of a society. However, there exist different segments within this national culture, and one can identify various groups, within the larger society, that possess unique cultural characteristics of their own. These segments are called subcultures. They have distinct beliefs, values, customs and traditions that distinguish them from the larger cultural mainstream. Although the subcultural members follow most of the dominant cultural values and behaviors of the society as a whole, they do manifest some features that are somewhat deviant from the mainstream behavioral patterns and unique to a specific population.

Among the many identifiable subcultures, only some are important in terms of advertising and marketing, because they orientate the advertisers and marketers to the right market segments. For example, cosmetics are usually popular among ladies, household appliances are important for housewives, and supplements draw the attention of the elderly people. Obviously, the product category tends to indicate which particular subculture needs to be explored and proper advertising and marketing campaigns will be launched accordingly. However, the relevance between product category and subcultures are not static but dynamic. For example, although cosmetics are conventionally believed to be appealing exclusively to women, these years have seen the increasing interest of men in them. Even the subcultures themselves are evolving. For instance, in the early days of new China, the average life expectancy of Chinese people was about 40 years, but nowadays, this number has increased to about 70. Thus, the definition of an old age has to be modified according to the social context.

Gender subcultures

In all cultures, males and females are naturally endowed with certain physical characteristics, which are the ground for the assignment of certain personal attributes and social roles. Males, with a stronger physique, are generally expected to be independent, aggressive, dominating and self-confident in almost all societies. They are usually the bread earners in families and leaders in organizations. Females, on the other hand, are supposed to be quiet, submissive, tender, compassionate, tactful and talkative. They have typically been brought up as homemakers, giving birth to children and taking care of the whole family. Nevertheless, individuals may display different levels of masculinity and femininity. Some biological males, for example, may be possessed of feminine traits and even choose to transform their sex to obtain a physical appearance typical of a female. The same is true of some biological females.

Advertisers and marketers should be gender-sensitive. Apparently, many products are typically associated with either males or females. For example, razors, lighters, cigarettes, ties and motorcycles are male products; lipsticks, jewelries, sanitary towels and miniskirts are products for females. However, gender typing is losing its grip and many products now are attracting consumers from the opposite sex. For example, the boyfriend style is receiving favor from some women; plastic surgeries are no longer foreign to men.

The male or female market segment is not as homogenous as we may believe. A typical example is the subtle segmentation of the female market. With the development of society, especially the awakening of feminine consciousness, advertising and marketing strategies cannot neglect female consumers. Currently, they are not only spenders, but also earners and participants or decision makers of household budget. Some researchers have identified four significant female market segments: the traditional housewife who prefers to stay at home, feels supported by family, and is generally content with her role; the trapped housewife who prefers to work outside but has to stay at home due to family duties and has mixed feelings about the current status and is concerned about lost opportunities; the trapped working woman who, married or single, prefers to stay at home but has to work for economic necessity, feels conflict about her role, and is proud of her financial contribution to the family; the career working woman who, married or single, prefers to work, derives satisfaction and meaning from employment rather than home and family, and feels pressed for time.

Every year, more and more products and services are targeted at women. In China, online shopping, paired with massive campaigns, seems to have set off a frenzy of consumption on the part of women. Some promise youth and beauty, like skin care products, cosmetics and slimming products. Some help to facilitate household maintenance, such as high-tech kitchen utensils and domestic services. Despite the similar consumption tendency, working women spend less time shopping than nonworking women. They economize their time by shopping less often and by being brand and store loyal. They are also likely to shop during evening hours and on weekends, as well as to buy through direct-mail catalogue. (Schiffman, 2017: 419) Recognition of the different consumer behavior within the female market usually indicates effectiveness and profitability.

Age subcultures

It is not difficult to understand why age grouping is a critical factor in advertising and marketing. In all societies, young people display different physical and social characteristics from older members. They are more energetic, rebellious and eager to show their uniqueness. For example, they listen to different music and dress differently from their parents and grandparents. A few age cohorts have been identified as subcultures because they are associated with unique shared values and behaviors. An age cohort, or a generation, is a group of people who are born and brought up over a relatively short and continuous period of time, and thus share similar social, political, historical and economic experiences. In this section, we will explore the youth market and the mature market, respectively.

Youth is widely celebrated as the source of creation and revolution. Among those who can be labeled as young, there are usually tweens, teenagers and college students. The global youth market contains substantial profits. Tweens are those standing between childhood and adolescence, and they possess characteristics of both age groups. In public, they may act like cool teenagers but in private, they resume their childish characteristics. They are mostly interested in clothes, CDs, movies, and other products that make them feel right. To communicate with tweens is quite challenging because they are not children but not yet adults, or even real teenagers. Teenagers are transmitting from childhood to adulthood. This transmission is both exciting and confusing. It is exciting because one will soon assume the role of an adult. It is confusing due to the uncertainty of self. It is urgent that they find cues for the right way to look and behave. Peers and advertisements serve as the ready reference. Teenagers have to cope with problems like insecurity, parental authority and peer pressure. Their life is characterized by a series of conflicts:

- Autonomy versus belonging—Teens need to acquire independence, so they try to break away from their families. However, they need to attach themselves to a support structure, such as peers, to avoid being alone.

- Rebellion versus conformity—Teens need to rebel against social standards of appearance and behavior, yet they still need to fit in and be accepted by others. They prize "in-your-face" products that cultivate a rebellious image.

- Idealism versus pragmatism—Teens tend to view adults as hypocrites, whereas they see themselves as being sincere. They have to struggle to reconcile their view of how the world should be with the realities they perceive around them.

- Narcissism versus intimacy—Teens tend to be obsessed with their appearance and needs. However, they also feel the desire to connect with others on a meaningful level. (qtd from Solomon, 2018: 349)

Teenagers have developed their own consumption style. For example, most teenagers prefer to wear modern casual dresses, sports shoes of known brands, want to own autos that project a macho image, listen to pop music, and watch MTV. They spend family money and often influence family purchases. For many products, friends are the most significant influence. Nevertheless, parents are still an important factor affecting many buying decisions. Their brand and store preferences tend to be enduring. This market is particularly attractive to marketers because preferences and tastes formed during these years can significantly influence purchases throughout their life. To influence them as consumers, marketers need to use appropriate language, music, images, and media. College students capture the interest of advertisers and marketers because of their great buying power. It is reported that every year American students spend about $11 billion on snacks and beverages, $4 billion on personal care products, and $3 billion on CDs and tapes (Solomon, 2018: 352). Different from teenagers, who somewhat depend on parents to make purchase decisions, college students have developed independent consumption styles because they are finally away from home. Researchers believe that during the college years, they are willing to try new products and the formation of desired brand loyalty is promising. However, advertisers and marketers have to understand that college students cannot be reached through conventional media such as newspapers. Nowadays, going online via smart phones is commonplace among college students. So online advertising is very effective.

Old age is traditionally associated with wrinkles, grey hair, clumsy motion, chronic diseases, loneliness, poverty, and dwindling purchasing desires. Nevertheless, this stereotype has to be altered. With the development of economy and medical science, populations around the world are enjoying longer life span and better physical conditions. An elderly person, currently, is one who is curious about what life means, interested in buying good-quality products and services and loyal to favorite brands for years. Some are engaged in the daily care of grandchildren or short-term hired labor, and some are devoted to volunteer work. Considering the large sum of discretionary income they own, they constitute a profitable market. They spend generously on exercise facilities, skin treatments, vacations, financial products, and even university courses to enhance their retirement life. Behind this thriving grey market is a belief that age is not a state of body but of mind. When it comes to longevity and quality of life, it is not one's chronological age but his/her mental outlook that really matters. Thus, perceived age, or how old one feels about himself/herself, is a more appropriate standard to judge one's overall state of being. Many marketers, aware of this, will focus on product benefits, rather than the claim that the product is suitable to a particular age. As a matter of fact, many elderly people opt not to buy the products targeted at their chronological age. Marketers who want to communicate successfully with mature consumers have to grasp their psyche. The following key words deserve special attention: autonomy (mature consumers want to lead active lives and to be self-sufficient); connectedness (mature consumers value the bonds they have with friends and family), and altruism (mature consumers want to give something back to the world). (Solomon, 2018: 357)

Geographic and regional subcultures

Populations distributed in different geographic and regional areas may display distinct and homogenous lifestyles, needs, tastes, and values, thus forming various geographic and regional subcultures. Take China as one example. China, with a vast territory, includes a wide range of climatic and geographic conditions that give rise to various natural environments and resources. Generations living in a particular area have developed unique local preferences in food and drink. For example, peppers are the key ingredient in Sichuan cuisine not because people there are addicted to the burning pain, but because peppers can help the human body to repel moisture that penetrates the mountainous province.

It is simply natural that many people have developed a sense of regional identification. For instance, in China, they may call themselves or others as southerners or northerners. These labels are usually helpful in portraying and understanding the person in question. For advertisers, geographic and regional subcultures usually indicate different consumption behaviors. In China, southerners prefer rice while northerners prefer wheaten food. Heating equipment sells well in the north but rarely arouses interest in the south, especially in the subtropic or tropic provinces like Guangdong, Guangxi and Hainan. Regional differences also indicate brand preferences. According to a report posted on Sohu, the most popular car brands in Guangdong are Dongfeng Nissan, Guangqi Honda, FAW Toyota, and Guangqi Toyota; those in Shandong are Shanghai Volkswagen, FAW Volkswagen, SAIC, and SGMW.

Geographic and regional subcultures are also associated with the consumption patterns of urban and rural areas. In China, a substantial gap has been in existence between urban and rural residents in terms of income, consumption level and consumption structure. Although the distance is decreasing, due to the overall economic development and the poverty alleviation policy oriented at impoverished areas, urban and rural residents prioritize different consumption items. According to a research by Li Nana and others, from 2006 to 2015, rural residents spend more on food and clothing than their urban counterpart whose expenditure on housing is currently increasing. They have also found that rural areas have witnessed a sluggish increase of the expenditure on household appliances, transportation, telecommunication, entertainment and education; but in rural areas, medicine and health care account for a larger proportion of the total expenditure than in urban areas. These observations offer cues for how advertisers and marketers may successfully reach their rural and urban audiences.

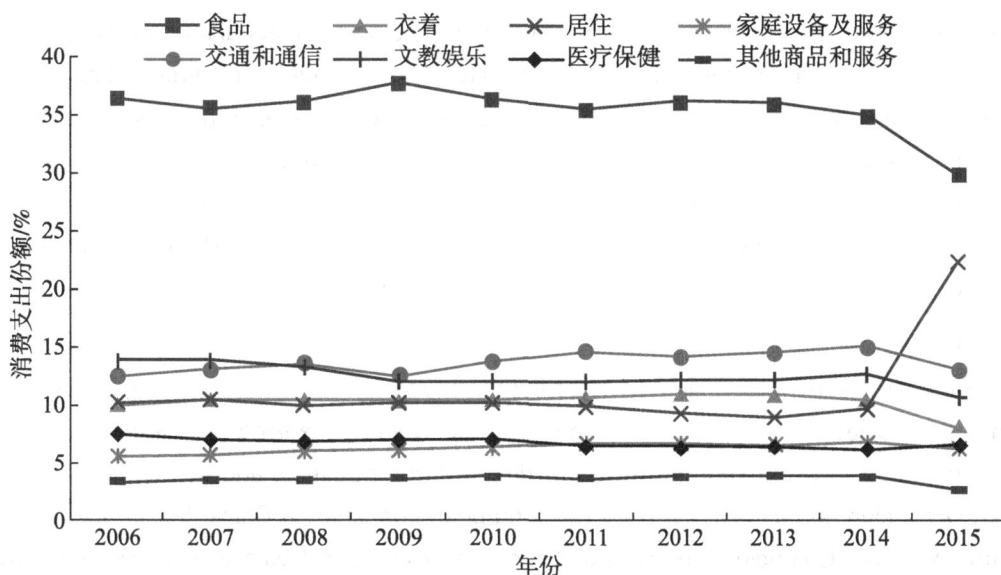

图 3-1 2006—2015 年城镇各类消费支出份额

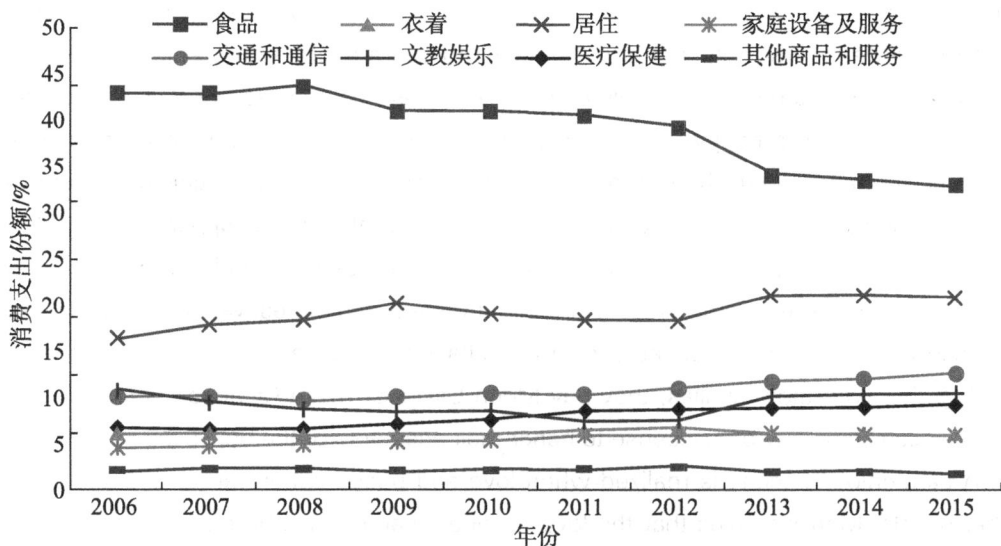

图 3-2 2006—2015 年农村各类消费支出份额

3.2 Values

In this section, we explore how Chinese culture is correlated with consumer behavior. We will identify a number of core values that both reflect and affect Chinese society and culture. However, this is not an easy task to accomplish. The reasons are as follows: First, China, with its huge population and 55 ethnicities, is a diverse country, within which people hold various and even conflicting beliefs, values and customs. Second, cultural values are evolving. Values that used to be dominant may be losing their popularity among people as time goes by. Finally, the introduction of cultural characteristics of other countries, to some extent, makes some Chinese values blurred and vague. For example, being reserved, traditionally perceived to be a Chinese value, is somewhat foreign to the post-90s youngsters. They have been encouraged to and also learned to express themselves explicitly. The values that will be examined are pervasive, enduring and consumption related. Some values are unique to Chinese culture and others are widely embraced in the world.

Harmony

Harmony means "proper and balanced coordination between things". (Zhang Lihua) This kind of coordination means the balanced relation between humankind and nature; between people and society; between members of different communities; and between mind and body. As a high social ideal, harmony has long been cherished in China. In the Spring and Autumn Period, Confucius proposed that the role of Li (rituals) was to maintain harmony among people (礼之用，和为贵). Harmony, in this case, is the sublime goal people strive for. In daily life, it has been taken as a guiding principle for social interaction. Even conflicts may dissolve when the parties involved resort to the principle of harmony. In advertising and marketing, products and services that strengthen social bonds and accord with the spirit of harmony may attract a large audience.

Harmony originates from the peace of family. As the saying goes, a peaceful family will prosper (家和万事兴). Chinese people believe a harmonious family is the key to a worthwhile life. In advertising, it is not unusual to see a happy family enjoying a certain product and strengthening the family bonds. Real estate companies, for example, usually project the ideal of a happy family into their marketing designs and thus render their audience to identify with them immediately. Besides, the growth of children, a mutual understanding of couples, keeping pets, company of parents, or the support for the elderly are often presented in advertising to create the desired security and warmth of family. Traditional festivals, especially Mid-Autumn Festival and Spring Festival, see how the ideal of a harmonious family influences consumer behavior—they travel thousands of miles to get together with their families; they buy Moon Cakes or make Chinese dumplings; they stick red couplets; they burn incense to honor their ancestors or the deceased.

A harmonious society is realized when love and peace within family is extended to other people. Mencius holds that the love for one's parents can be extended to the love for the people, then to everything (亲亲而仁民，仁民而爱物). This idea, in a way, advocates universal love on the part of all the social members. It is still having its impact on modern

China. In advertising, brotherhood, a form of universal love, is a popular theme. In China, Chinese spirits is an important medium to build and maintain connections among males. A famous saying, "good friends, bottoms up (感情深，一口闷)", is often heard when one is at the table and endeavors to attain the recognition of his counterpart. Sharing the joy of success and celebrating everlasting friendship often appear in the advertising claims.

Filial piety

Filial piety means being dutiful to parents. When they are alive, one should take care of them; when they pass away, one should mourn them according to local customs. This duty stems from the profound relationship that has been established during the early childhood of a person. As The *Analects* says, "a child should not leave his parents' bosom until he is three years old (子生三年，然后免于父母之怀). Parents give birth to children, bring them up, educate them, and lead them to the journey of life. Naturally, they should be rewarded for what they have done for their children. Mostly, the reward may take the form of financial, material and emotional support from children. Sometimes, obedience on the part of children is also required. According to Confucius, "the greatest love for people is the love for one's parents (仁者，人也，亲亲为大)". Until today, filial piety is conceived to be the most fundamental virtue of a person. In the Chinese market, there are plenty of products and services that help people to conduct filial piety.

Concerned with their parents' well-being and health, consumers are willing to buy them products or services that are said to be conducive to their physical and mental state. Among the most popular items are clothing, accessories, home healthcare products, and supplements. Some people send their parents on a package tour and others reserve physical examinations for parents. Interestingly, China has got a special day to honor the elderly—Double Ninth Festival. Although not all the parents are old enough to be categorized as "elderly", this festival offers a good opportunity for people to show their love and gratitude to parents. Around this day, a great number of consumers involve themselves in gift purchasing. Besides, Mothers' Day and Fathers' Day, though imported from the west, have also promoted consumption in the Chinese market. These two days have won the heart of Chinese consumers partly because they have been properly localized and partly because their connotations somewhat embody filial piety.

When parents pass away, grand funerals, especially those in rural places, are commonplace. This will propel massive consumption. It is believed that the deceased will live another life in the underworld and thus need all the necessities as the alive. This notion brings consumers to the funeral supply stores to buy the required items. In many places, buying and selling graveyards with favorable fengshui (or geomantic omen, an old belief that the location and structure of the grave might influence the fortune of the deceased and the family) has become a thriving business. What is more, funerals offer a scenario to manifest the social networks developed by the deceased. Apart from family members, neighbors, relatives, friends, colleagues, and classmates are also present. So a series of receptions will be held. The consumption of foods, drinks, vegetables and fruits are predictable. For some people, grand funerals represent their close connection to and reluctant departure from their deceased parents; for others, funerals provide the chance to declare to the public that they are conducting the conventional practice of loving parents. In either case, filial piety, a deep-rooted cultural value, has a great impact on consumption.

Achievement and success

Different from Daoism, which is characterized by reclusion from the secular world, Confucianism advocates engagement in social activities. A motto by Mencius, "Preserve your dignity as a nobody; promote the social welfare as a somebody"(穷则独善其身，达则兼济天下), appeals men of insight to involve themselves in the well-being and development of the whole society. The Confucian doctrine of cultivating a moral self, regulating a decent family, administrating a righteous state and making a peaceful world(修身、齐家、治国、平天下), has been a standard against which the worth of a person is determined. Those who have played a role in the social dynamics are perceived to have realized their value. While devoting themselves in the social activities, they obtain the social recognition, and this is taken as the genuine achievement.

In old times, one's position in the bureaucratic institution indicated the height of his achievement. The higher his official position was, the more successful he was. The official position may be inherited from one's ancestors, or obtained because of one's battlefield feats. Academic success may send one to the top of the social ladder, too. The imperial civil examination system has served as an efficient approach to select governmental officials. Since the Ming and Qing Dynasties, good command of Confucian classics was the prerequisite for one's political success. Even today, it is still widely accepted that he who excels in study can follow an official career(学而优则仕). The college entrance examination has helped thousands of people to ascend to higher classes or at least secure their current class. Pursuit for academic success has greatly impacted advertising styles and consumer behavior. Infant formulas never fail to remind their audience of the intelligence-stimulating substances they contain. The early education centers that are targeted at young children claim their courses will enhance the balanced development of the brain. After-school classes are providing rich resources to improve the examination scores of your children. Parents are never reluctant to pay the bills. Anyway, overwhelmed by the eagerness for academic achievement, the whole society seems to have entered a large-scale intelligence competition.

Since the introduction of the reform and open-up policy in 1978, China has developed into the second largest economy in the world. Over the years, the standard for one's achievement has been shifted to economic success. Those that have gained substantial wealth are considered to be capable and respectable. This influences consumption a lot. People believe that, after years of hard work, they deserve high-quality products and services. The advertising claims, like "You owe it to yourself" or "You worked for it", are quite seditious to consumers. Purchase of material or spiritual comfort is like a compensation for their previous hardships.

Face

The term "face" possesses rich and subtle connotations, among which self-esteem and unwillingness to admit one's own disadvantage cannot be neglected. In reality, it is a very subjective experience, because what denotes value and dignity for one person may be insignificant for others. It is notable that people care for their face only when confronted with acquaintances. Presence of strangers does not cause concerns for face. Chinese people are so obsessed with face that it has almost become a national pet phrase. What has given rise to this obsession? Many cultural researches have attributed it to collectivism, a deep-seated belief in China. High interdependence is universally admitted among social members, producing the interdependent self, as opposed to the independent self nurtured by individualism. Individuals, living in a complicated social network, depend on others to clarify their identity. They are much concerned about who they are in the eyes of other people. They strive to establish a positive image, acquire wide recognition and get a favorable position in communities. What they fear most is to be despised by fellows. So, they may disguise the negative aspects of their personality and life.

Face has greatly influenced consumption in the Chinese market. A typical example is conspicuous consumption, lavish or wasteful spending thought to enhance social prestige. Many consumers choose items with conspicuous famous brand logos because this allows them to display symbolically their economic and social power. For example, numerous consumers are crazy for handbags with eye-catching logos of Hermès, Louis Vuitton and Chanel. Some, with a limited budget, even opt for counterfeit products. What's more, super-luxury wristwatches, cars, yachts and private jets have won the heart of the new rich in China. The real estate market has never failed to witness the thriving selling and buying of mansions. High-end artistic exhibitions are the dream destinations of those who expect to cultivate an elite taste. The sky-high price is not a burden but a threshold across which one will be identified as a member of the distinguished class. Chinese people not only gain face for themselves but they also grant face to other people by giving them luxurious gifts. Receiving luxurious gifts, as a matter of fact, indicates that the receiver has been admitted into the exclusive circle. Anyway, consumption of luxurious products is linked to the prominence Chinese people give to the value of face.

Health

Chinese people have long been preoccupied with fitness and health. The First Emperor of Qin is said to have been obsessed with the idea of immortality. According to a legend, he once sent thousands of virgin boys and girls, led by the alchemist Xu Fu, to the islands of Penglai, Fangzhang and Yingzhou, to search for elixirs. Unfortunately, his dream had never been realized. Although modern Chinese people never hope for immortality, the eagerness for health and longevity has always been in existence. The advertising claims that attract a large audience are probably associated with fitness and health.

With the passage of time, the traditional Chinese medicine (TCM) has gradually developed into a standard set of principles and practices, that have been proved to be functional in both treatment and prevention. For thousands of years, Chinese people have been guided by TCM and survived numerous fatal diseases. Today, when it comes to health and longevity, TCM still influences consumer behaviors. First, edible and medicinable plants are introduced into Chinese diets, because Chinese people believe in homology of medicine and food. Housewives are familiar with the function and medicinal value of common ingredients in their kitchens. For example, Chinese dates nourish blood and mung beans reduce internal heat. In the Cantonese supermarket, it is not unusual to find shelves loaded with medicinal plants for making soup. Second, Chinese medicine physiotherapy centers are widely embedded in residential communities. The most common services offered are acupuncture, massage, moxibustion, and Guasha. Third, healthcare guides and lessons are in great demand. There are many professional publications on Chinese health preservation. Some newspapers and magazines offer healthcare tips to attract more readers. The registration for online and offline courses on Chinese health preservation is on the increase.

Recently, while enjoying the benefits of thriving economy, Chinese people have been brought under unprecedented pressure. Cases of death from overwork are often reported. Besides TCM, people begin to resort to modern medical or healthcare products and services. They buy household medical equipment like sphygmomanometers and glucometers; they buy organic food; they consider the content of calory and sugar while making their purchase decisions. Many people are taking supplements to cope with their subhealth. Others go to the fitness clubs or gyms regularly.

Summary

Culture can be regarded as the sum total of learned beliefs, values, and customs that serve to direct the consumer behavior of members of a particular society. Within a national culture, there exist different cultural segments called subcultures, which are formed based on distinct and homogenous characteristics. Beliefs, values and customs are factors influencing consumers to choose what ways to satisfy their needs. Culture provides reliable reference by which people behave properly and acceptably while striving to satisfy their needs in a particular situation. Apart from satisfying personal needs, culture also shapes the framework within which people interact with other members in a society.

Culture keeps evolving rather than remaining static, leading to altered beliefs, values and customs, one typical example is the acceptance of cosmetic surgery, which contradicts the traditional value of keeping your body intact as a way of respecting nature and your parents.

Marketers can adopt two ways to communicate with consumers and thus swing their behavior. On one hand, they share beliefs, values and customs with consumers. Cultural messages are included in the marketing claims, and then become internalized and popularized among consumers. On the other hand, they teach beliefs, values and customs to consumers. This strategy is applied frequently to those products or services that involve specialty such as high-tech products and medical consultation. Producers or marketers are usually at a superior position, knowing more and better than consumers. Thus, they automatically have the advantage to influence consumers.

Members in a society need to use a common language to communicate with each other in order to acquire a common culture. Marketers also need to communicate with their audience effectively with a "language", which are usually symbols that help convey the desired product images or features. Apart from the verbal or nonverbal symbols, advertisers can use ritualized experiences to communicate with their audience so as to influence their behavior.

Depending on different theoretical preferences and standards, people may adopt different approaches to examine culture. A convenient way would be to take into account the common cultural characteristics shared by a particular population and position culture at different levels.

Subcultures have distinct beliefs, values, customs, and traditions that distinguish them from the larger cultural mainstream, only some of which are important in terms of advertising and marketing, because they orientate the advertisers and marketers to the right market segments. Gender subcultures, age subcultures, and geographic and regional subcultures all possess distinctive characteristics and have significant implications for marketers.

Harmony, filial piety, achievement and success, face and health are essential values upheld by most Chinese, which are pervasive, enduring and consumption-related.

Exercises

(1) The debate on the status of TCM and Western medicine is getting more heated recently. Simultaneously, health awareness of Chinese people is on the increase. Which medicine will you adopt to maintain your health? Why? How, do you think, should the advertisers and marketers adjust their strategies to meet consumers' demands for better health conditions?

(2) Interview two or more people from two different foreign cultures. Ask them what major differences they see between the cultural values in their country and those in the Chinese culture. Ask the students to explain these to the class.

(3) Groups of students compare a list of rituals that will probably be performed (or that were performed) at their friends' or families' wedding ceremony and reception. What are the marketing implications of these rituals? Another important question might be asked: How are wedding plans affected when people from different subcultures get married?

Case Analysis

Observe the hanfu culture among your friends and on social media platforms, and summarize the characteristics of this trend. Suppose you were the owner of a Taobao store specializing in hanfu, how would you devise your advertising and marketing strategies to attract more college students? Present your findings and strategies to the class.

Classical Dress on the Rise Notably with Gen Z

Women in traditional hanfu attire take a selfie at Nanjing Forestry University, March 22, 2018.

China's hanfu market has been attracting big investment in recent years, as the sector finds increasing favor with young consumers. Hanfu, the traditional clothing worn by the Han ethnicity for thousands of years, is growing in popularity as Chinese people become more confident about their national culture.

This is causing capital to flow into the hanfu sector. In April, Shanghai-based hanfu manufacturing enterprise Shisanyu completed a financing round of over 100 million yuan ($15.72 million). The company said that with the investment, it plans to continue to promote traditional Chinese culture and expand the product chain. Likewise, the Chengdu-based hanfu brand CNWear and Hangzhou-based hanfu retail platform Dozen Sunshine, received investments in September and November, respectively. Dozen Sunshine said that the investment will be used to establish new physical stores and expand its supply chain.

An increasing number of hanfu enthusiasts are driving the investment surge. A recent report from Guangzhou-based consultancy iiMedia Research said China's hanfu-related industry maintained rapid growth in 2020, with the number of hanfu fans rising by over 70 percent on an annualized basis between 2017 and 2020.

Among surveyed hanfu consumers, 40.5 percent purchased hanfu products because they were fascinated by the cultural origins, 36.9 percent of consumers purchased them because of the appearance of the clothing, while 33.6 percent hoped to carry forward traditional Chinese culture, said the report.

With the rapidly expanding market, industry players are actively looking to diversify their product portfolios by making inroads in areas such as hanfu experience houses, integrating daily wear with hanfu elements and hanfu-themed animations, comics and games. For example, Shisanyu teamed up with Tencent's popular smartphone-based video game King of Glory, NetEase's role-playing game Justice Online and Chinese TV drama Serenade of Peaceful Joy, and launched co-branded hanfu. It also inked a deal with West Lake scenic spot officials in Hangzhou, Zhejiang province, and established a brick-and-mortar experience hall.

"In recent years, the hanfu sector has evolved into a greater one. Hanfu-related industries include activities like wearing hanfu, hanfu cosmetics, hanfu picture taking and traditional Chinese etiquette training. The hanfu-related scenarios have extended to shopping malls, scenic spots, hotels and wedding ceremonies," Tian Tian, founder of a hanfu media platform, said during an interview with Economic View, a new media platform of China News Service.

CHAPTER FOUR
Sensation and Perception

Learning objectives

After learning this chapter, you will be able to:

- identify sensation and perception in customer behavior;
- know the factors influencing customer perception;
- understand the three-stage process of perception;
- make marketing strategies with customer perception.

Lead-in Case
The Secret Recipe of HeyTea's Buzz in China

It is nothing unusual to see hundreds of customers waiting in queues for globally anticipated products such as the latest iPhone. However, the Chinese brand HeyTea had convinced clients to line up for more than five hours—and for quite a different type of product: tea with cheese-topping.

Since February 2017, HeyTea's buzz in China has changed the brand into a phenomenal food trend. The brand's turnover has reached, in average, over 1 million yuan per month per store—roughly 2000 cups per day. The highest turnover is realized in a single Shenzen shop, at 1.5 million to 1.7 million yuan per month. So, what made those consumers stand hours in line for a cup of HeyTea?

China's middle class has become richer. They are increasingly willing to pay more for brand names, differentiated features, and higher quality. Younger consumers are more curious than their parents. As they have more choices than previous generations have ever seen, they are often willing to try new experiences, technologies, platforms, and foreign brands or products. This observation is especially true for the dinning industry. Consequentially, one of the best ways to emerge above competitors in the food and drink sector is to place emphasis on forging not just a product, but a new experience. HeyTea's strategy aimed to incite in consumers a sense that they are privileged. This strategy successfully meets Chinese Millennials' expectations for food and beverages. The founder of HeyTea, Nie Yunchen understood this pattern, and in order to create HeyTea's buzz in China, he attempted to develop the impression of a novel experience surrounding HeyTea beverages.

One of its popular drinks is a tea with two layers, composed 20 percent of a cream cheese topping and 80 percent of a green or fruit tea-base. The cream layer is sometimes sweet, sometimes salty and sometimes sprinkled with salt, flower sprinkles or chocolate powder, etc. To enhance the sensory experience of trying a new beverage, an eye-catching packaging has also been developed. Through a transparent cup, the customer is able to observe two differently coloured layers, sometimes topped by mint leaves. The only thing that is truly new to this product, however, is its adjustable plastic cover. This design allows the consumer to concurrently savour both layers of the tea, thus maximizing the product's taste. In stores, employees were instructed to ask the new customers if they knew how to drink the brand's teas before serving them. According to the brand, its tea is supposed to be tasted in a certain way. Stirring or using a straw, for instance, is not recommended. This way of drinking is also recommended by the brand, as it creates a mustache of cream on the consumer's upper lips. Through the experience of a new product, the brand sought to make customers feel as if they are a part of something big.

Moreover, HeyTea has managed to boost the perceived value of its products through intangible features. Its menu has been revised by changing some of the item names to bring a brand new experience to customers. For example, a product previously named "Cheese and milk green tea" (芝士奶霜绿茶) is later called "Green beauty" (绿妍). Similarly, each of the brand's products was given a "fancier" new name in place of their more descriptive former names.

The brand reached exceptional popularity in Shanghai and Shenzhen, the success of which is likely a result of the KOL groups' influence. HeyTea has obtained credibility and visibility by relaying word of their unique product online. Then, the brand supported its high product pricing by locating its stores in top-quality malls associated to luxury brands. Together, these marketing strategies successfully solidified the brand's image of merit in the minds of consumers. As a result, many consumers are incentivized to share photographs of their experience on social media, adding to the popularity of the brand in China. This strategy succeeded in attracting buyers to line up in front of HeyTea shops, realizing the online buzz in Shanghai.

In China, it is common for social media "friends" to discuss their purchases with each other even if they may not be familiar in real life. This occurrence motivated Chinese netizens to share pictures as they shop, which in turn led to trends that created sizable queues in front of stores. While the long wait for a single product may come across as unusual to the foreigner, many Chinese consumers view the practice as a statement of their social status and fancy lifestyle.

Introduction

In the case of HeyTea, we can see a totally fresh and enjoyable experience can be the key driver for Chinese young consumers to try, follow and share. The impact on sensations is all-around: the taste of the tea or fruit juice, the look of the double layers through a transparent cup, the texture of the cheese topping, the smell of the combined fragrances of natural ingredients. What's worth mentioning is that HeyTea keeps launching seasonal new items to maintain popularity among young consumers, e.g. cheery and tea slush with cheese topping, longan mixed with rice wine topped with cream sprinkled with osmanthus, which are perceived as trendy and novel. This constitutes another essential element for the success of HeyTea: the new product is eye-catching material to post on social media, indicating the people who share it are the trend setters. All of these add up to the image of a brand constantly bringing newness and uniqueness to consumers, which caters for young people's pursuit of particularity in the food and beverage category.

4.1 Sensation

4.1.1 What is sensation?

Sensation is a mental process (such as seeing, hearing, or smelling) resulting from the immediate external stimulation of a sense organ, which is often distinct from conscious awareness of the sensory process. A stimulus may be any unit of input to any of these senses. In the daily life, there are many stimuli affecting our sensory system. Various sensations impact the brain through the process of nervous system. In the field of consumer behavior, products, packages, brand names, advertisements and commercials are the common marketing examples of stimuli.

Imagine your phone rings. You take it out and see that it's an unfamiliar number. You're wary of telemarketers, but you're also procrastinating doing homework, so you pick up the call anyway. You hear a voice say, "hello"; you perceive that the voice is your friend Philip's. He explains that he's calling from a different number because his phone is dead, and you make plans to see a movie. Even though you didn't recognize the number Philip is calling from, you heard his voice and recognized it as his. Hearing his voice was sensation; recognizing it was perception. Sensation is passively receiving information through sensory inputs, and perception is interpreting this information.

Sensory organs have at least 5 categories, which are vision (our eyes), sound (our ears), taste (our tongues), touch (our skin), and taste (our noses). Although sensation is a simple psychology phenomenon, it plays a vital role in human's psychology activities. We use our sensory organs to get senses: seeing, hearing, smelling, touching and tasting, which is our proprioception to be aware of the body's motions and position. All of these senses give us information (sensation) which our brains have to interpret (perception).

4.1.2 The categories of sensation

Sensation can be categorised as external senses and internal senses. **The external senses** are seeing, hearing, smelling, tasting, and touching. **The internal senses** are common sense, memory (storage and retrieval of information), imagination, and evaluation. We will mainly introduce five external senses related closely with consumer behavior.

1. Vision

Vision is the special sense by which the qualities of an object (such as

> **感觉：**是外部即时刺激作用于感觉器官导致的精神过程（如看见、听见或闻到），通常有别于感官过程有意识的感知。

> **外部感觉：** 包括视觉、听觉、嗅觉、味觉和触觉。
>
> **内部感觉：** 包括常识、记忆（信息的存储和回溯）、想象力和评价。

color, luminosity, shape, and size) constituting its appearance are perceived through a process in which light rays entering the eye are transformed by the retina into electrical signals that are transmitted to the brain via the optic nerve. Vision is the most complicated, sophisticated and principal sense in both human beings and other creatures. Marketers apply visual stimuli to communicate and convey advertising information frequently. A product's package such as colour, shape and size are conducted to consumers through the visual channel.

Colour, equipped with important sensory connotation, can influence our emotional feelings directly. Some primal color associations remain and are deeply powerful, while others are relatively new and exciting. Colors in the red area of the color spectrum are known as warm colors, including red, orange, and yellow. These warm colors evoke emotions ranging from feelings of warmth and comfort to feelings of anger and hostility. For example, scientists believe that red associates with arousal as well as power in the human mind unconsciously. Colors on the blue side of the spectrum are known as cool colors and include blue, purple and green. These colors are often described as calm, but can also call to mind feelings of sadness or indifference. Blue is believed to soothe illnesses and treat pain for instance.

Studies have shown that colors can impact people in various ways. Black uniforms are more likely to receive penalties. Additionally, students were more likely to associate negative qualities with a player wearing a black uniform according to a study that looked at historical data of sports teams and what they were dressed. While the color red is often described as threatening, arousing or exciting, many previous studies on the impact of

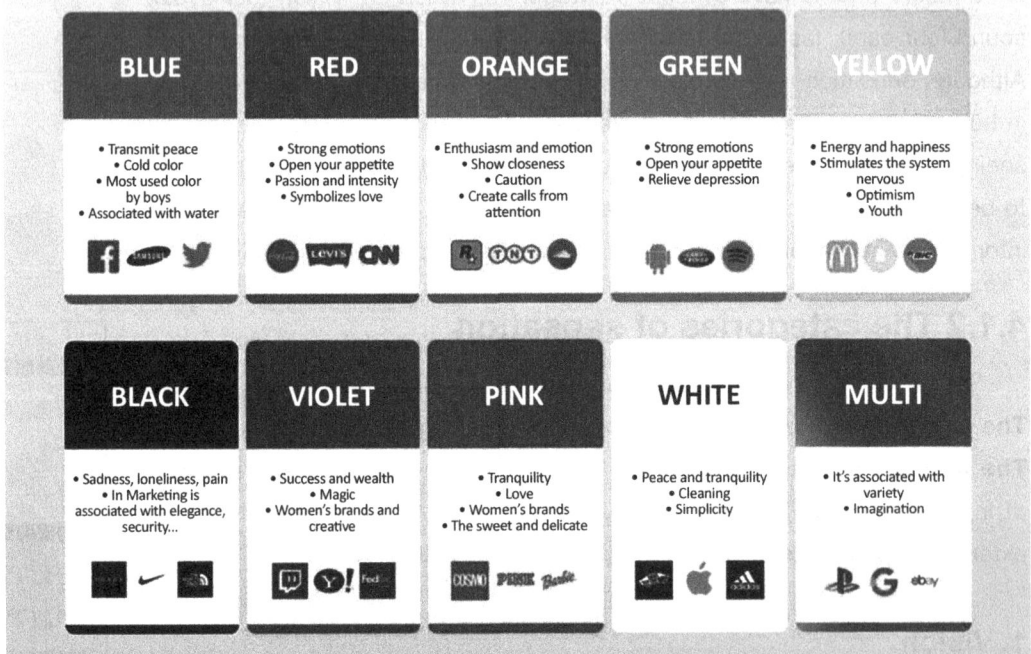

Figure 4-1 Psychology of using colors and marketing

the color red have been largely inconclusive. The study found, however, that exposing students to the color red prior to an exam has been shown to have a negative impact on test performance. Sometimes one color in a brand is so important that it becomes its own entity, like Coca-Cola Red or Tiffany Blue.

Besides, colors also have different meanings in different cultures. For example, while the color white is used in many Western countries to represent purity and innocence, it is seen as a symbol of mourning in many Eastern countries. Research has demonstrated that purple is mostly related with costly products, and grey means cheap and low-quality in China and Japan, while it is opposite in the US.

Color psychology suggests that various shades can have a wide range of effects, from boosting our moods to causing anxiety. Color preferences, from the clothes you wear to the car you drive, can sometimes make a statement about how we want other people to perceive us. For example, purchasing a white vehicle might be less about wanting people to think that you are young and modern and more about the climate you live in; people who live in hot climates typically prefer light-colored vehicles to dark ones.

2. Sound

Sound (music, songs, the spoken words or noises) also plays an important role in sensory marketing, which focuses on all of the human senses. Sound can be the complementary action of vision in our experiences of the world. People hear the stimulus before they see it, especially when the stimulus occurs behind you or on the other side of opaque objects (such as walls). As visual marketing is ubiquitous, sound marketing gives businesses the opportunity to differentiate their marketing from others who just focus on visual promotional activities. Bayerische Motoren Werke (BMW) used a technique known as audio watermarking in the end of its global TV and radio advertisements. The company claimed that BMW wants to create the sound of brand and the unique sonic signature is a sign of The Ultimate Driving Machine.

Music and sounds can always be used to affect consumers' sensations, emotions and actions by marketers. Advertising professionals rely heavily on sound as the background to build up the positive association of brands. Today, brands spend huge sums of money and time choosing the music, jingles, and spoken words that consumers will come to associate with their products. Major retail outlets such as Gap, Bed Bath & Beyond, and Outdoor World, for example, use customized in-store music programs to appeal to the senses of their anticipated customer groups.

Abercrombie and Fitch knows, for example, that their typically younger customers spend more money when loud and upbeat dance music is being played in the store. As Emily Anthese of Psychology Today wrote, "Shoppers make more impulsive purchases when they're over-stimulated. Loud volume leads to sensory overload, which weakens self-control."

According to *the Harvard Business Review*, the familiar Intel "Bong" is played somewhere in the world once every five minutes. The simple five-note tone, along with the memorable slogan—"Intel inside"—has helped Intel become one of the most recognized brands in the world.

3. Smell

Researchers believe that smell is the sense most powerfully linked to emotion, with over 75% of our feelings being generated by odors. Today's fragrance industry is increasingly focused on perfecting perfumes for the brain—specifically, the brains of customers. According to Harold Vogt, co-founder of the Scent Marketing Institute in Scarsdale, New York, at least 20 scent-marketing companies worldwide are developing scents and aromas for companies to help them enhance their marketing and reinforce their brand identity with customers.

The consumer scent industry is currently a billion-dollar business. The fragrance industry is moving into the conditioning of indoor environments using aromatherapy infusion technology. Natural and chemical substances are released into the air to improve feelings of well-being and even increase human performance.

Scent conditioning systems are now found in homes, hotels, resorts, healthcare institutions, and retail stores. In-house bakery and coffee chains like Starbucks, Dunkin' Donuts, and Bread Talk, recognize the importance of the smell of fresh-brewed coffee in attracting customers. Scent marketing researchers say that aromas of lavender, basil, cinnamon, and citrus flavors are relaxing, whereas peppermint, thyme, and rosemary are invigorating. Ginger, cardamom, licorice, and chocolate tend to stir romantic feelings, while rose promotes positivity and happiness. Another recent study showed that the smell of oranges tends to calm the fears of dental patients awaiting major procedures.

Singapore Airlines is in the sensory marketing hall of fame for its patented scent called Stefan Floridian Waters. Now a registered trademark of the airline, Stefan Floridian Waters is used in the perfume worn by flight attendants, blended into the hotel towels served before takeoff, and diffused throughout the cabins of all Singapore Airlines planes.

4. Taste

Taste is considered the most intimate of the senses, mainly because flavors cannot be tasted from a distance. Taste is also considered the hardest sense to cater to because it differs so widely from person to person. Researchers have found that our individual taste preferences are 78% dependent on our genes.

Despite the difficulties of generating mass "taste appeal", it has been attempted. In 2007, the Swedish food retail chain City Gross began delivering grocery bags containing samples of bread, beverages, sandwich spreads, and fruits directly to customers' homes. As a result, City Gross' customers felt a more intimate and memorable connection with the brand's products compared to those of brands who used more traditional marketing tactics such as coupons and discounts.

5. Touch

The first rule of retail sales is, "Get the customer to hold the product." As an important aspect of sensory marketing, touch enhances customers' interaction with a brand's products. Physically holding products can create a sense of ownership, triggering "must-have" purchase decisions. Medical research has proven that pleasant touching experiences cause the brain to release the so-called "love hormone"—oxytocin, which leads to feelings of calmness and well-being.

As with the sense of taste, tactile marketing cannot be done at a distance. It requires that the customer interact directly with the brand, usually through in-store experiences. This has led many retailers to display un-boxed products on open shelves, rather than in closed-display cases. Major customer electronics retailers like Best Buy and the Apple Store are known for encouraging shoppers to handle high-end items.

Research cited by *the Harvard Business Review* shows that actual interpersonal touch, such as a handshake or a light pat on the shoulder, leads people to feel safer and spend more money. Studies have shown that waitresses who touch the diners they are serving earn more in tips.

4.1.3 Sensory thresholds

1. Sensitivity and sensory thresholds

Sensitivity is the property of being perceptible by the mind or the senses, where the sensitivity to stimuli varies with the quality of an individual's sensory receptors and the amount or intensity of the stimuli to which he is exposed. Schiffman et al. (1991) note that sensation is the immediate and direct response of the sensory organs to simple stimuli (e.g. an advertisement, a brand name, etc.). In other words, whether a stimulus can be sensed has something to do with how sensitive the receptors are and how intense the stimulus is. "The ability of consumers to detect variations in light, sound, smell, or other stimuli is determined by their threshold levels." (Assael 1992: 131) Every sensation has two sensitivity and sensory thresholds, namely, the absolute sensitivity and the absolute threshold, the differential sensitivity and the differential threshold.

1) The absolute sensitivity and the absolute threshold

Various factors influence the sensory absolute threshold, stimulus sensory adaptation and individual expectations or motivation (the cognitive processes). Not every input stimulus can arouse human sense in everyday life. The **absolute threshold** is the lowest level of stimulus that an individual can perceive using their senses such as sight, taste, hearing, touch, and smell. The term is often used in neuroscience and experimental research and

绝对阈限：个体通过视觉、味觉、听觉、触觉和嗅觉等感官所能感知到的最低刺激量。

can be applied to any stimulus that can be detected by the human senses. At this point an individual can detect a difference between "something" and "nothing", and it would be this individual's absolute threshold for that stimulus. For instance, in an experiment on sound detention, researchers may present a sound with varying levels of volume. The smallest level that a participant is able to hear is the absolute threshold. However, it is important to note that at such low levels, participants may only detect the stimulus part of the time. Because of this, the absolute threshold is usually defined as the smallest level of a stimulus that a person is able to detect 50% of the time.

But what is that "50% of the time" part of the definition for? Why not 100% of the time?

That is because our absolute threshold can vary according to external and internal factors like background noise, expectation, motivation, and physical condition. It is easier to hear a sound when we are in perfect health, expecting to hear it in a quiet room than when we are tired, unaware of it and in a noisy street.

The affirmation that there is no single absolute threshold is called the signal detection theory. Because our perception responses may vary, to find a person's absolute threshold researchers conduct multiple tests until they find the amount that is perceived 50% of the time.

Presently, the absolute sensitivity is often in inverse proportion to the absolute threshold in number. The relationship between the absolute sensitivity and the absolute threshold can be presented as follows:

$E=1/R$

Where $E=$ the absolute sensitivity

$R=$ the absolute threshold

The absolute threshold varies from different sensories. For example, young children generally have a lower absolute threshold for sounds since the ability to detect sounds at the lowest and highest ranges tends to decrease with age. In one classic experiment, researchers found that after controlling for dark adaptation, wavelength, location, and stimulus size, the human eye was able to detect a stimulus between the range of 54 and 148 photons.

2) The differential sensitivity and the differential threshold

The **differential threshold** is the smallest change in stimulation that a person can detect, also known as the just noticeable difference (JND). The capability to sense the minimum difference is called the differential sensitivity.

To measure the differential threshold for a stimulus, one commonly changes its intensity in very small amounts. An individual's threshold exists when he/she first notices that the stimulus has changed. The difference between this value and the starting value is JND. To quantify the differential threshold, in 1834, a German psycho-physicist Ernst Heinrich Weber stated that JND is an amount relative to the intensity of the initial stimulus. Weber also developed what is known as Weber's Law. The law was proposed by Weber and another German experimental psychologist, Gustav Theodor

> **差别阈限：**个体能察觉刺激变化的最小量，也称为最小可觉差。

Fechner. The law is actually a combination of the Weber law and the Fechner law. According to Weber's Law, this differential threshold is a constant proportion of the original threshold size. In other words, the higher the intensity of a stimulus, the more it will need to change so we can notice a difference. In mathematical terms, the equation for the Weber's Law is:

$\Delta R/R=K$

Where $\Delta R=$ the smallest increase in stimulus intensity that will be perceived as different from the existing intensity;

$R=$ the existing stimulus intensity;

$K=$ a constant that varies across senses.

Meanwhile, the Fechner theory holds that subjective sensation is proportional to the logarithm of the intensity of the stimulus. It is expressed as:

$S = K \log R+C$

Where $S =$ the allocation of the stimulus to the psychological or discriminal continuum;

$R =$ the stimulus magnitude;

$C =$ a constant.

Thus, this combined law presents the relationship between the intensity or degree of physical stimulus and its perceptual effects in quantifiable terms. For instance, the law can be used to calculate how much the volume of a radio should be decreased before the perceiver notices.

For example, if I were to give you a pile of five apples and then give you one more, you'd probably notice the difference. It only took adding one apple for you to notice a change, so the difference threshold was one apple. However, it's important to not just look at the difference threshold as a flat number, but also as a percentage of change. If you had started with 100 apples, one more would not have produced a noticeable difference. So, if I added 20% to your pile of 100 apples, you would definitely notice a difference of 20 apples. In these examples, the difference thresholds were 1, 20 or 20%.

3) Subliminal perception

Another aspect of sensory perception, subliminal perception (perception without awareness), has been of interest in recent years. Although most marketers worry about whether their offers will be perceived at all, some consumers worry that they will be affected by marketing messages without even knowing it. The concept of the perceptual threshold is important for another phenomenon "subliminal perception". People can also perceive stimuli which are below their level of conscious awareness. In this situation, the stimuli which are otherwise too weak or brief to be consciously seen or heard prove strong enough to be perceived. When the stimulus is below the threshold of awareness and is perceived, the process is called subliminal perception. This shows that the threshold of conscious awareness is higher than the absolute threshold for effective perception. Disguised stimuli, not readily recognised by consumers are called "embeds". These embeds are believed to be planted in print advertisement to influence consumers' purchase behavior. A number of research studies suggest that individuals differ in their susceptibility to subliminal stimuli and that subliminal messages can trigger basic drives such as hunger, but stimulation does not necessarily precipitate action. Suppose we are sitting at a movie and are exposed in this case through a "subliminal advertisement". In 1957 a researcher announced that he had flashed the phrases "Eat Popcorn" and "Drink Coca-Cola" on the theater screen every 5seconds for 1/300th of a second.

Numerous studies by psychologists and consumers researchers have found no link between subliminal messages and consumer behavior. It appears that subliminal advertising simply doesn't have the power attributed to it by it's critics. Such stimuli have found that these advertisements won't arouse motives like hunger, nor the subliminally presented sexual stimuli affect consumers' attitudes or preferences.

4) Sensory adaption

If you are exposed to a stimulus that doesn't change over a period of time, sensory adaptation takes places, and you become less sensitive to the stimulus. Sensory adaptation can take place with any of our senses just like thresholds. It is also called as neural adaptation and can be explained as a gradual reduction or a fall in the sensory response because of the repeated exposure of a particular stimulus over a period of time. This change can be both positive and negative and does not necessarily involve ignoring of the stimulus completely. When you leave a room or place with bright light and get into a poorly lit or completely dark room, it will be hard for you to see anything at first. But with time, you get used to the darkness and soon you start seeing shiny objects in the dark room, and then you are able to see a few things in there which are fairly bright. If you have to study in a room with a constant noise outside, for example, you will usually eventually adapt to the noise, and it will become less offensive.

Sensory adaptation also happens when certain stimuli are decreased and the receptors increase their sensitivity, such as when someone walks into a dark building and their pupils dilate to take in as much light as possible.

2. Sensory threshold and marketing

The sensory threshold is an important consideration in designing marketing stimuli. There are two main reasons why marketers make great efforts to confirm the consumer's sensory threshold related with their products: (1) negative changes (e.g. reductions in the product size or quality or increases in product prices) are not discernible to the public (i.e. remain below JND) and (2) product improvements (e.g. improved or updated packaging, a larger size or a lower price) are very apparent to consumers without being wastefully extravagant (i.e. they are at or just above the JND). When it comes to product improvements, marketers very much want to meet or exceed the consumer's differential threshold; that is, they want consumers to readily perceive any improvements made in the original product comparing these implications for marketing, it is obvious that the differential threshold is more important to marketers.

The marketing implication of the absolute threshold is that consumers will only perceive a marketing stimulus when it is higher than the absolute threshold. In other words, if images or words in a commercial are too small, the consumer's sensory receptors will not be activated and the stimulus will not be perceived. The differential threshold measures the limits of product similarities and brand redundancies to judge how much of a gap is required between them to be successful. This judgement can help to determine whether your marketing message delineates these differences and changes clearly enough to be understood by the consumer, and whether the differences listed are significant to the customer.

When the threshold is reached, your message may begin to blend with the messages of your competitors, leaving the consumer unclear as to why your product or service should be considered. Separation from others and a clear product or brand identity are two goals of good marketing. The differential threshold helps to achieve and maintain those goals.

4.2 Perception
4.2.1 What is perception?

> **知觉：** 个体选择性地吸收环境中的刺激物，从认知上对感知的信息以特定的方式进行组织，并对该信息进行解读的过程。

Perception is determined by both physiological and psychological characteristics of the human being whereas sensation is conceived with only the physiological features. Thus, perception is much more complex than what one sees with the eyes. Perception is the process by which an individual selectively absorbs or assimilates the stimuli in the environment, cognitively organizes the perceived information in a specific fashion and then interprets the information to make an assessment about what is going on in one's environment.

Perception is a subjective process, therefore, different people may perceive the same environment differently based on what particular aspects of the situation they choose to selectively absorb, how they organize this information and the manner in which they interpret it to obtain a grasp of the situation.

As a consumer, as an employee, as a parent, as a friend, as a person—perception is the most important psychological factor in all human behavior. According to Radhika Duggal at Forbes, "Perception is defined as the process by which individuals select, organize and interpret stimuli into a meaningful and coherent picture of the world." There are numerous definitions in literature explaining perception from a consumer behavior perspective. Joseph Reitz states, "Perception includes all those processes by which an individual receives information about his environment—seeing, hearing, feeling, tasting and smelling. The study of these perpetual processes shows that their functioning is affected by three classes of variables—the objects or events being perceived, the environment in which perception occurs and the individual doing the perceiving."

Perception has been explained by Ajit Singh as follows, "Perception refers to the interpretation of sensory data." In other words, sensation involves detecting the presence of a stimulus whereas perception involves understanding what the stimulus means. For example, when we see something, the visual stimulus is the light energy reflected from the external world and the eye becomes the sensor. This visual image of the external thing becomes perception when it is interpreted in the visual cortex of the brain. Thus, visual perception refers to interpreting the image of the external world projected on the retina of the eye and constructing a model of the three dimensional world."

4.2.2 Characteristics of perception

感知者： 意识集中在刺激物上，从而开始感知该刺激物的人。

目标： 感知的对象。

情形： 包括环境的因素、时间、刺激的程度。

Perception comprises three components according to Alan Saks and Gary Johns (2011), namely the **perceiver**, the **target** (stimulus), and the **situation**. The characteristics of each of these components influence the perceptual processes of selection, organization, and interpretation.

(1) The perceiver. This refers to a person whose awareness is focused on the stimulus, and thus begins to perceive it. There are many factors that may influence the perceptions of the perceiver. The three major factors include the motivational state, the emotional state, and the experience. All of these factors, especially motivation and emotion, greatly contribute to how the person perceives a situation. Oftentimes, he or she may employ the so-called "perceptual defense", which means that the person only perceives what he wants to perceive, even though the stimulus acts on his or her senses.

(2)The target (stimulus). This includes the object of perception. It is something or someone that is being perceived. The amount of information gathered by the sensory organs of the perceiver affects the interpretation and understanding of the target.

(3) The situation. The environmental factors, timing, and the degree of stimulation also affect the process of perception. These factors may render a single stimulus to be left as merely a stimulus, not a percept that is subject for brain interpretation. However, ambiguous stimulus may sometimes be transduced into one or more percepts. When this occurs, a process called "multistable perception" occurs.

Perception is a complex process. After a stimulus is detected by the sense organs, the perceptual process comes into play and involves the interplay of three processes, namely selection, organization, and interpretation. It involves a series of mental function in giving meaning to sensation. They include assimilation, discrimination, association, objectification, and unification of knowledge. On the accomplishment of these activities, only our mind can derive the meaning of the given object. In this way, perception is a dynamic process.

Perception is also an intellectual process, as it involves a lot of cognitive effort. Once sensation takes place, the cognitive processes take over and assign meaning to the stimulus. Consumers possess varying cognitive capacities and capabilities; their backgrounds are diverse, and psychological processes (needs, motivation, learning, attitudes, and values) and sociological factors (culture, sub-culture, and social class) are different. The cognitive processes have a bearing on not only the perceptual mechanism, but also on the resultant output and the behavioural response of the perceiver.

Perception is broad in nature. It includes a physiological component (through sensation), as well as cognitive, sociological, and psychological components.

Perception is a subjective process, as it is unique to each person. Different people may perceive the same environment differently based on what particular aspects of the situation they choose to selectively absorb, how they organize this information, and the manner in which they interpret it to obtain a grasp of the situation.

4.2.3 Importance of perception

Perception is very important in understanding human behavior, because every person perceives the world and approaches the life problems differently—whatever we see or feel is not necessarily the same as it really is. It is because what we hear is not what is really said, but what we perceive as being said. When we buy something, it is not because it is the best, but because we take it to be the best. Thus, it is because of perception, we can find out why one individual finds a job satisfying while another one may not be satisfied with it. If people behave on the basis of their perception, we can predict their behavior in the changed circumstances by understanding their present perception of the environment.

As a consumer, perception becomes shaped by advertising, word of mouth, past experiences, social media, pricing, quality, and customer service. Through these efforts, brands can redefine themselves as not just a product but also as a part of the consumer's lifestyle choices. Consumers make choices based on price, need, opportunity, packaging, brand ethics, and more. Shifting how consumers perceive these things can dramatically impact whether they purchase any given brand and why. If consumers perceive that a product or a brand is a bad choice, whether it's based on ethos, quality or price, then it really doesn't matter if it actually is a bad choice because customer perception dictates consumer action, and that action becomes reality.

"If you want to win the heart of a person, first win the perception." Those are the wise words of author Santosh Avvannavar, and it's true for brands, too. If brands can create a public perception that their product is of high quality, their prices are fair, their service is responsible and attentive, and that the brand stands behind what they do, they'll gain more customers and enjoy great loyalty. It's that simple—and that hard.

Consumer perception can make or break your brand. When customers had a pleasant experience of getting their products delivered on time, they form a perception. Getting the products that were as described in the product description also creates a positive customer perception. When customers experienced a great after-sale service, it is going to develop a positive opinion about the brand.

But when customers had a bad experience such as broken products, no returns, no after-sales service, etc., the customers build a negative perception about the brand.

When companies work towards strengthening the bond between customers and the company, customer perception improves, and this gives way for a better competitive edge.

Customer perception is also important to determine the kind of image a brand wants to build.

For example, when a retail clothing store has displayed clothes in crowded racks using low-quality plastic hangers, customers get a perception that it is a low-quality brand. But when the same clothes are presented well with back-lit mannequins, neatly arranged, on good-quality attractive hangers, etc., the customers build a different perception about the brand.

4.2.4 The process of consumer perception

While the process of perception is thought to generally have three stages, it is possible to extend this to five (These five stages include stimulation, organization, interpretation, memory, and recall), especially where human beings are concerned. When a person receives information, he tries to process it through the following sub processes of selection, organisation and interpretation.

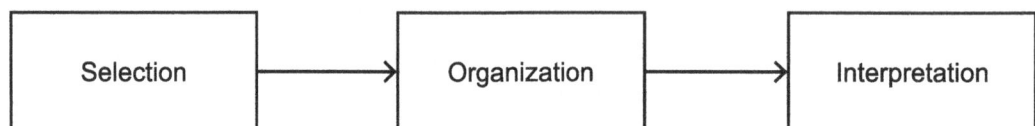

Figure 4-2 The perception process

1. Perceptual selection

Many things are taking place in the environment simultaneously. However, one cannot pay equal attention to all these things, and thus the need of perceptual selectivity emerges. Perceptual selectivity refers to the tendency to select certain objects from the environment for attention. The objects which are selected are those relevant and appropriate for an individual or those consistent with our existing beliefs, values and needs. Perception is a selective process. Usually, people are able to sense and receive only limited information from the environment and hence are characteristically selective. During this process of selection, certain aspects of stimuli are screened out and others admitted. These aspects of the stimuli which are admitted remain and fall within the threshold of the person, while those which are screened out fall out or below the threshold limit.

Consumers will identify and choose marketing stimuli based on their needs and attitudes. A consumer intending to buy a sports bike will be more attentive to motor bikes ads, a style conscious person will be more receptive to ads for fashionable clothes while another consumer who is a habitual soft drink lover will be more attentive to advertisements portraying the various soft drink brands. In all the above instances the consumer will process stimuli selectively by picking and choosing them based on his or her psychological set. For example, one consumer may believe that the Tide washing powder washes and makes clothes whiter than other washing powders. Whereas, there could be another consumer who may not agree with this claim, for she may believe that all the washing powders are the same.

Perceptual selection occurs at every stage in the perceptual process. Selective exposure takes place because each individual's belief will influence what she decides to read or hear. Selective organisation occurs because each person will organize information so that it is consistent to her beliefs. And selective interpretation will take place such that perception will conform to prior beliefs and attitudes.

For example, Oral B Toothbrush claims that its toothbrush will indicate when the user has to purchase a new toothbrush. This, the marketer assumed would be consistent to the consumers beliefs that such a toothbrush will be helpful. However, dentists, in general, may not concur with the claim. Such consumers' perception can be influenced by brand name associations arrived at from advertising and social stimuli, where the association tends to conform to the consumer's current knowledge and past experiences.

There are three processes which define selection: exposure, attention and selective perception.

1) Exposure

When a consumer's senses—sight, hearing, smell, taste, touch are activated by a stimulus, exposure is said to have occurred. Wells (1989) proposed that exposure, as the first step of the perception, happens when stimuli come within the range of our senses. Hence, exposure is the minimum requirement of perception. No matter how great a message is, it will not be perceived unless a person is exposed to the stimulus.

There are two basic ways of exposure to stimuli, which are conscious exposure and unconscious exposure.

In conscious exposure, consumers will explore information which can help them to get the process of purchasing products. For instance, based on their need which is active at that point of time, people will be selective and choose to listen to certain aspects of the advertising message, and decide to see and hear only a part of what is being communicated. For instance, if a person's need is to purchase a refrigerator, his mind will be ready to receive only those stimuli which will give him some information related to refrigerators. He will exercise a great deal of selectivity and look out for information messages that will help him to increase his knowledge about the retail refrigerators.

Researches showed that most of the consumers are exposed to the various ads unconsciously in everyday life. For example the sportswear brand Adidas had used the suburban underground railway system to tie in with the brand's tagline. "Impossible is Nothing". Although those marketing messages are exposed to consumers unconsciously, they can also affect the consumer buying behavior.

2) Attention

People will be selective in their choice of receiving various kinds of information for different products or services based on what interests them rather than the message content and also the selection of the media. Attention is defined as the momentary focusing of a consumer's cognitive capacity on a specific stimulus. For example, when consumers take notice of a TV ad, a new product displayed in the retail outlet or a new vehicle in the company showroom, it is said that attention has taken place. There are various external and internal factors which influence selective attention.

(1) External factors

These factors may be further classified as sensory elements and structural elements. Sensory elements are characteristics in the stimulus, which are sensed immediately, such as smell and sound, taste and feel, and colours and visuals. The structural elements also pertain to the stimulus and comprise characteristics that make a stimulus stand out and apart from others.

① Size: The bigger the size of the stimulus, the more likely it is to be noticed. Size always attracts the attention, because it establishes dominance. The size may be the height or weight of an individual, sign board of a shop, or the space devoted to an advertisement in the newspaper. For example, headlines in the newspaper are in a larger font size and immediately catch our attention. Similarly, the brand name on the packaging of a product is again in a larger font size, and is meant to draw our attention. In addition, a full-page print advertisement is more likely to be noticed than a half-page or a quarter-page advertisement.

② Intensity: The larger the force or power of a stimulus, the greater will be the chances of it getting noticed and perceived. A few examples of intensity are yelling or whispering, very bright colours, very bright or very dim lights. Intensity will also include behavioral intensity. If the office order says "Report to the boss immediately," it will be more intense and effective as compared to the office order which says "Make it convenient to meet the boss today."

③ Repetition: The repetition principle states that a repeated external stimulus is more attention-drawing than a single one. Because of this principle, supervisors make it a point to give the necessary directions again and again to the workers. Similarly, the same advertisement or different advertisements but for the same product shown again and again on the TV will have more attention as compared to an advertisement which is shown once a day.

④ Status: High-status people exert greater influence on the perception of the employees than low-status people. There will always be different reactions to the orders given by the foreman, the supervisor or the production manager.

⑤ Contrast: Any stimulus that stands out from the rest of the environment receives greater attention. For example, the "Exit" signs in the cinema halls which have red lettering on a black background are attention drawing or a warning sign in a factory, such as Danger, written in black against a red or yellow background will be easily noticeable. In a room if there are twenty men and one woman, the woman will be noticed first because of the contrast.

⑥ Movement: The principle of motion states that a moving object receives more attention than an object which is standing still. A moving car among the parked cars catches our attention faster. A flashing neon-sign is more easily noticed.

⑦ Novelty and Familiarity: This principle states that either a novel or a familiar external situation can serve as an attention getter. New objects in the familiar settings or familiar objects in new settings will draw the attention of the perceiver. A familiar face on a crowded railway platform will immediately catch attention. Because of this principle, the managers change the workers' jobs from time to time, because it will increase the attention they give to their jobs.

⑧ Nature: By nature we mean, whether the object is visual or auditory and whether it involves pictures, people or animals. It is well known that pictures attract more attention than words. Videoes attract more attention than still pictures. A picture with human beings attracts more attention than a picture with animals.

(2) Internal factors

Internal factors also affect perceptual selectivity. These factors are those factors that relate to an individual and would differ from person to person. Factors like motivation, learning, personality and self-image, past experience, expectations, etc.

① Needs and Motivation: The selection of a stimulus depends on our needs, wants, and motivation, and what we think is relevant to us. For example, if a person wants to buy a flat (for safety and security need), and if he is high on the esteem need too, he will be quick to notice advertisements for availability of a flat in the posh areas of the city. He will be receptive to such stimuli that support this need.

Similarly, if a person is strong on the need for achievement, he will be receptive to inputs or stimuli that support the need for achievement. Thus, people with different needs select different stimuli (i.e., items) to respond to. The stronger the need is, the greater will be the tendency to select related stimuli and ignore unrelated stimuli in the environment. Interest and involvement with a product category also impact the level of attention that a person would give to the goods and services and/or brands.

② Learning: Learning influences the development of perceptual sets within an individual. People have a tendency to perceive things based on their perceptual sets and beliefs.

As individuals, we learn from our experiences and store such learning in our memory bank. The selectivity of stimuli is based on what and how we would like and/or expect things to be. For example, consumers are attracted to a particular brand(s) because they have heard or read good reviews and expect it to be good. A person who has heard something positive about a Dell laptop or who has had pleasant experiences with it in the past will be attracted towards reading and watching anything positive about it, so that it conforms to his attitudes and beliefs.

③ Personality and Self-Image: Personality traits and characteristics have a bearing on an individual's nature to perceive or not to perceive. They also affect the dynamics of perception, that is, the manner in which they select (what), organize, and interpret (how) their sensory impressions to give meaning to a stimulus. Further, a person will be attracted to a stimulus that closely relates to his/her personality and self-image.

For example, a person will be attracted to a product and/or a brand where the product and/or brand personality is in congruence with his own. Thus, while some people prefer plain and simple two-wheelers, others prefer trendy, stylish, and more powerful ones.

3) Selective perception

Consumers will perceive marketing experiences stimuli selectively because each person will be unique in terms of individual needs, attitudes, experiences and personal characteristics. Selective perception means that different persons may perceive the same product, advertisement package in a different way.

2. Perceptual organisation

The second sub-process in the perceptual process is referred to as perceptual organization. According to Assael (1992), perceptual organization is the organization of disparate information so that it can be comprehended and retained. After having selectively absorbed the data from the range of stimuli we are exposed to at any given time, we then try to organize the perceptual inputs in such a manner that would facilitate us to extract meaning out of what we perceive. Or in other words, a person's perceptual process organizes the incoming information into a meaningful whole. While selection is a subjective process, organizing is a cognitive process. Perceptual organization arranges the stimulus into meaningful, recognizable, and understandable patterns. When exposed to various stimuli, human beings do not select them as separate and unrelated identities, but group them and perceive them as "a unified or meaningful whole".

Aaker et al. (1987) claimed that stimuli are perceived not as a set of elements but as a whole, it can be concluded that this total has a meaning of its own that is not necessarily deductible from its individual components. This phenomenon is termed as the Gestalt theory. The Gestalt theory explains how people assemble and organize visually independent stimuli (objects, persons, things, and information) into a group or a 'unified whole'.

3. Perceptual interpretation

The last stage is perceptual interpretation, which happens after we have attended to a stimulus. Mowen (1993) noted that interpretation is a process whereby people draw upon their experience, memory, and expectations to interpret and attach meaning to a stimulus.

After the input has been given attention, and has been organized into a coherent form, a meaning is extracted out of it. As processes, both perceptual organization and interpretation are intertwined, as both have to do with the deriving sense and assigning meaning to the stimulus to which a person has been exposed. The difference between the two lies is the fact that while, in most of the cases, the laws of perceptual organization are applied sub-consciously, and perceptual organization is a sub-conscious process, while perceptual interpretation is a conscious process.

In the context of marketing, when a consumer makes a purchase decision, it is a function of not only how the stimuli (any or all of the elements of the marketing mix) are presented, but also the manner in which such stimuli are organized and interpreted. This has relevance for marketing communication, where decisions with respect to both the message strategy (content and context) and the media strategy has an impact on perceptual selectivity, organization, and interpretation.

4.3 Marketing strategies and consumer perception

Perception in marketing is crucial because what consumers feel and believe about a product can be just as important as what that product actually delivers in terms of performance. It's significant for entrepreneurs to understand how their target market perceives their company.

There are several main marketing factors which are related with consumer perception.

1. Pricing

Establishing the right price for a product is a huge factor in how the public perceives a brand. Consumers want to save money, yes, but if a product is priced too low, it can be perceived as "cheap" and consumers may question what's wrong with it — were corners cut, is quality lacking, why is it being sold at such a crazy price? Pricing is an art, not a science. Too low, the public gets suspicious; too high, the public resents the brand.

2. Quality

This is a no-brainer; bad quality makes consumers angry. End of story. Quality is key to success or failure, and if a brand starts selling products that don't live up to their past reputation, they won't just lose sales, they'll lose trust and damage their reputation — things that can take years to rebuild.

3. Packaging

How products are packaged definitely impacts consumer perception; look at the first-generation iPod through to the iPhones. The look defined the user experience, but then the packaging clinched how unique it was. Just opening the box felt amazing — high-quality cardboard, carefully packaged, a beautifully printed user manual on heavy-gauge paper. Soon iPod, then iPhone, took over the device market around the world.

4. Brand reputation/history

Having a good reputation can take years to build, but losing it can happen overnight. One of the companies considered to have among the world's best reputations right now is Netflix, whose brand soared after they sacrificed one of their most successful series by killing off the character of Frank Underwood in "House of Cards" after disturbing sexual assault allegations were made against Kevin Spacey.

5. Responsibility and ethics

Responsibility, environmental practices and political allegiances can all define how companies are perceived. Just ask Nike, whose Colin Kaepernick sponsorships and other social justice stances have made buying Nike a political act that transcends consumerism. How companies behave on the world stage matters to the bottom line. Another example is Patagonia, the outdoor clothing company, who has taken strong political stances on protecting parklands in North America and through establishing parks worldwide, like buying thousands of square miles of land to make parks in its namesake region Patagonia.

6. Advertising, messaging and perception

Great marketing and brand messaging understand what drives perception and try to skew it in a way that benefits a brand. Music in commercials is a perfect example. The right song can connect a product to a feeling, a lifestyle, a social cause and so much more, creating a subconscious or even conscious association between all of those things and the brand. The importance of consumer perception in marketing can't be overstated.

While more has been known about the psychology of selling and perception than ever before, commercials of the 1980s, like drinking 7-Up as the first post-drought rain falls, the Dr. Pepper "Be a Pepper" campaign and the Foster's beer "It's what's inside that counts" ads are all part of when beverage campaigns took adverting to the next level. They made beverage choice resonate with the idea of choosing a lifestyle, of being yourself, of living life on your terms and not society's – a tall order for a can of soda, but it worked because it created momentum in the coveted 18- to 34-year-old consumer demographic.

Similarly, Dove beauty and skin products launched one of the greatest advertising campaigns ever in shaping consumer perception. Their "Campaign for Real Beauty" began in 2004 after their researchers traveled to 10 countries, talking to 3,000 women and learning that only 2 percent felt beautiful. The campaign highlighted how individuality was beautiful, and in doing so, Dove became more than just a beauty product, it became a lifestyle choice. In buying Dove, some women felt they were supporting a kinder, gentler company that sought to banish body image issues.

The good news about perception is that most brands and companies are perceived as being somewhat neutral. The bad news is that no one gets an overwhelming urge to be loyal to a neutral experience.

To ramp up perception from meh to meaningful, there are several ways to do it:

(1) Cohesive Identity: Whatever your identity is, be sure it's the same across all channels. Think in terms of logo, brand voice, typography, images and colors. Have a cohesive idea of what the branding should look and sound like, and then get behind that across all channels of advertising, PR and social media.

(2) Strong Web Presence: Many companies, particularly restaurants and other food services, are giving up control over their brand by forsaking a website in trade for a Facebook page. Owning your own identity and creating a visual web domain are as important as having a social media presence. By having an attentive, clear, easily navigated website and accessible customer service through both social media and possibly helpful bots on your branded site, consumers will feel like you value their experience throughout all stages of business.

(3) Satisfying Customer Service: The easier you make it for consumers to contact you, ask questions and get information, the more likely you are to change their perception of how loyal your company is to customers and how much you value their experience. A majority of today's customers now say they will pay more for brands that have attentive, fast, easy customer service, and an equal majority say they'll buy from a brand again if they have great, quick service. This is, in fact, the best and fastest way to improve consumer perception of your brand.

Summary

Sensation is a mental process (such as seeing, hearing, or smelling) resulting from the immediate external stimulation of a sense organ often as distinguished from a conscious awareness of the sensory process.

Sensation can be categorised as external senses and internal senses. The External Senses are seeing, hearing, smelling, tasting and touching.

Every sensation has two sensitivity and sensory thresholds, i.e. the absolute sensitivity and the absolute threshold, the differential sensitivity and the differential threshold. The absolute threshold is the lowest level of stimulus that an individual can perceive. The differential threshold, the minimum level of stimulation that a person can detect 50 percent of the time, is also known as the just noticeable difference (JND) .

Perception refers to the set of processes we use to make sense of the different stimuli we're presented with. Our perceptions are based on how we interpret different sensations.

Perception is the process of selecting, organizing, and interpreting information. There are three processes which define selection: exposure, attention and selective perception.

Perception in marketing is crucial. Pricing, quality, packaging, brand reputation or history, responsibility and ethics, advertising, messaging and perception are the main marketing factors which are related with consumer perception.

Exercises

(1) What is the difference between sensation and perception?

(2) Outline and explain the parts of the perceptual process that would allow a shopper to recognize Nestlé coffee in a supermarket.

(3) Blind taste tests in the 1980s showed that most Coke drinkers preferred a cola that was sweeter than the current product. When Coca-Cola attempted to make its product sweeter, brand loyal customers revolted and demanded the old product be returned. Explain how Coca-Cola marketers could have used the principles of psychophysics to introduce the new coke without creating these problems.

(4) At a business meeting, a consultant states that "perception is reality, because a customer never works with the actual product, but only with his or her perception of that product." In a university lab, researchers determine that when a rat is looking at a brightly colored rectangle, a close inspection of the rat's optic nerves (that connect the eyes to the cortex) show no visible change from when the rat is looking at a green circle; however, electrodes placed in the nerve show a different pattern of transmitted codes. How are these two events related, and what does this relationship tell us about perception?

Case Analysis

Read the following introduction about the popularity of luosifen and analyze why it has become a commercial success, using the knowledge learned in this chapter. Is there any local specialty in your hometown that has the potential to gain nationwide attention? Adopt the luosifen model and formulate a promotion strategy for it.

Taste Treat That Will First Hit Your Nose

In the world of Chinese gastronomy few things are renowned for their pungent — and for some, repellent-smell, but each is a classic and is loved by millions, including Anhui stinky mandarin fish, Changsha stinky tofu, Beijing mung bean juice and luosifen.

In recent years luosifen, also called as snail noodles, have grown in popularity, even though you could not say they had taken off across the country. But then came COVID-19 and a greater reliance of hundreds of millions of Chinese on online shopping over the first half of 2020, and the renown or notoriety-of luosifen, rocketed. Among the monickers attached to it on the internet were "King of Darkness" "gastronomic bioweapon", the food "that puts your friendship with your roommates to the test", and the food "with the smell of a broken toilet". However, rather than driving away would-be customers, and perhaps future connoisseurs, of the noodles, it has transformed in 2020 into a nationwide sensation.

The Liuzhou Municipal Bureau of Commerce says daily production and sales of the noodles doubled from before the pandemic to 3 million bags. Those surging sales have fed growing interest on the internet in the noodles, which in turn has no doubt generated growing sales.

In May the People's Daily and Li Ziqi, a video blogger with 11.9 million followers on YouTube and 26 million on Sina Weibo, released their collaboration luosifen, and hit newspaper headlines.

"The result has been good business traffic and exposure. Because of being unable to go out for dinner during the epidemic and because of a lack of foodstuffs, instant food has become a popular necessity. Coupled with the catalytic push of internet celebrities, the sales of snail noodles have ushered in explosive growth, and hundreds of thousands of searches have been posted on Weibo and TikTok." says Guo Xin, a marketing professor at Beijing Technology and Business University.

In February the value of sales of snail noodles on the internet shopping platform Taobao exceeded 390 million yuan. Since then, monthly sales have more than doubled compared with the corresponding period last year, the Taobao Foodstuffs Big Data Report says. Ele.me (饿了么), one of China's major online food delivery services, says take-away orders for luosifen have risen 58 percent after Feb 25.

No matter what manufacturer or brand of snail noodles you come across, a distinct smell is destined to hit your soul, the progenitor of that smell being sour bamboo shoots. In humid Guangxi sourness is integral to local food. In addition, because bamboo is abundant in the region, and it is difficult to keep bamboo shoots fresh, sour bamboo shoots have naturally become the local staple side dish, one that depends on fermentation to prolong its usefulness.

"I don't think it's smelly at all," says Wang Jing, who regards himself as a connoisseur. "If luosifen is just about a foul smell, it might be on 'hot sell' for a short time because of those hunting for a novelty, but the foul sour bamboo shoots are the magic. As long as you put it in your mouth only the savory taste lingers. It's the taste of a past and present life."

According to the Guangxi University study, this is because while the smelly substances are produced by the fermentation of bamboo shoots, short peptides, amino acids and sugars are dissociated. As a typical high-protein aquatic product, the snail soup is also rich in nucleotides and polysaccharides, which all have high melting points, and are nonvolatile with their umami substance. We can't smell but we can taste it.

So those who appreciate snail noodles have really tasted the sweetness. It is precisely with this strange taste that snail noodles have torn many people's traditional dietary views beyond Guangxi.

CHAPTER FIVE
Learning and Memory

Learning objectives

After learning this chapter, you will be able to:

- understand behavioral learning theories and the cognitive learning theory;
- master the basic theories of classical conditioning and instrumental conditioning;
- learn about ways to measure consumer learning;
- apply theories of learning and memory into marketing strategies.

Lead-in Case

D2C Brand Perfect Diary Is Disrupting China's Beauty Market

In China, the development of D2C brands has been built on similar strategies to brands globally, however, the strategies have been adapted for the local market and focus heavily on user platforms and customer care. Perfect Diary has paved the way, becoming one of China's first beauty disruptors.

(Perfect Diary's cosmetic products showcased backstage at Masha Ma's show.)

Perfect Diary is one of China's most innovative D2C brands and is now valued at US$1 billion. It has proved itself to be a fast-learning, dynamic brand that stands out among the stiff competition in the beauty sector. It has dominated the sector by implementing dedicated KOL strategies applied to product by to product.

Since its launch in 2016, China's homegrown beauty brand Perfect Diary is now the hottest cosmetics brand on Tmall. During Singles Day 2019, Perfect Diary broke the first brand breaking the 100 million RMB (US$14 million) sales record

in one day—ahead of other international cosmetic brands. Moreover, in September 2019, the brand raised a new round of funding and was valued at US$1 billion. Chinese media reports it is planning to use this capital to grow its offline store counts from 40 to 300 and to enter the perfume market. What attributed their astonishing growth? And what are some concerns behind? We took to the Internet to find out what consumers thought and spoke with experts in marketing, influencer strategy, and beauty sectors.

WeChat-first response

Traditionally in the west, D2C (Direct-to-Consumer) brands' path of development has been quite clear: They manufacture and ship products directly to consumers without relying on physical stores. Companies like Glossier, Allbirds, and Everlane are the flagship D2C brands; whether building slack groups or repurposing user-generated content, they are disrupting the traditional industry by being user-centric.

In China, the development of D2C brands is built on similar strategies to the aforementioned but have a local twist. For example, by leveraging private traffic on WeChat, Perfect Diary has become a trailblazer in engaging with consumers on a one-on-one basis. This includes the creation of a fictional avatar "Xiao Wanzi" that be friends and chats with customers.

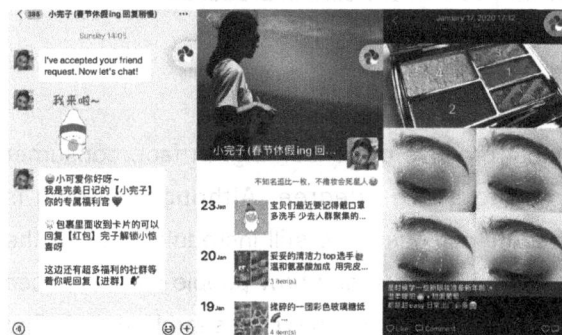

(Once a friend is added on WeChat, the virtual avatar sends discount codes and shares makeup tutorials on her moments. Photo: screenshots/WeChat)

"Today there are hundreds of 'Xiao Wanzi' personal WeChat accounts run by Perfect Diary employees, all with the same profile image and WeChat Moments posts. Each of these accounts operates dozens, if not hundreds, of WeChat groups filled with the brand's customers," wrote marketing expert and a China trend watcher Lauren Hallanan. These WeChat groups contain daily chat updates on the latest Brand products, makeup tips and more.

Little Red Book KOLs

Besides establishing WeChat touch points, Perfect Diary was initially known for building viral campaigns on the Little Red Book app. Such popularity was achieved by their bulletproof KOL strategy. Kim Leitzes, founder and CEO of China's influencer marketing platform Parklu, notes, "they activate across the entire spectrum—celebrity, top-tier, mid-tier, micro and KOC." These beauty KOLs' product reviews ultimately attracted consumers. And, because the product pricing is relatively low and accessible, ranging from about $8 (52rmb) for a lipstick to $19 (129rmb) for a twelve-color eyeshadow plate, Perfect Diary easily grew its first set of consumers from Little Red Book.

As the company distributed their KOL budgets one product at a time, it built "It items" like the Little Diamond lipstick and the twelve-color eyeshadow collaboration with the Discovery channel while their consumer base snowballed. Within the first year of the brand's launch, it became the top mentioned beauty brand on Little Red Book, ahead of luxury brands like L'Oreal, Tom Ford, and Estee Lauder.

The average media value of Perfect Diary's KOL mentions is 36% more than other domestic brands, but the frequency of repeated mentions is much lower.

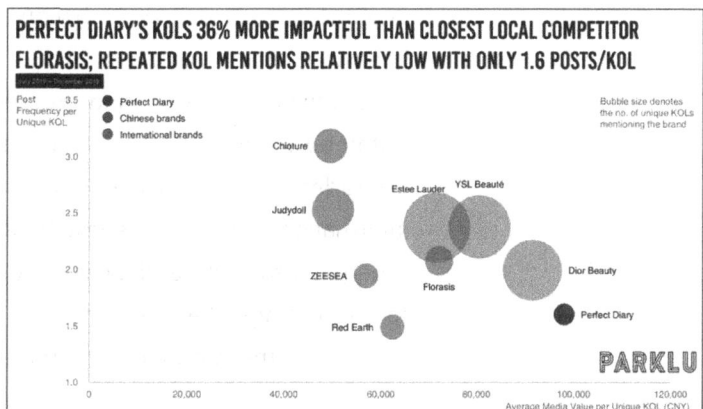

PERFECT DIARY'S KOLS 36% MORE IMPACTFUL THAN CLOSEST LOCAL COMPETITOR FLORASIS; REPEATED KOL MENTIONS RELATIVELY LOW WITH ONLY 1.6 POSTS/KOL

Introduction

With WeChat groups, video streams and low prices for foundation, China's Perfect Diary has emerged from nowhere four years ago to become a cosmetics giant in the digital age, trailing only L'Oreal and LVMH in the world's No. 2 market for make-up. Perfect Diary's rise has been fuelled by blending low prices and social media platforms like Douyin—TikTok for China—and WeChat, collecting customer data it can use to design and roll out new products rapidly, helped by charismatic influencers with huge online followings.

By using innovative marketing tactics—from private WeChat groups to sophisticated KOL strategies on Little Red Book—Perfect Diary has proved to be a fast-learning, dynamic D2C brand that customers perceive as standing out among the stiff competition. It has created diverse products that amassed users' attention on social media. On Weibo, the tag #perfectdiarymonthlynewdrop had over 649,300 views and attracted a constant follower growth. Analysts said Perfect Diary's rise has been boosted by younger, "Generation Z" consumers' willingness to embrace homegrown products.

We can attribute Perfect Diary's success to its KOL (Key Opinion Leaders) strategies in China as well as consumer socialization. In this chapter, we will discuss about how an individual learns to be a consumer and how they remember certain products.

消费者的学习: 个体获取购物和消费知识和体验的过程,并会在将来应用于相关行为。

5.1 Learning

Learning is an indispensable process of consuming. In fact, consumer behavior depends on learning to a large degree. Although learning is everywhere in our daily life, some scientists are still incredulous about the process of how the new behavior is acquired and how people are influenced by any other individuals' behavior through learning. Research shows that learning is a relatively permanent change in individuals' behavior occurring as a consequence of experience. Schiffman and Kanuk defined learning, from a marketing perspective, as "the process by which individuals acquire the purchase and consumption knowledge and experience that they apply to future related behavior". Simply, learning is the acquisition of new behaviors. It is agreed that learning involves changes in the behavior that we practice in our daily lives and which becomes a permanent part of our existing set of behaviors.

Learning is an enduring process, i.e. learning, as the result of recently obtained knowledge and practical experiences, constantly updates and upgrades. Specifically, consumers learn from observational and social information, which can renew their beliefs about the quality levels and then determine the future choices they make. Marketers must teach consumers to learn things like where to buy, how to use, how to maintain, and how to dispose the products. But more importantly, embarking on a revolution in consumers' concepts would enable marketers to gain an upper hand among fierce competition. Apple introduced the idea of smartphones when most of the users perceived mobile phones simply as the devices to send and receive texts and make phone calls.

Learning can also occur when no changes happen in individuals' own observable behavior. For example, we can recognize many brands even though we have never used them by ourselves. Those non-observable behavior of consumers are called incidental learning.

There are several theories of learning to explain the learning process. Many theories of learning are old and well established while many other theories are in its evolutionary stage. Regarding the process of learning, two distinctive schools of thought exist, namely, behavioral learning theories and cognitive learning theory.

5.1.1 Elements of consumer learning

Different scholars have different descriptions about learning, but it is agreed that there are several common elements in the consumer learning process.

1. Motivation

Motivation refers to the processes that lead people to behave as they do. It occurs when a need arises that a consumer wishes to satisfy. Motivation is based on needs and goals. It acts as a spur of learning. Uncovering consumer motives is one of the prime tasks of marketers, who then try to teach motivated consumer segments why and how their products will fulfill the consumer's needs. If an individual has strong motivation to get to know and be good at something, there is increased possibility that learning will happen. For example, people who want to become outstanding basketball players would be motivated to learn knowledge concerning basketball. Conversely, people who are not interested are unlikely to pay any attention or ignore all information about basketball. Marketers use motivation research to excavate consumer motives and use it in developing marketing campaigns. Knowledge and theories regarding consumers' motivation will be elaborated in Chapter Six.

> **驱动力：**引领人们行为的过程。

2. Cues

Cue is a stimulus that suggests a specific way to satisfy a silent motive. If motives serve to stimulate learning, cues are the stimuli that give direction to these motives. In the marketplace, price, styling, packaging, advertising and store displays all serve as cues to help consumers fulfill their needs in product-specific ways. Cues serve to direct consumer drives when they are consistent with their expectations. Marketers must be careful to provide cues that do not upset those expectations.

> **提示：**暗示满足隐性动机的特定方式的刺激物。

3. Response

Response means how individuals react to a drive or cue or how they behave. Response can lead to learning which could be physical or mental in nature. Learning can occur even when responses are not explicit. The automobile manufacturer that provides consistent cues to a consumer may not always succeed in stimulating a purchase. A response is not tied to a need in a one-to-one fashion. If the manufacturer succeeds in forming a favorable image of a particular automobile model in the consumer's mind, when the consumer is ready to buy, it is likely that he or she will consider that make or model. Actually, as a result of response-reinforcement, the responses to particular cues or stimuli may be significantly influenced by earlier learning.

> **响应：** 个体对驱动力或提示的反应，或者他们的行为。

4. Reinforcement

Most scholars agree that reinforcement is a positive or negative outcome that influences the likelihood that a specific behavior will be repeated in the future in response to a particular cue or stimulus. It increases the likelihood that a specific response will occur in the future as the result of particular cues or stimuli. Through positive reinforcement, learning has taken place. For instance, if a consumer learns that an advertised facial serum could help brighten her skin, she is more likely to buy the brand for a try, and then repurchase if needed in future, because the effectiveness lived up to expectations. Had the advertised brand failed to deliver expected or promised results after using for a period of time, the individual would be less likely to buy that brand again, no matter how often she gets exposed to advertising or other promotions for the same brand.

> **强化：** 影响特定行为在将来是否会被重复的积极或负面的结果，该行为是对特定提示或刺激物的响应。

5.1.2 Behavioural learning theories

Behavioral learning theories are sometimes referred to as stimulus-response theories because they are based on the premise that observable responses to specific external stimuli signal that learning has taken place. It is believed that an individual's experience is shaped due to the feedback he/she receives from the daily life. When an individual responds in a predictable manner to a known stimulus, the person is said to have "learned."

There are two main theories under the umbrella of behavioral approaches about learning: classical conditioning (sometimes called respondent conditioning) and instrumental conditioning (also called operant conditioning).

1. Classical conditioning

Classical conditioning suggest that when two stimuli are closely linked together and produce a specific learned result then even in the absence of one of the stimuli the remaining one produces the same resultant behavior. Early classical conditioning theorists regarded all organisms as related entities that could be taught certain behaviors through repetition or conditioning. The word **conditioning** means a kind of "knee-jerk" or automatic response to a situation built up through repeated exposure. For example, if you get a headache every time you think of visiting a doctor, the reaction may be conditioned from visiting the doctor. Pavlov's demonstration of conditioned learning in his studies with dogs is also a good example of it.

In the famous experiments that Ivan Pavlov conducted with his dogs, he found that objects or events could trigger a conditioned response. The experiments began with Pavlov demonstrating how the presence of a bowl of dog food (stimulus) would trigger an unconditioned response (salivation). But Pavlov noticed that the dogs started to associate his lab assistant with food, creating a learned and conditioned response. This was an important scientific discovery.

Pavlov then designed an experiment using a bell as a neutral stimulus. As he gave food to the dogs, he rang the bell. Then, after repeating this procedure, he tried ringing the bell without providing food to the dogs. On its own, an increase in salivation occurred. The result of the experiment was a new conditioned response in the dogs.

调节： 对通过反复暴露构建的情形产生"下意识"或自动的响应。

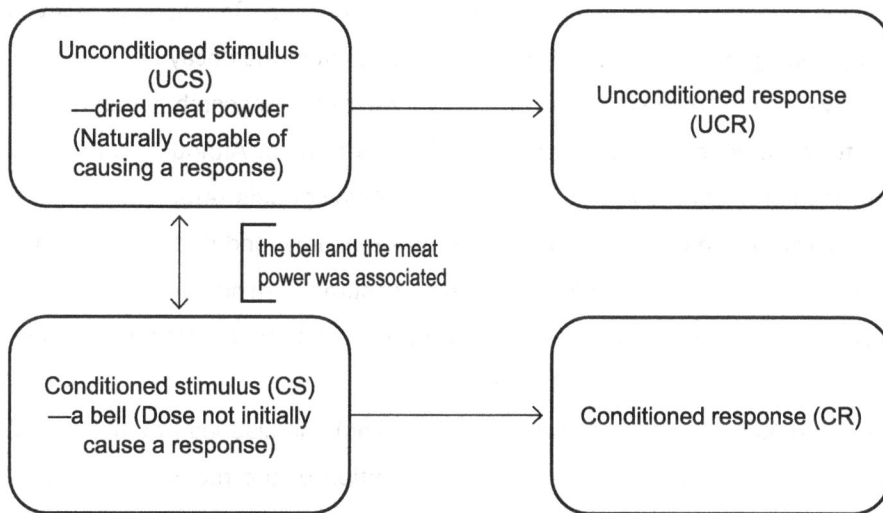

Figure 5-1 Ivan Pavlov's dogs experiment

As we can see from the figure above, response is generated by repeated paired exposures to UCS and CS. Eventually, through learned association and repetition, the CS will cause the CR.

Pavlov's theory was later developed into **classical conditioning**, which refers to learning that associates an unconditioned stimulus that already results in a response (such as a reflex) with a new, conditioned stimulus. As a result, the new stimulus brings about the same response. Under the Neo-Pavlovian theory, the consumer can be viewed as an information seeker who uses logical and perceptual relations among events, along with his or her own preconceptions, to form a sophisticated representation of the world.

Mackintosh (1983) stated that classical conditioning is viewed as the learning of associations among events that allows the organism to anticipate

经典条件反射： 将已经产生反应（如反射）的无条件刺激与新的条件刺激联系起来的学习。

and represent its environment. From this viewpoint, classical conditioning is not reflexive action, but rather the acquisition of new knowledge. According to this view, the relationship or contiguity between the conditioned stimulus and the unconditioned stimulus influences expectations, which in turn influences consumers' behavior.

An unconditioned stimulus might consist of a well-known brand symbol (such as a skin care product brand name Neutrogena) that implies representation of dermatologists' endorsement and pure. This previously acquired consumer perception of Neutrogena is the unconditioned response.

Conditioned stimuli might consist of new products bearing this well-known symbol (such as the items depicted in new products bearing the familiar brand name and logo); and the conditioned response would be trying these products because of the belief that they embody the same attributes with which the Neutrogena name is associated.

The three basic concepts derived from classical conditioning are: repetition, stimulus generalisation, and stimulus discrimination.

1) Repetition

Consumers tend to forget most of the messages they receive. One proven method of increasing retention of learning is repeated exposures, i.e. repetition. Repetition is believed to work by strengthening the bond of association and thus prevent the decay of association in memory, but over time it may cause advertising to wear out. Research suggests that there is a limit to the amount of repetition that will aid retention. Although some over learning (i.e., repetition beyond what is necessary for learning) aids retention, at some point, an individual can become fed up with numerous exposures, and both attention and retention will decline. In order to etch their brands into consumers' mind, some advertisers are willing to repeat their brand names a number of times in just one advertisement, such as the Naobaijin ads broadcasted again and again.

However, overexposure (too much repetitive advertising) can also lead to individuals' boredom, disinterest and decreased attention and retention of the message. David W Schumann, Richard E Petty and D Scott Clemons have proved that varying the ad message can decrease the advertising wear-out effect. This means the effective promotion strategy would be repeated exposures of similar communication content with moderate intervals via alternated media, e.g. transmitting the same message in social media and public transportation advertising. In this way, consumers are well aware but not too annoyed.

2) Stimulus generalisation

刺激泛化： 由某种刺激引起的反应能够由另一种有差别但相类似的其他刺激引起。

Stimulus generalisation occurs when an organism responds to a stimulus in the same way that it responds to a similar stimulus. This occurs during the classical conditioning process. It is the inability to perceive differences between slightly dissimilar stimuli. It is defined as making of the same response with slightly different stimuli—not much learning takes place. For instance, in Pavlov's experiments, dogs could learn to salivate when they heard a similar sound such as keys jangling.

Stimulus generalization can also explain why some "me too" products succeed in the marketplace. It is proved that a new but similar stimulus or stimulus situation will lead to much the same reactions consumers responded to the original stimulus. The more the new stimulus is like the conditioned stimulus, the more probable it is that the new stimulus will produce the same conditioned response. Consumers always confuse the "me-too" products with the original product they have been advertised. It also explains why manufacturers of private-label brands try to make their packaging closely resemble the national brand leaders.

According to Bernard Brelson and Gary A Steiner, the process of stimulus generalisation seems to occur automatically unless stopped by discrimination learning. Stimulus generalisation makes consumers' life easier and allows them to simplify the process of evaluation because they do not have to make separate judgements for each and every stimulus. For example, Air Jordan, a shoe and apparel brand created by basketball legend Michael Jordan in the year 1985, has become one of the most successful campaigns for Nike because consumers will connect Air Jordan shoes with the "best player in the universe"—Michael Jordan. Thus Nike made Air Jordan as a "status symbol" i.e., owning AJ shoes became a very big thing in a social group.

For matching or identical stimuli just one response can be used, unless there is a strong reason to discriminate between them. With more dissimilarities between two stimuli, there is less likelihood that stimulus generalisation will occur. As an increasing number of new products are introduced in the market, consumers use stimulus generalisation from past experience to put them in categories. Properly utilizing this mechanism can drive sales of new products of well-established brands, accelerating the process of entering the market, and thus reducing promotional fees. However, corporations should be vigilant that this also gives competitors opportunities to create counterfeit products. Some local or regional marketers make use of this principle by using look-alike packaging for their products so that they resemble some well-known brands in appearance. Under this circumstance, marketers should remind consumers to identify different products using the stimulus discrimination theory, which will be stated later.

Nowadays, a bunch of new products are introduced to the market rapidly, and there are several strategies that marketers often use based on stimulus generalisation.

(1) Product Line, Form, and Category Extensions: **Product line extension** is the strategy of introducing variants of the same product. The variation may be simply of colour, packaging, size, benefit or flavour, etc., but the core product value remains the same. For example, different flavours can be found among Nongfu Spring's Farmer's Orchard mixed fruit and vegetable juice product portfolio, in packages of several colors, such as the orange mix (orange, carrot, apple and cherry plum), the red mix (tomato, strawberry,

> **产品线延伸：**对同一产品引入各个相关品种的策略。

blackcurrant and apple), and the yellow mix (mango, pineapple, guava and grapefruit). Product form extension means that the same product is available in different physical forms such as Liby laundry soap, powder and liquid. Many drugs are available as tablet, syrup, injections, or as inhalers. Product category extension means diversifying into producing products in different categories and using the same established brand name. For example, Maggi noodles and Maggi tomato chilli sauce. Similarly there are Dove body wash and shampoo; LG home appliances like washing machine and TV, as well as personal care products like toothpastes, etc. The success of the product category extension strategy depends on the quality image of the parent brand because only then consumers are more likely to bring positive associations to the new category extensions.

家族品牌： 在同一品牌名称下售卖数种相关产品的营销策略。

(2) <u>Family Branding</u>: Family branding is a marketing strategy that involves selling several related products under one brand name. Family branding is also known as umbrella branding. It contrasts with individual product branding, in which each product in a portfolio is given a unique brand name and identity. It is another strategy that capitalizes on the consumer's ability to generalize favorable brand associations from one product to another. In other words, the aim is to take advantage of consumers' tendency to extend positive feelings for the brand from one successful product to the next. For example, L'Oréal uses one brand to market soap, lotion, hair shampoo, nail polish, etc. Some consumers are more likely to choose a product with a familiar name over one that is less well-known, even if the known brand is more expensive.

品牌授权： 知名品牌允许其他制造商的产品贴上该品牌的营销策略。

(3) **Licensing**: Allowing a well-known brand name to be affixed to products of another manufacturer is a marketing strategy that operates on the principle of stimulus generalization. The names of designers, manufacturers, celebrities, corporations and even cartoon characters are attached for a fee (i.e. "rented") to a variety of products, enabling the licensees to achieve instant recognition and implied quality for the licensed products, e.g. Calvin Kline or McDonalds.

(4) <u>Look-alike packaging</u>: Some local or regional marketers make use of look-alike packaging to create strong associations for their products with some well-known brands in appearance. This practice can also be seen, for example, in case of various brands of cooking oils prepared from sunflower or soybean, or different brands of iodised table salt. Some companies follow the

policy of stimulus generalisation and some others avoid it.

3) Stimulus discrimination

Stimulus discrimination is just opposite to stimulus generalisation. Unlike reaction to similarity of stimuli, discrimination is a reaction to differences among similar stimuli. The ability to discriminate among stimuli is learned. For example, frequent users of a brand are better able to notice relatively small differences among brands in the same product category. Not taking any chances, marketers use advertisements to communicate brand differences that physical characteristics alone would not convey. The concept of "product or brand positioning" is based on stimulus discrimination, which strives to create a brand's unique image in the consumers' minds. Marketers who offer the me-two type of products attempt to encourage stimulus generalisation among consumers while innovators and market leaders strive to convince consumers to discriminate and consider their brands as different from the generic-type of products and other brands in the same product category. For example, China's herbal tea war between two seemingly same but different companies, Wanglaoji and Jiaduobao (JDB). The famous brand battle has led to some changes in the packaging and marketing of the herbal tea products. Besides the red cans having already differentiating itself in name, the JDB cans are now solid gold in color for the China market.

刺激分化： 对相似刺激物的差异作出的反应。

(1) <u>Positioning</u>: The image or position that a product or service holds in the mind of the consumer is critical to its success. The core objective of "positioning" is to create a brand's unique image in the consumers' minds and "teach" consumers to discriminate or distinguish among similar products based on stimulus discrimination. The outstanding image a product or service holds in the mind of the consumer is critical to its success. When a marketer targets consumers with a strong communication message that stresses the unique ways in which its product will satisfy the consumer's needs, it wants the consumer to differentiate its product from competitive products on the shelf. For example, the entire ad campaign of Mengniu Dairy Company Limited's Deluxe Milk series focused on convincing consumers that "not all the milk products can be called Deluxe" and thereby differentiate its products by delivering superior quality and establishing a premium brand image.

In this case, the company encouraged the consumers to tell their own products apart from its competitors. In most situations, it is very difficult to unsettle a leader brand from its position after stimulus discrimination has occurred. For example, there is nothing unique or secret as far as the ingredient in Vicks VapoRub or Nissin instant noodles are concerned. They are leaders because they were the first to be introduced and got a longer period to "teach" consumers through various marketing communications to associate the brand name with a product. In general, it is more likely that consumers learn to discriminate, if the period of learning is longer, and associate a brand name with a product. Every day consumers are exposed to numerous marketing stimuli, some encouraging stimulus generalisation and others discrimination. The key to achieve stimulus discrimination is effective product or brand positioning.

(2) Product Differentiation: Most product differentiation strategies are designed to distinguish a product or brand from that of competitors based on an attribute that is relevant, meaningful, and valuable to consumers. Many marketers successfully differentiate their brands on an attribute that may actually be irrelevant to creating the implied benefit, such as a noncontributing ingredient or a color. It is often difficult for a marketer to unseat a brand once stimulus discrimination has occurred. One explanation is that the leader was usually the first to enter the market and had to teach customers for a longer period to associate with the brand name. Apple is a prominent example of differentiating a product. Its early ads explicitly stated that Apple's innovative products represent a distinctive and extraordinary way of thinking. These ads' tagline was "Think Different", and they brilliantly conveyed this notion by featuring famous geniuses like Pablo Picasso, Albert Einstein and business magnate Richard Branson, who thought "outside the box" and came up with ideas that changed the world.

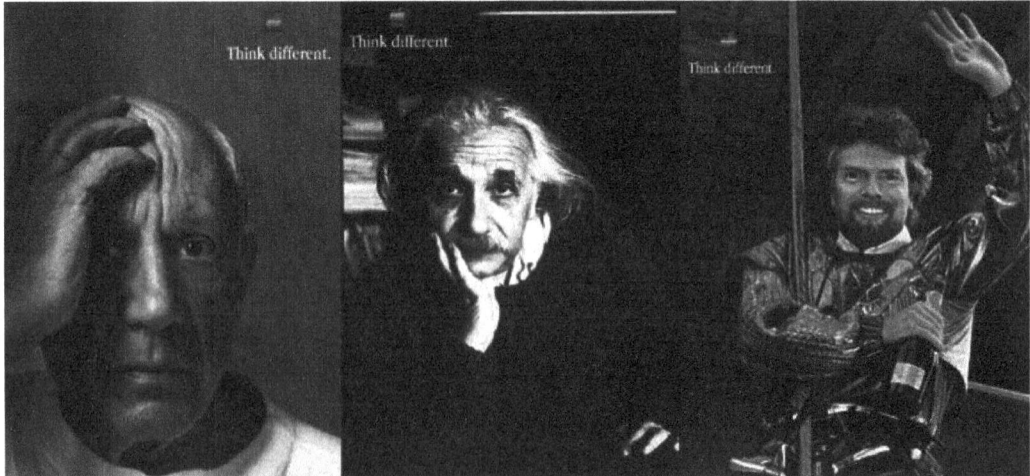

Every day consumers are exposed to numerous marketing stimuli, some encouraging stimulus generalisation and others discrimination. The key to achieve stimulus discrimination is effective product or brand positioning.

工具性条件反射：消费者通过试错过程进行学习，在此过程中，有些购买行为比其他购买行为更能获得良好的结果。

2. Instrumental conditioning (operant conditioning)

Instrumental conditioning (also known as operant conditioning) is a behavioral theory of learning based on a trial-and-error process, with habits forced as the result of positive experiences (reinforcement) resulting from certain responses or behaviors. Psychologist B.F. Skinner is considered the father of this theory.

Like the classical approach, instrumental theory endorses the link between stimulus and the response (i.e. inputs and outputs). But this theory further elaborates the fact that the stimulus that produces the most satisfactory result for the respondent is learned. In consumer behavior terms, it suggests that consumers learn by a trial-and-error process in which some purchase behaviors result in more favorable outcomes (i.e., rewards) than other purchase behaviors. A favorable experience is "instrumental" in teaching the individual to repeat a specific behavior. In the best-known example, a rat in a laboratory learns to press a lever in a cage (called a "Skinner box") to receive food. Because the rat has no "natural" association between pressing a lever and getting food, the rat has to learn this connection. At first, the rat simply explored its cage, climbing on top of things, burrowing under things, in search of food. Eventually while poking around its cage, the rat accidentally pressed the lever, and a food pellet dropped in. This voluntary behavior is called an operant behaviour, because it "operates" in the environment (i.e., it is an action that the animal itself makes). Once the rat recognized that it could receive a piece of food every time it pressed the lever, the behavior of lever-pressing has become reinforced. That is, the food pellets serve as reinforcers because they strengthen the rat's desire to engage with the environment in this particular manner. Classical conditioning depends on an already established stimulus-response connection, while the learner in instrumental conditioning is required to discover a "correct" or appropriate behavior through a trial-and-error process that will be reinforced. Over a number of reinforced trials, the experimental animal learns a connection between the lever (unconditioned stimulus) and pushing it (response).

According to the instrumental conditioning learning theory, behavior is a function of its consequences. Learning occurs because the consequence of a repeated behavior is rewarding. With respect to consumer behavior, instrumental conditioning deems that most learning takes place by means of a trial-and-error process and consumers experience more satisfying results (outcomes or rewards) in case of some purchases than others.

Favourable consequences reinforce the behavior and increase the likelihood of its repetition, that is, the consumer will purchase the product again; unfavourable outcomes will decrease that likelihood.

Reinforcement is a term used in operant conditioning to refer to anything that increases the likelihood that a response will occur. For example, reinforcement might involve giving praise (the reinforcer) immediately after a child puts away her toys (the response). By reinforcing the desired behavior with praise, the child will be more likely to perform the same actions again in the future. Reinforcement can include anything that strengthens or increases a behavior, including specific tangible rewards, events, and situations.

> **强化:** 增强某种刺激与个体某种反应之间的联系。

积极强化：增强特定反应发生的可能性的事件。

消极强化：鼓励某一特定行为发生的负面结果。

惩罚：行为发生后导致的有害或负面事件，降低同样行为在将来发生的可能性。

Skinner distinguished two types of reinforcement. The first type, **positive reinforcement,** consists of events that strengthen the likelihood of a specific response. For example, using a shampoo that leaves your hairs silky and clean is likely to result in a repeated purchase of the shampoo. **Negative reinforcement** is an unpleasant or negative outcome that also serves to encourage a specific behavior. Slathering sunscreen lotion on your face and four limbs can prevent an aversive outcome (getting sunburnt). It is an example of negative reinforcement. Because engaging in the behavior minimizes an aversive outcome, you will be more likely to use sunscreen lotion again in the future.

Either positive or negative reinforcement can be used to elicit a desired response. However, negative reinforcement should not be confused with **punishment**, which is designed to discourage behavior. For example, receiving a fine ticket when you park the car in the wrong place is a form of punishment.

When a learned response is no longer reinforced, it diminishes to the point of extinction, that is, to the point at which the link between the stimulus and the expected reward is eliminated. If a consumer is no longer satisfied with the service a retail store provides, the link between the stimulus (the store) and the response (expected satisfaction) is no longer reinforced, it is "unlearned". There is a difference, however, between extinction and forgetting. Forgetting is often related to the passage of time; this is known as the process of decay. Marketers can overcome forgetting through repetition and can combat extinction through the deliberate enhancement of consumer satisfaction. Marketers effectively utilize the concept of consumer instrumental learning when they provide positive reinforcement by assuring customer satisfaction with the product, the service, and the total buying experience.

The objective of all marketing efforts should be to maximize customer satisfaction. Marketers must be certain to provide the best possible product for the money and to avoid raising consumer expectations for product (or services) performance beyond what the product can deliver. Aside from the experience of using the product itself, consumers can receive reinforcement from other elements in the purchase situation, such as the environment in which the transaction or service takes place, the attention and service provided by employees, and the amenities provided. For instance, most frequent shopper programs are based on enhancing positive reinforcement and encouraging continued patronage. The more a consumer uses the service, the greater the rewards.

Relationships marketers develop an intimate personalized relationship with customers are another form of non-product reinforcement. Knowing that selected merchandise will be advised of a forthcoming sale, or that selected merchandise will be set aside for his/her next visit cements the loyalty that a customer may have for a retail store.

Marketers have found that product quality must be consistently high each time the customer uses it to provide satisfaction. Desired consumer rewards do not have to be offered each time the transaction takes place, and even an occasional reward provides reinforcement and encourages consumer patronage. Marketers have identified three types of reinforcement schedules as follows.

(1) <u>Total or Continuous Reinforcement</u>: An example of a total or continuous reinforcement schedule is the free after-dinner drink or fruit plate always served to patrons at certain restaurants. The basic product or service rendered is expected to provide total satisfaction (reinforcement) each time it is used.

(2) <u>Systematic (Fixed Ratio) Reinforcement</u>: A fixed ratio reinforcement schedule provides reinforcement every time the product or service is purchased (say every third time). For example, a retailer may send a credit voucher to account holders every three months based on a percentage of the previous quarter's purchases.

(3) <u>Random or Variable Ratio Reinforcement</u>: This schedule rewards consumers on a random basis or an average frequency basis (such as every third or tenth transaction). Variable ratios tend to engender high rates of desired behavior and are somewhat resistant to extinction—perhaps because, for many consumers, hope springs eternity. Other examples of variable ratio require certain consumer behaviors for eligibility.

It can be learned from instrumental conditioning that when a learned behavior is no longer reinforced, it diminishes to the point of extinction and the consumer ceases buying by habit. Marketers can combat forgetting by repetition of advertising, preferably not the same ad again and again because this may prove to be boring or annoying, but conveying the same core message and changing only the communication channels.

5.1.3 Cognitive learning theory

The cognitive learning theory explains how internal and external factors influence an individual's mental processes to supplement learning. A considerable amount of learning takes place as a result of consumer thinking and problem solving. Sudden learning is also a reality. When confronted with a problem, we sometimes see the solution instantly. We are likely to search for information based on which to make decisions possible for our purposes. Learning based on the mental activity is called "cognitive learning". It is used to describe the kind of learning that its most distinctive characteristic is problem solving, which enables individuals to gain some control over their environment.

> **认知学习理论:** 是个体对整个问题情景进行感知和理解,领悟其中各种条件之间的关系以及条件和问题之间的关系,并在此基础上产生新的行为的过程。

Typically, consumer behavior involves choices and decision-making, cognitive theorists hold that learning is an intellectual activity based on complex mental processes involving motivation, perception, formation of brand beliefs, attitude development and change, problem solving and insight. Even sudden learning may also happen when someone is faced with a problem. As we acquire more experience and familiarity with different products and services, our cognitive ability to compare various product attributes increases and improves.

One important aspect of a cognitive learning perspective is **observational learning**, which occurs when people change their own attitudes or behaviors simply by watching the actions of others. In this case, learning occurs as a result of indirect rather than direct experience.

> **观察学习：** 通过观察他人及他人的行为结果而改变自身态度或行为的过程。

1. Observational learning

Observational learning is a form of social learning. It takes place by watching the behavior of others. It can occur in a number of different ways and does not require reinforcement in order to be successful. This type of learning often involves observing the behavior of a parent, friend, teacher, sibling, or another person who has a perceived authority or status in a given area. Also, observational learning is a complex process. People store these observations in memory as they accumulate knowledge, perhaps using this information at a later point to guide their own behavior. Imagine a child walking up to a group of children playing a game on the playground. The game looks fun, but it is new and unfamiliar. Rather than joining the game immediately, the child opts to sit back and watch the other children play a round or two. By observing the others, the child takes note of the ways in which they behave while playing the game. In this way, the child can figure out the rules of the game and even some strategies for doing well at the game.

Observational learning doesn't involve reinforcements or repetition. Therefore, it differs from the previously discussed learning theories. Psychologist Albert Bandura (1999) suggested that people often learn through observation, modeling, and imitation. According to Bandura, the observational learning process consists of four parts. The first is *attention*—as, quite simply, one must pay attention to what they are observing in order to learn. The second part is retention: to learn one must be able to retain the behavior they are observing in memory. The third part of observational learning, *reproduction*, acknowledges that the learner must be able to execute (or initiate) the learned behavior. Lastly, the observer must possess the *motivation* to engage in observational learning.

> **树立榜样：** 模仿其他人的行为的过程。

2. Modeling

Modeling is the process of imitating the behavior of others. It can play an important factor in a consumer's decision-making process since it plays into our desires to imitate the behavior of others. Modeling as a marketing strategy can be particularly effective when the models are the individuals (or more appropriately, "influencers") who consumers admire. Marketers utilize the learning theory of modeling by featuring individuals whom consumers aspire to be like or imitate into their advertising campaigns (Dahl, White, & Solomon, 2015).

This is a particularly common form of learning for young consumers, who often observe the behavior of others (individuals whom they look up to or admire, such as an online influencer) and imitate their behavior. Naturally, when speaking of young consumers, the negative effects of this learning model are clear: smoking, high-risk behavior, violence, self-harm, etc. are behaviors that children are not only observing in others, but also perceiving these behaviors as being cool and learning how to copy and perform on their own. The responsibility of advertisers with regard to their influence and impact on children and young consumers has been brought into question, what should be marketed to kids and what should not? Remember advertisements for smoking? No? I do.—But that's because I grew up at a time when there was little consideration about the effects (role) models had on children. Often seen in smoking commercials and billboards, attractive and idealized adults modeled to a young audience the perceived joy and sophistication that came along with being a smoker. After years of scrutiny, activism, and eventually legislation, tobacco companies were no longer permitted to advertise their products to children and young consumers.

5.2 Memory

5.2.1 Memory systems

Memory refers to the retention process of the information about past events or ideas. There are three stages of memory. The first stage is the encoding stage, which means information is entered in a recognizable way. **Encoding** is the process by which we select a word or visual image to represent a perceived object. When consumers are presented with too much information (called information overload), they may encounter difficulties in encoding and storing it all. In the *storage* stage, i.e., the second stage, knowledge is integrated into what is already there and stored. Information does not just sit in long-term storage waiting for *retrieval*. Instead, information is constantly organized and reorganized as new links between chunks of information are forged. In fact, many information-processing theorists view the long-term store as a network consisting of nodes (i.e., concepts), with links between and among them. The total package of associations brought to mind when a cue is activated is called a *schema*.

> **记忆:** 保留关于过去事件和想法的信息的过程。
>
> ···········
>
> **编码:** 选择文字或视觉映像以代表被感知的物件的过程。

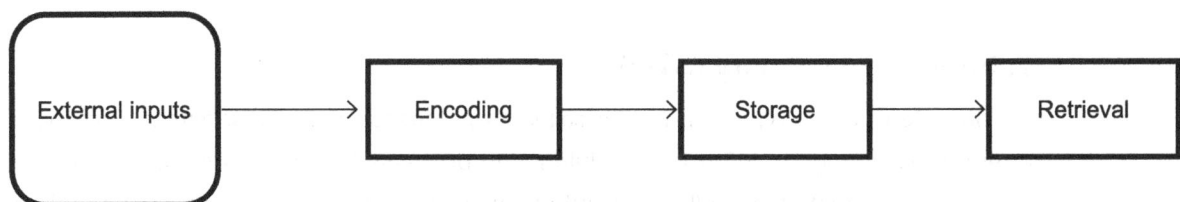

Figure 5-2 The memory process (Soloman 2017:66)

Product information stored in memory tends to be brand based, and consumers interpret new information in a manner consistent with the way in which it is already organized. Consumers are confronted with thousands of new products each year and their information search is often dependent upon how similar or dissimilar (discrepant) these products are to product categories already stored in memory. Consumers recode what they have already encoded to include larger amounts of information (chunking). Information is stored in long-term memory in two ways: episodically (by the order in which it is acquired) and semantically (according to significant concepts). During the last stage, the retrieval stage, individuals access the desired information. It is the process by which we recover information from long-term storage. Marketers maintain that consumers tend to remember the product's benefits rather than its attributes, suggesting that advertising messages are most effective when they link the product's attributes with the benefits that consumers seek from the product. Incongruent elements that are not relevant to an ad also pierce the consumer's perceptual screen but provide no memorable elements for the product.

The information chosen through the processes of attention and perception among the sensory record goes into the short memory, which is the second element of the system, the first being sensory memory. A basic research concern most cognitive scientists have discovered is how information gets stored in memory, how it is retained, and how it is retrieved. Consumers have prior learning experiences, which are accumulated in their minds. Thus it's proved that memory ranges in duration on a continuum from extremely short to very long term. Researchers found that there are three memory systems, which are *sensory memory*, *short-term memory* and *long-term memory*. Every system has its own influence in process in brand-related information.

1. Sensory memory

Sensory memory is a very temporary storage of information individuals receive through senses. However, the senses of human beings do not transmit whole images as a camera does. Instead, each sense receives a fragmented piece of information (such as the smell, color, shape, and feel of a flower) and transmits it to the brain in parallel, where the perceptions of a single incident are synchronized and perceived as a single image, in a single moment of time. The image of a sensory input lasts for just a second or two in the mind's sensory store. If it is not processed, it is lost immediately. For example, when a picture is passed in front of the eyes quickly, its sign stays in the eyes for a second, or when a fly touches on cheek, it is felt at the very moment. The stimuli on sensors need to be transferred to short-term memory by means of the processes of attention and perception in order to be conscious and meaningful pieces.

2. Short-term memory (STM)

Short-term memory, which is also called as processor memory or active memory, is a temporary storage of information while being processed which holds about 7 (plus or minus 2) units of information (letter, number, shape, sentence, photograph, etc.) at a time. Short-term memory can be recalled immediately and it can give continued repetition of a piece of information that can be used for problem solving. It has a limited capacity that may lead to information overload. Previously stored experiences, values, attitudes, beliefs and feelings could be used by complex activities to interpret and evaluate information and add new elements to memory. Both sensory record and long-term memory are connected with short-term memory. If information in the short-term store undergoes the process known as *Rehearsal* (i.e., the silent, mental repetition of information), it is then transferred to the long-term store. The transfer process takes from 2 to 10 seconds. If information is not rehearsed and transferred, it is lost in about 30 seconds or less. The amount of information that can be held in short-term storage is limited to about four or five items.

Moreover, it is important to use some strategies such as repetition, memorization, making sense, associating and grouping to increase the capacity of short-term memory.

3. Long-term memory (LTM)

Long-term memory is transferred from short-term memory and can retain information for a long period of time. Although it is possible to forget something within a few minutes after the information has reached long-term storage to last for days, weeks, or even years. The information is facilitated by chunking, rehearsal, recirculation, and elaboration. For example, pictures are more memorable than words. It is active and can store a variety of information consisting of concepts, decisions, rules, processes, affective states, etc. This is important to marketers because an image of a brand and the concepts that a consumer had heard about a brand, are made up of various elements and the consumer can have a lot of meanings attached to the brand, when the particular brand is mentioned. The amount of information available for delivery from short-term storage to long-term storage depends on the amount of rehearsal it is given. Failure to rehearse an input, either by repeating it or by relating it to other data, can result in fading and eventual loss of the information. Information can also be lost because of competition for attention.

5.2.2 Memory storage

When information comes into our memory system (from sensory input), it needs to be changed into a form that the system can cope with, so that it can be stored. As we learned before, memory is defined as the encoding, storage, and retrieval of an experience, which is a recollection of the past. The relationship between short-term memory and long-term memory can be seen as follow.

> **记忆储存：** 信息以感觉输入的形式进入记忆系统，转变成大脑系统能处理的方式从而保存的过程。

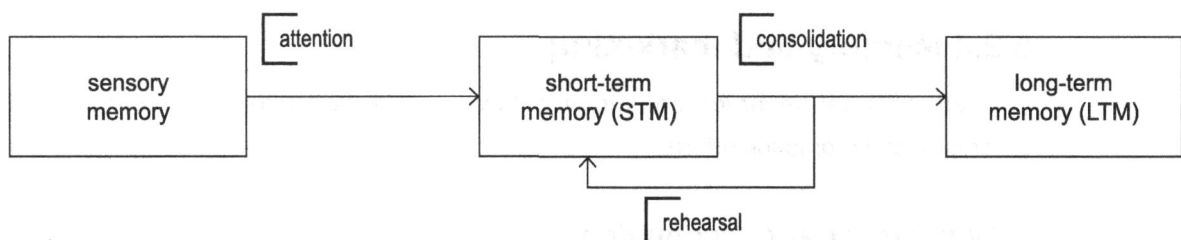

Figure 5-3 The relationship between different types of memory

Individuals do not need to maintain every perceived detail of life in their brain. The forte of memory is not only about keeping things as it is, but it is also a far complex process having various stages through which the information is passed and processed, so it can be used to facilitate the processes of adaptation and learning. For example, whenever you are walking, driving, scrolling on your phone, or just simply sitting somewhere, you are in connection with your environment. Sometimes this connection is so passive that you do not even realize it. The human brain is continuously making thoughts that are created by some sort of sensory information. As soon as we intercept the sensory information, the information is encoded into the STM. Once this information is processed, two different things can happen: the information can be lost or it can be transferred into LTM. Many researchers have proved that the more efforts an individual has done to process the information, the more likely the information will transfer into LTM.

5.2.3 Memory retrieval

记忆检索：个体从记忆储存中调取信息的过程。

Retrieval refers to the process in which individuals getting information out of storage. If a consumer can not remember a specific ad, it may be because he/she is unable to retrieve it. The information simply fails to get to the LTM. There are obvious differences between STM and LTM when consumers are asked to retrieve a particular memory.

STM is stored and retrieved in regular succession without gaps. For example, if a group of participants are given a list of words to remember, and then asked to recall the fourth word on the list, participants go through the list in the order they heard it to retrieve the information.

However, LTM is stored and retrieved by association. For example, consumers can remember brands, products, manufacturers and stores which were saved in their memories according to their own unique experiences. This is why you can remember what you went to the stores for if you go back to the place where you first thought about it.

Organizing information can help aid retrieval. You can organize information in sequences (such as alphabetically, by size or by time). Imagine a patient being discharged from hospital whose treatment involved taking various pills at different times, if the doctor gives instructions according to the order which they must be carried out throughout the day (i.e., in the sequence of time), it will help the patient remember them.

5.2.4 Memory and marketing

Marketers can leverage consumer behaviors and psychologies to add in their advertising and promotion efforts.

1. Brand recall and recognition

In order to facilitate the repeated purchase of customers, marketers would use the brand recall strategy, which plays a crucial role in getting more customers to stick with a specific brand. When a customer buys a certain product, once the product is finished or deteriorated, instinctively they would like to purchase from the same brand, as the experience it has offered was pleasant. Also when a brand is out of the market and then reappears, it is highly possible that you would purchase it again if there had been a nice experience.

The purpose of marketing is to get people to remember your company when they are in need of the products or services that you provide. We spend money to make the brand information relayed in a memorable way so that consumers' mind can store it for easy retrieval at a later date. That is brand recall, a qualitative measure of how well a brand name is connected with a product type or class of products by consumers.

In order to remain competitive in today's highly challenging business environment, marketers are focusing on *brand recall*, as it would mean a competitive advantage against their rivals. By this we mean that if the consumer can remember the brand without having it previously mentioned, then the brand has a great impact on the consumer and he/she recalls the brand very well. Therefore, marketers would work hard to place their brand messages in front of consumers so that consumers would actually remember the ads and transfer the information into LTM.

Brand recognition and brand recall are two ways to analyze whether a consumer will choose a brand because of recall.

Recognition of a brand can happen, for example, when watching different movies where *product placement* has been used. Once you notice the presence of a known product in one of the scenes, you recognize the brand and become aware of the brand immediately. Now when you are in the supermarket, your brain looks at the same brand and immediately makes a decision. Brand recognition is how we access information in our memory to identify a brand. It could also be negative: you recognize a terrible ice cream brand just by looking at the logo or by not having very good memories about it. Brand recognition highly influences the decision process of the customers, and the factors that help in brand recognition include identity, packaging and advertising.

Brand recall, however, does not come from external incentives. Consider that your shower gel is used up and you need to buy a new one. Different brands are going to pop up in your mind. That would be brand recall. However, without brand recognition, there can be no brand recall. We usually recall brands when we think about some category and these brands come to mind. Therefore, this process is connected with our own memory and not from the environment around us. The stronger the brand, the easier it will be for the customers to recall. A brand's value is directly connected to its presence in the memory of consumers. Quite simply, if a consumer remembers a brand, he/she is likely to buy that brand. If he/she doesn't remember it, he/she will buy the ones he/she remembers. Thus, for a brand, it is important to set itself in customers' memory.

2. Nostalgia

Marketers often use autobiographical advertising as a means to create nostalgia for their products. As the years go by, we all develop a certain degree of nostalgic feelings for our younger days. Brands from all industries are experimenting with nostalgia marketing tapping into positive cultural memories from previous decades, designed to drive energy to modern campaigns. Coca-Cola, Microsoft, Lego, even Herbal Essences haircare products are just some of the brands that are trying their hands at stepping back in time to reignite campaign strategies of the past. Whether it's bringing Colonel Sanders back to KFC or engaging millennial gamers with a new Nintendo console, smart brands are maximizing nostalgia marketing and enjoying tremendous results.

Unless you live under a rock, chances are you've heard something about the interactive mobile game that's taking the country by storm. "White Rabbit" is an extraordinary example of nostalgia marketing done well. In an age of impersonal digital media, building social connectedness through nostalgia is an easy way for companies to leverage the optimistic feelings that often accompany walks down the memory lane. Associating brand messaging with positive references from the 00s, 90s, 80s and even the 70s, humanizes brands, forging meaningful connections between the past and present.

Summary

Learning is an enduring process and there are two distinctive theories, i.e., behavioral learning theories and cognitive learning theories can explain the learning process.

Four components appear to be fundamental to almost all learning situations and include motivation, cues, response and reinforcement.

There are two forms of conditioned learning: classical and instrumental. Classical conditioning refers to the process of using an existent relationship between a stimulus and a response to bring about the learning of the same response to a different stimulus.

There are three basic concepts derived from classical conditioning, which are repetition, stimulus generalisation, and stimulus discrimination.

In instrumental conditioning, reinforcement plays a more important role than in classical conditioning.

Memory storage is the process by which the brain can store facts or events so that they can be helpful in the future. It is the process by which life experiences are stored and different skill sets are learned and retained in the brain.

Based on the time for which information is stored in the brain, memories are of the following types:

Sensory memory is created when sensory information is received and processed by the brain. It is either associated with some previous memory and is stored or is either discarded after its processing.

Short-term memory is the one which is stored in the brain for some seconds to minutes;

Long-term memory is stored for months to years. It includes memories about facts and life events as well as memories related to some skills such as writing, typing, etc.

Exercises

(1) Visit a grocery store or a supermarket or a hyper market in your neighborhood and *silently* observe the behavior of individual shoppers and groups of shoppers for an extended period. Record any behaviors that you witness that could be examples of the following concepts: incidental learning, classical conditioning, and instrumental conditioning. Present your findings to the class or discuss them in groups.

(2) Locate a print/digital advertisement that is a clear example of a marketer employing the concepts of stimulus generalization or stimulus discrimination. Present the ads to the class and explain how it works.

(3) [In-class activity] Write down your favorite brand name, and then draw an associative network around the brand that includes three attributes/features, three benefits, three competitors, attributes, and benefits for the competing brands, etc. You can add personal opinions and feelings about the brand to the network.

(4) Create a long list of brand slogans from the past 10 or more years. Divide the class into teams or simply in half. Read the brand slogans one at a time, omitting the brand name. Award points to the first team to correctly identify the brand associated with each slogan. Afterward, point out how memory was strong, even for older slogans (some may be able to identify slogans from when they were very young children). Discuss why this is the case according to the principles of memory in the chapter.

Case Analysis

For most Chinese, coffee is an acquired taste, which means most people are not accustomed to the taste of black coffee at first, and then develop ways to appreciate it. On the other hand, the number of sophisticated coffee lovers in China has been growing in recent years. Adopting what has been learned about consumers' learning in this chapter, read the following news report, find out the triggers for trial of freshly ground coffee, analyze how the accumulation of knowledge about coffee contributes to the enjoyment and constant consumption of the beverage.

Coffee Culture Steaming Hot in China

Coffee has become a lifestyle choice for urban Chinese consumers, with multiple types of the brewed beverage entering the fray, said a recent report from consultancy CBNData. In a survey polling 2,000 consumers in May from China's first-and second-tier cities, over 60 percent said they drink three cups of coffee per week or more. Such cities, exemplified by Shanghai and Hangzhou, Zhejiang province, usually indicate higher levels of economic development and disposable income.

The study found that first-tier city dwellers consume 326 cups of coffee on an annual basis, a level comparable to that of developed economies. The result dwarfed 280 in Japan, was comparable to 329 in the United States and was lower than the Republic of Korea's 367. The findings are surprising on the surface because it wasn't like this until 1988 when Nestle first sold instant coffee in China, with tastes entirely new to most Chinese. And it was in 1999 that Starbucks began offering fresh ground coffee to local consumers who were by then becoming increasingly accustomed to evolving consumption lifestyles.

"Chinese millennials and Gen Z are particularly open-minded and hungry for new experiences," said Wei Yutong, a CBNData analyst. "This is a major factor in the Chinese coffee boom seen throughout the last decade. Millions of young coffee aficionados have been searching for new types of coffees and cafes to try."

Like many consumer goods, online purchases saw the fastest growth, registering 60 percent sales growth in the past year and a 50 percent surge in the number of buyers. Among them, freeze-dried coffees and capsule coffees posted higher growth than coffee concentrates or drip coffees, despite the first two varieties' average higher retail prices. Female shoppers were three times more inclined to try out novel coffee products than conventional ones like instant coffee packages.

Oat milk and other plant-based dairy alternatives are fast rising to become the new darlings of coffee lovers who either suffer from lactose intolerance or simply want healthier options. Nearly 90 percent of those who choose oat milk are female customers, the survey found.

Sophisticated buyers are also taking a closer look at the origins of coffee beans. While established sources like Brazil and Vietnam still lead the way, those from China, Costa Rica, Jamaica and elsewhere are quickly gaining popularity among consumers seeking novel experiences with the beverage.

For offline coffee shops, customers are anticipating a more comprehensive overall experience. The study found that 72 percent of white-collar workers typically go to chain stores for cost-effective drinks that are convenient and consistent in quality. Meanwhile, other avant-garde coffee lovers normally aspire to the uniqueness discovered in standalone boutique shops, or immersive experiences both fun and photogenic.

Also, delivery services have become a staple of life in China. The strategy to support a delivery service for single cups of low-price coffee was immediately accepted by local customers. Nearly all major chain stores have adopted delivery models, while concerns that transport may affect coffee taste have been kept at bay. "With deliveries in place, you do see this rising awareness of freshly ground coffee being promoted as an affordable yet necessary daily pleasure," Wei said.

Coffee has quickly become an iconic venture capital-investing target in China. Of late, tech company ByteDance is smelling opportunities in brewing, backing coffee chain Manner Coffee, which is known for its cost-effective deals and minimalist sleek design of shops. Following suit is Tim Hortons, a Canadian coffee shop that has thrived in China since debuting in 2019. Its Chinese unit, which has also been injected with funds by Tencent, has vowed to open some 1,500 outlets in the country. Domestic chains such as Luckin Coffee have also played a key role in driving up the numbers. Founded in 2017, it is now the second-largest coffee chain in Shanghai, with 499 stores. It runs 4,507 direct-sale stores in China, the most of any brand, foreign or domestic.

CHAPTER SIX
Motivation

Learning objectives

After learning this chapter, you will be able to:

● comprehend the types of human needs and motives and the meanings of goal;

● understand the dynamics of motivation, the selection of goals, the arousal of needs, and the interrelationship between needs and goals;

● learn about several systems of needs developed by researchers;

● master the effective ways of motives measurement and research.

Lead-in Case

China's Alternative Meat Market Heats Up

Fungus-based meat may become a new choice for China's meat substitute lovers as more and more Chinese companies are tapping into the growing plant-based meat market amid rising consumer appetites for healthy and nutritious foods.

"Besides soy and pea proteins that have been widely used to produce meat alternatives in China, fungus protein is also a high-quality ingredient, which can improve food taste and nutrition," said Yang Yongping, chairman of Shanghai Xuerong Biotechnology Co., Ltd.

Xuerong, a leading edible fungus supplier in China with a history of over 20 years, has recently invested in the field of plant-based meat to produce fungus-based meat substitutes, making full use of its expertise in fungus production.

In July, Xuerong announced a capital increase of 14 million yuan ($2.04 million) in cash for Vesta Food Lab, a Beijing-based food technology company dedicated to producing plant-based meat.

Xuerong also announced it will found a joint venture with a Chinese snack company, with a registered capital of 10 million yuan, which will focus on the research and development (R&D), production, and sales of plant-based protein snacks.

The company is not alone in biting into China's expanding protein-based meat market.

Compared with real meat, plant-based meat is high-protein, with low cholesterol and fat, and contributes to environmental protection and animal welfare, which has triggered a food trend that various food companies and capital markets worldwide have been following.

Since US plant-based food manufacturer Beyond Meat went public last year, competition in the plant-based meat substitutes industry has been heating up worldwide.

In China, many start-ups are rolling out products such as mooncakes, glutinous rice dumplings, and noodles containing meat substitutes to lure consumers.

Ramen Talk, a Chinese noodle brand, has recently cooperated with a domestic meat manufacturer to launch a product featuring a plant-based meat sauce similar to Bolognese sauce in flavor.

The first batch of 20,000 packages were sold out in just one minute when the product was released through livestreaming on China's e-commerce platform Tmall, according to company data.

"This is a major trend in the development of China's food industry these days, and it also represents a direction for future food technology," said He Chuchu, product manager of Ramen Talk.

Meat substitutes are nothing new for Chinese consumers, as the country has a long history of eating "mock meat" made from soybeans, usually called "vegetarian meat" in traditional Chinese cuisine.

In recent years, meatless diets have become more popular due to rising concerns over fitness and food quality and safety, driving meat substitute producers to target not only niche vegetarian consumers but also mainstream meat lovers.

The COVID-19 pandemic has further accelerated Chinese consumers' pursuit of healthier diets.

In a McKinsey report on "How COVID-19 is accelerating five key trends shaping the Chinese economy," more than 70 percent of respondents to its COVID-19 consumer survey will continue to spend more time and money purchasing safe and eco-friendly products, while three-quarters want to eat more healthily after the pandemic.

China's plant-based meat market has also attracted many overseas meat substitute producers. Impossible Foods, a US plant-based meat company, brought plant-based meat alternatives from the US to serve about 50,000 meat lovers at the second China International Import Expo in 2019.

Traditional food companies like Xuerong view plant-based meat as an opportunity to expand their existing industry chain.

According to Yang Yongping, Xuerong will explore the meatless meat industry from two aspects. It will use fungus directly in products that taste like real meat, and it will also extract proteins from fungus to produce fungus-based meat substitutes.

"The meatless meat industry for us is a step further into the deep processing of edible fungus. Plant-based meat start-ups have their advantage in R&D, while we have over 20 years of factory management experience. The cooperation is win-win and will contribute to the development of plant-based meat," Yang said.

Introduction

The force that drives vegetarians to purchase and consume plant-based products is crystal clear, that is, to stay healthy and make contribution to the environment protection and animal welfare. The diet of vegetarians is related to their beliefs about what is appropriate or worthwhile, while these emotional reactions will bring a high degree of loyalty to the product.

Human needs, namely consumer needs, are the foundation of all modern marketing. Needs are the essence of marketing philosophy. Under a highly competitive marketplace, it is of great significance of a company to possess its ability in the identification and satisfaction with unslaked consumers' needs, for the sake of survival, profitability and growth.

The comprehension of customer needs is one of the main basic structures of marketing concepts. The nature of being market-oriented rather than product-oriented calls for organizations to consider who their best customers might be, where they are, how to target them and with what. A significant starting point is to understand what they really want.

This chapter discusses human needs that motivate behavior and explore the influence that such needs have on consumption behavior.

6.1 Basic concept

Motivation: Motivation is the driving force within individuals that impels them to action.

动机：推动个体行动的内在驱动力。

Discounts usually encourage consumers to buy.

Needs: The need is a basic biological motive. Needs are the essence of the marketing concept. Marketers do not create needs but can make consumers aware of needs.

需要：基本的生物动机。

Certain products and/or services are created to satisfy unfulfilled consumer needs.

Goals: The sought-after results of motivated behavior.

目标：驱动行为所追求的结果。

Consumers buy face cream for skin care.

6.2 Model of the motivation process

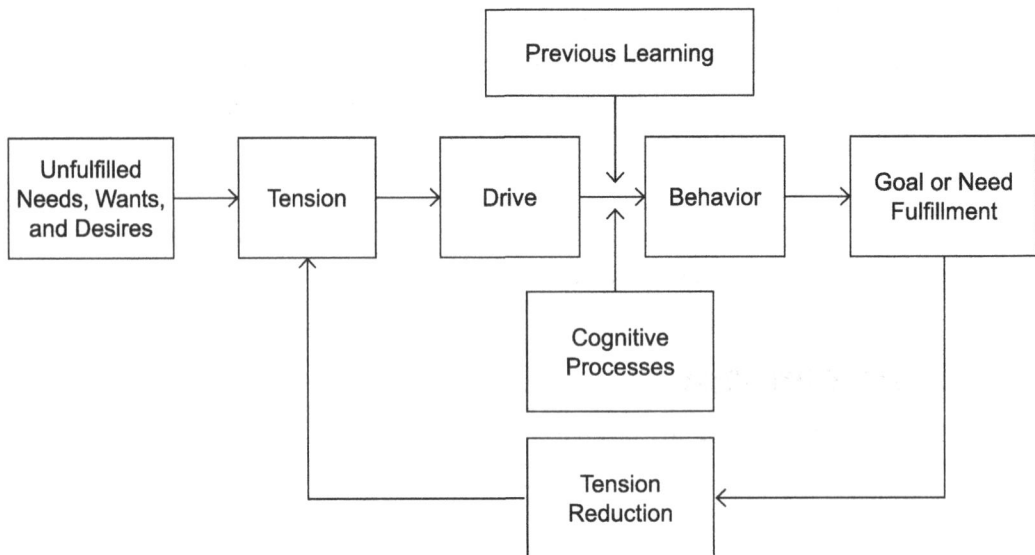

Figure 6-1 Model of the motivation process
(*Consumer Behavior* written by Leon G. Schiffman & Leslie Lazar Kanuk)

As it can be seen in Figure 6-1, motivation is the process of guiding people to act. Motivation arises when the requirements that consumers wish to meet are to be activated. The *need* will create a state of *tension*, driving consumers to try to reduce or eliminate this tension. This need may be utilitarian or hedonic. The final state of this need is the consumer's *goal*. Marketers try to create products and services that can provide consumers with the benefits they want and reduce their tension.

6.2.1 Motivation as a psychological force

Motivation is the basic drive of human behavior and even consumer behavior. Motivation can be described as the internal driving force of individuals that prompts them to take specific actions. This driving force is generated by a state of tension, which is caused by the unfulfilled need that keeps us away from psychological equilibrium or homeostasis (Figure 6-2).

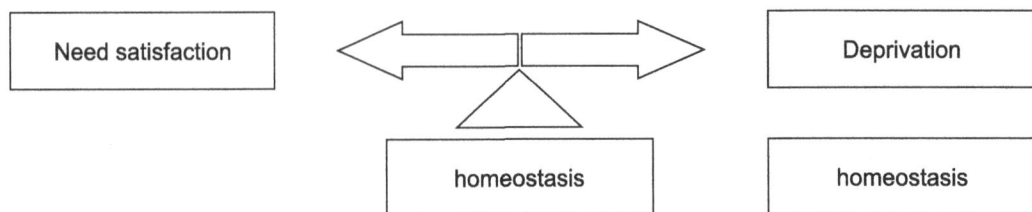

We strive for a state of equilibrium (Homeostasis)
Physiological needs (e.g. hunger) move us away from this
But so do social and psychological needs

Figure 6-2 The homeostasis see-saw
(*Consumer Behaviour* written by Martin Evans, Ahmad Jamal and Gordon Foxall)

In fact, motivated behavior is an activity that is aimed at the achievement of a goal or objective. Not all motives come from physical drives. After satisfying their hunger and other physical needs, people may be found buying such items as fashionable clothes or cosmetics. Obviously, the motives behind this behavior are completely separated from those that involve the satisfaction from physiological drives, for example, keeping warm and the need to eat and drink to sustain life. All kinds of psychogenic drives (e.g. the desire to be appreciated or to have status or feel "at one with one's self") stem from our social environment, culture and the interaction of social groups. Every individual has similar need structure, but at various points in time, under diverse cultural and social contexts, discrete individuals will have distinct specific needs.

6.2.2 Needs

Everyone has needs. Some are innate; others are acquired. *Innate needs* are physiological, which include the need for food, water, air, clothing, shelter, and sex. Because their tasks are to sustain biological life, biological needs are regarded as primary needs or motivation.

Acquired needs are needs that we learn to adapt to the culture or environment. These may include needs for self-esteem, prestige, emotion, strength, and learning. Because acquired needs are usually psychological, they are treated as secondary needs or motivation. They stem from the individual's subjective psychological state and the relationship with others. For example, shelter is needed by all individuals. Therefore, finding a place to live can meet the important basic needs of a young, upwardly mobile couple. However, the type of housing they rent or buy may be the product of secondary needs. The couple may be looking for a place to entertain large numbers of people. They may want to live in a unique community to establish prominent personal images to impress their friends and family. Therefore, the place where individuals ultimately choose to live can meet the primary and secondary needs.

Motivation or need can have positive or negative directions. We may sense a driving force towards a certain object or state or a driving force away from a certain object or state. For example, to avoid health problems or to look more attractive and energetic, a person may proactively start exercising.

6.2.3 Goals

Goals are the sought-after results of motivated behavior. Goals are different from motivation, because goals are external and pull people in a given direction; motivation is internal and pushes the individual. That is to say, the goal is the driving force for action. Having goals can improve task performance: when people have a distinctive, challenging goal, they are more willing to take risks. If someone has a drive that is addressed, there may be several possible goals for that drive. For example, the need for entertainment is felt by an individual, and this may result in a drive to find something to do, which in turn causes the person to set some goals, which lead to some kind of pastime.

The basic results, needs or values that consumers want to achieve are called *end goals*. These end goals can be concrete or abstract. A concrete end goal comes directly from product purchase, while an abstract end goal comes indirectly from the purchase. For example, someone might buy a bottle of wine to go to a party. Partying is the end goal, not drinking the wine. The goal is abstract: it is intangible and involves hedonic and even irrational motives. Abstract goals are not necessarily irrational or hedonic: someone buying a new suit in order to achieve the end goal of passing a job interview embodies the purchaser's practical purpose in mind. A concrete end goal is to buy a new car because of a need for transportation to get to work, while buying a car to manifest your taste is an abstract goal. In most cases, abstract goals can be achieved in multiple ways, just like a new swimming pool or expensive vacations may also leave a great impression on neighbors.

6.3 Motivational conflict

When a need conflict and/or a motivational conflict occurs, it can take one of three basic forms, as follows:

(1) Approach-approach conflict: This occurs when the individual is faced with two or more desirable alternatives. For example, an individual may be invited to a party on a weekend when his or her football team is playing a game 300 miles away. The two events are equally desirable for this person. Approach-approach conflicts are common, because most individuals have limited financial resources or insufficient time, and often have to make a choice between spending money/time on one product/event or spending it on another product/event.

(2) Avoidance-avoidance conflict: This happens when the individual is faced with two or more equally disagreeable options. For instance, someone might be confronted with the choice of having to spend money on buying new shoes to replace the old but comfortable ones, or continuing to wear the old shoes regardless of the fact that they are now draining water and separating at the seams.

(3) Approach-avoidance conflict: This happens when the course of action has both positive and negative consequences. For example, certain drugs have dangerous side-effects. Most purchases have an element of approach-avoidance conflicts because they involve spending money or giving up other things. Many purchases of new products involve a switching cost, namely, the effort and sometimes cash expenditure involved in moving from the old product to the new one. Anyone who has bought a new BluRay player to replace their DVD player knows the switching cost, and researchers have discovered that people are unwilling to spend large-denomination banknotes, because "breaking a 100 banknote" will let people sense the loss about the entire amount.

The relationship between these motivational conflicts is displayed as follows (Figure 6-3).

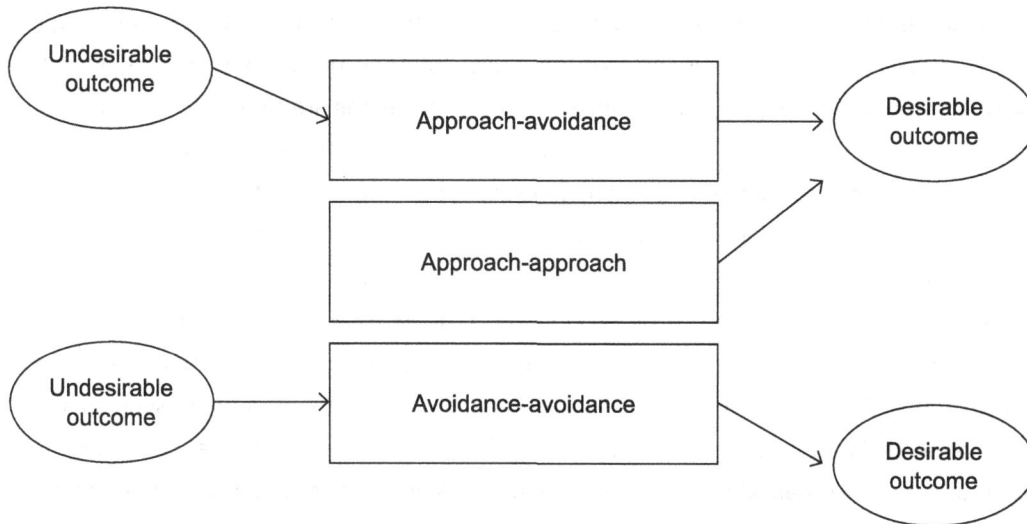

Figure 6-3 Motivational conflict (*Consumer Behaviour* written by Jim Blythe)

In many cases, this situation is far more complicated than a simple dichotomy. This is because we are usually faced with several possible courses of action, each of which with positive and negative consequences. If the conflict of motivation is to be resolved, the individual needs to assign a priority to his or her needs.

The intensity of motivation is sometimes strong enough to overturn all other considerations; while at other times, it may be much weaker. Sometimes, the intensity of motivation is high due to a high level of drive (for instance, a thirteen-year-old who is being mocked at school for wearing the wrong sports shoes will be highly motivated to get the right kind next time). In addition, sometimes motivational intensity is high on account of personal *involvement* with the product category. Involvement implies that the individual attaches great importance to having exactly the right product: for example, a pilot would pay special attention to acquiring the correct spares, fuel and oil for the aircraft, as this will affect the safety of the aircraft. Likewise, a musician might be extremely anxious of acquiring the right instrument; a film star may be very worried about not wearing appropriate clothes, etc. Having to put in some effort into the consumer experience will usually boost consumer satisfaction with the product. This is clearly the case for sports equipment, but this may even be the case for ordinary items such as self-assembled furniture. Each of us has at least some products in which we are highly involved.

From a marketing perspective, producing involvement is obviously essential to cultivating loyal customers. The greater the involvement, the greater the consumer's efforts to meet the need, and the greater the tendency to remain loyal in the future. In some cases, companies can run loyalty programs to keep consumers involved: common examples are loyalty cards in supermarkets and frequent flyer programs in airlines. In other cases, product promotion or celebrity endorsement will also generate involvement.

Motivation can be subdivided into positive and negative categories. People may take action to get a reward, or they may act to avoid an unnecessary consequence. For example, someone may buy aspirin to treat a headache (obtain a positive outcome) or take a dose of medicine every day to prevent a heart attack (negative motivation). Other psychologists divide motivation into internal and external ones. Internal motivations are the ones that originate from within the individual, while external motivations are those that result from an external stimulus or reward. An internal motivation may come from self-actualization needs, (such as the desire to acquire a new language), while an external motivation may arise from social needs or physical needs (such as a need to be recognized by a new group of people, or to move to a larger house).

Alternatively, motivation can be divided into rational motivation, emotional motivation and instinctive motivation. Rational motivations are produced by a conscious thinking process; emotional motivations are those resulting from an irrational source, such as anger, love, pride, jealousy, and so on. Instinctive motivations come from deeper drives and may lead to compulsive behavior: although in most cases, instinctive motivations only drive the occasional impulse purchase.

6.4 The dynamics of motivation

Motivation is a highly dynamic construct, and its reaction to life experience is constantly changing. Needs and goals will change and grow with the individual's physical condition, environment and interactions. When individuals achieve their goals, they will set new goals. If they failed to achieve their goals, they will continue to work for old goals or develop substitute goals. Some of the reasons why need-driven human activities never cease are as follows:

(1) Needs are never fully satisfied: Many needs are never fully satisfied; they continue to take actions aimed at achieving or maintaining satisfaction.

Needs of most people can never be fully or permanently satisfied. For example, everyone experiences hunger needs that must be satisfied, with fairly regular intervals every day. Most people constantly seek the company and recognition of others to satisfy their collective or social needs. Even more complex psychological needs are rarely fully met. For example, a person may act as an administrative assistant to a local politician, thereby partially satisfying the need for power, but this alternative taste of power may not fully satisfy his need. Therefore, he may work hard for a parliamentarian or even run for political office himself. In this case, the realization of temporary goals cannot fully meet the need for power, and individuals will work harder to satisfy this kind of need in a more active way.

(2) New needs emerge as old needs are satisfied: As needs are fulfilled, new and higher-level needs emerge, which can cause tension and induce activity.

Some motivational theorists point out that a hierarchy of needs no longer exists, and low-order needs are satisfied as new, higher-order needs appear. For example, a person whose basic physiological needs are fully met can redirect his efforts to gain acceptance among his neighbors by joining their civic club and supporting their candidate. Once he is convinced that he was being accepted, he can seek recognition by hosting a luxurious party or building a larger house.

(3) Success and failure influence goals: Individuals who achieve their goals set new and higher goals for themselves.

Many researchers have explored the nature of the goals that individuals lay down for themselves. In a nutshell, they concluded that people who successfully achieve their goals usually set new and higher goals for themselves. In other words, they raise their levels of aspiration. This may be explained by their success in reaching lower goals, making them more confident in their ability to reach higher goals. Conversely, those who do not reach their goals sometimes lower their expectations. Therefore, goal selection is usually a function of success and failure. For example, a senior who is not admitted to a medical school may try to become a dentist or a podiatrist.

The nature and continuity of an individual's behavior are usually affected by expectations of success and failure in achieving specified goals. In turn, these expectations are usually based on past experience. A person who takes decent snapshots with a low-cost camera may be motivated to buy a more high-tech camera because he believes that this will allow him to take better photos and eventually he may upgrade the camera for a few hundred dollars. On the other hand, people who are unable to take beautiful photos may keep the same camera or even lose all interest in photography.

These effects of success and failure on goal selection are of strategic significance to marketers: goals should be fairly achievable. Advertising should not make any promises to exceed the scope of benefit delivery. Products and services are generally evaluated by the size and direction of the gap between consumer expectations and objective performance. Therefore, if a good product cannot live up to the unrealistic expectations created by over-promising advertising, it will not be repurchased. Similarly, consumers may be more satisfied with a mediocre product than it warrants if its performance exceeds their expectations.

6.5 The selection of goals

For any given needs, there are a large number of various and appropriate goals. Individuals' selection of goals depends on their personal experience, physical ability, general cultural norms and values, and the accessibility of goals in the physical and social environment. For example, a young woman may wish to possess deep, or even tan skin, and likely to imagine spending some time in the sun to achieve her goal. However, if her dermatologist advised her to avoid direct exposure to the sun, she might end up in employing self-tanning cosmetics as an alternative. The goal must be socially acceptable and physically accessible. If cosmetics companies fail to provide effective alternatives for tanning, the young woman mentioned above will have to ignore the dermatologist's advice or choose an alternative target, such as tanned youthful-looking skin.

Like needs, goals can be positive or negative. A positive goal is a behavioral goal; therefore, it is often referred to as an approach object. A negative goal is a goal on which behavior will evade and is called an avoidance object. Since the approach goal and avoidance goal are both the result of motivational behavior, most researchers refer to them simply as goals. For example, a young person who really wants to get a higher degree takes college as a positive goal, and college represents an approach object. Another person may regard the lack of a higher degree and potential criticism from family and friends as a negative goal, and he or she tries to enroll in college to avoid such negative results. For this person, criticism is an avoidance object.

6.5.1 Substitute goals

When a person cannot achieve a specific goal or the type of goals that he or she is expected to satisfy, behavior may be directed to a substitute goal. Although the substitute goal may not fulfill the needs of the primary goal, it may be satisfactory enough to eliminate uncomfortable tension. Continuing to deprive the primary goal may lead to a substitute goal based on the primary goal. For example, a woman who has stopped drinking whole milk due to a diet may actually start to prefer skim milk. A man who can't afford BWM may convince himself that a new sporty and inexpensive Japanese car obviously has an image he likes.

6.5.2 Frustration

Failure to achieve a goal often leads to feelings of frustration. Every one of us has experienced the frustration of being unable to achieve our goals. The obstacle that precludes the achievement of goals may be personal to the individual, or it may be a barrier in the physical or social environment. Regardless of the cause, individuals react differently to frustrating circumstances. Some people strive to cope by finding their way around the obstacle, or if that fails, by choosing substitute goals. Others are less adaptable and may deem their failure to achieve a goal as a personal failure. These people may adopt a defense mechanism to protect their egos, lest they think that they are inadequate.

Products may represent creative responses to the concept of frustration. For example, consumers may feel frustrated by having to discard fresh, unconsumed agricultural products and fish a few days after purchase. The FoodSaver products include a vacuum sealing machine and corresponding bags and containers, allowing consumers to store perishable foods that cannot be frozen at all or lose a lot of flavor when frozen. Another example is the easy-to-access online help agents who chat with computer users to relieve a lot of frustration of having to go through interminable "frequently asked questions" or dedicated telephone lines with aggravating directions and long waits.

6.5.3 Defense mechanisms

People who fail to cope with frustration usually redefine their frustration psychologically in order to protect their self-images and self-esteem. For example, a young lady may be eager to take a vacation in Europe that she cannot afford. Those who cope may choose a less expensive trip to Disneyland or to a national park. An individual who can't get over it may get angry with the boss for not paying her enough salary to afford the vacation she desires, or she may convince herself that Europe is exceptionally hot this year. The last two possibilities are examples of aggression and rationalization, *defense mechanisms* that individuals sometimes adopt to protect their egos from feelings of failure when they fail to reach their goals. Other defense mechanisms include regression, withdrawal, projection, daydreaming, identification, and repression. The list of defense mechanisms is far from exhaustive, as individuals incline to develop their own ways to redefine frustrating situations to protect their self-esteem from the anxiety caused by failures in the attainment of their goals. Marketers usually consider this fact in their selection of advertisement appeals and create advertisements to portray an individual who solves a particular frustration by using the advertised product.

Defense Mechanism	Description and Illustration
Aggression	In the face of frustration, individuals may turn to their aggressive behavior in order to defend their self-esteem. A tennis player throws a tennis racket to the ground when he is disappointed with his game, or a baseball player frightens the referee for his call. These are examples of this kind of behavior. The same goes for consumers who boycott companies or stores.
Rationalization	People sometimes resolve frustration by conceiving acceptable reasons for not being able to achieve their goal (e.g., not having enough time to implement the project) or thinking that the goal is actually not worth pursuing (e.g., how important is it to get a straight A grade average in all courses?)
Regression	An individual may respond to frustration with naive or immature behavior. For example, a shopper participating in bargain sales may compete for merchandise and even tear up the clothing that another shopper will not give up rather than allowing others to own it.
Withdrawal	Frustration can sometimes be resolved by simply withdrawing from the situation. For example, a person who has difficulty in obtaining the senior management status in an organization may decide that he can spend more of his time on other leisure activities.
Projection	An individual may redefine a frustrating situation by blaming other objects or people for his own failure and inability. Therefore, a golfer who misses a stroke may blame his golf clubs or the caddy.
Daydreaming	Daydreaming or fantasizing may enable an individual to obtain imaginary indulgence of unsatisfied needs. For example, a shy and lonely person may daydream about a romantic relationship.
Identification	When faced with frustration, people may adjust themselves by subconsciously identifying with others or situations that they believe to be related. For example, slice-of-life commercials often characterize a stereotypical situation in which a person experiences a frustrating situation, and then he uses the advertised product to solve that problem. If the viewer can identify with the frustrating situation, he or she may be liable to adopt the suggested solution and purchase the same product.

Continued

Defense Mechanismt	Description and Illustration
Repression	Another way for individuals to avoid the tension arising from frustration is to repress the unsatisfied need. Therefore, individuals may force the need out of their own consciousness. Sometimes, repressed needs will manifest themselves in an indirect way. A wife who is unable to have children may teach in school or work in the library; her husband may do volunteer work in a boys' club. The repressed needs manifest themselves in a socially acceptable form, also known as sublimation, which is another type of defense mechanism.

6.5.4 Interdependence of needs and goals

Needs and goals are interdependent; there is no one without the other. However, people are usually unaware of their needs as they are of their goals. For example, a teenager may not consciously recognize his social needs but may join various online chat groups to meet new friends. A person may not consciously realize his power needs but may choose to run for public office when an elective position appears. College students may not be consciously aware of their need for accomplishments but may try to achieve a straight A grade point average.

Generally speaking, individuals are more aware of their bodily needs than they are of their psychological needs. Most people know when they are hungry, thirsty or have a cold, and they will take appropriate steps to meet these needs. The same person may be unconsciously aware of their needs for acceptance, self–esteem or status. However, they may subconsciously engage in behavior that fulfills their psychological needs.

6.6 Arousal of motives

In most cases, the specific needs of most individuals are dormant. The arousal of any specific set of needs at a specific occasion in time may be caused by internal stimuli in the individual's physiological conditions, emotional or cognitive processes, or stimuli in the external environment.

1. Physiological arousal

Physical needs at any given moment are based on physical conditions of the individual at that time. Lower blood sugar levels or stomach contractions trigger awareness of hunger. The secretion of sex hormones will arouse the sexual need. A drop in body temperature can cause shivering, which makes the individual conscious of the need to keep warm. Most of these physiological cues are involuntary. However, they cause related needs, which can lead to disturbing tensions until they are satisfied. For example, a person who feels cold may turn on the heat in the bedroom and also bear in mind that a warm cardigan sweater has to be purchased to wear around the house.

2. Emotional arousal

Sometimes daydreaming can trigger or stimulate potential needs. Those who are bored or frustrated with achieving their goals often engage in daydreams. They fantasize about being in various ideal situations. These thoughts often cause latent needs, which can create uncomfortable tensions and trap them in goal-oriented behaviors. A young woman who daydreams of a passionate romance may spend her free time in the singles' chat room on the Internet. A young man who dreams of becoming a famous novelist may attend a training course in writing.

3. Cognitive arousal

Sometimes, random thoughts lead to awareness of needs. Providing an advertisement to remind family members may trigger an instant yearning for a conversation with one's parents. This is the basis of the promotional activities of many long-distance telephone companies that emphasize the low cost of international calls. Advertisements are clues designed to stimulate needs. Without these prompts, the needs may remain dormant. Creative advertisings arouse needs and create psychological imbalances in consumers' minds.

When people live in a complex and changeable environment, they will encounter many opportunities for need arousal. On the contrary, when they live in a poor or deprived environment, the opportunity to activate needs will decrease. This explains why television has such a mixed impact on the lives of people in underdeveloped countries. It shows them various lifestyles and expensive products that they would not have seen before and awakens desires that they have little chance or no hope to satisfy. Therefore, although television has enriched many lives, it also frustrated people with little money, education or hope, and may lead to aggressive defense mechanisms such as robbery, boycott, and even uprising.

6.7 Maslow's hierarchy of needs

Clinical psychologist Dr. Abraham Maslow developed a widely accepted theory of human motivation founded on the conception of a universal hierarchy of human needs. Maslow's theory defines five basic levels of human needs, which are ranked in order of importance from lower-level needs to higher-level needs. The theory assumes that individuals strive to satisfy lower-level needs before the emergence of higher-level needs. The lowest level of long-term unsatisfied needs experienced by the individual can inspire his or her behavior. If this need is fairly well satisfied, there will be new needs that prompt the individual to take action. When this need is fulfilled, a new need will appear, and so on. Of course, if a lower-level need goes through some new deprivations, it may temporarily become dominant again.

The chart below shows an illustration of Maslow's hierarchy of needs. For the sake of clarity, each level is depicted as mutually exclusive. However, according to this theory, there is certain overlap between the levels, as no need is ever fully met. Therefore, although all levels of needs below the currently dominant level are still motivating behavior to a certain extent, the main driving force within the individual is the lowest level of need that has not yet been satisfied.

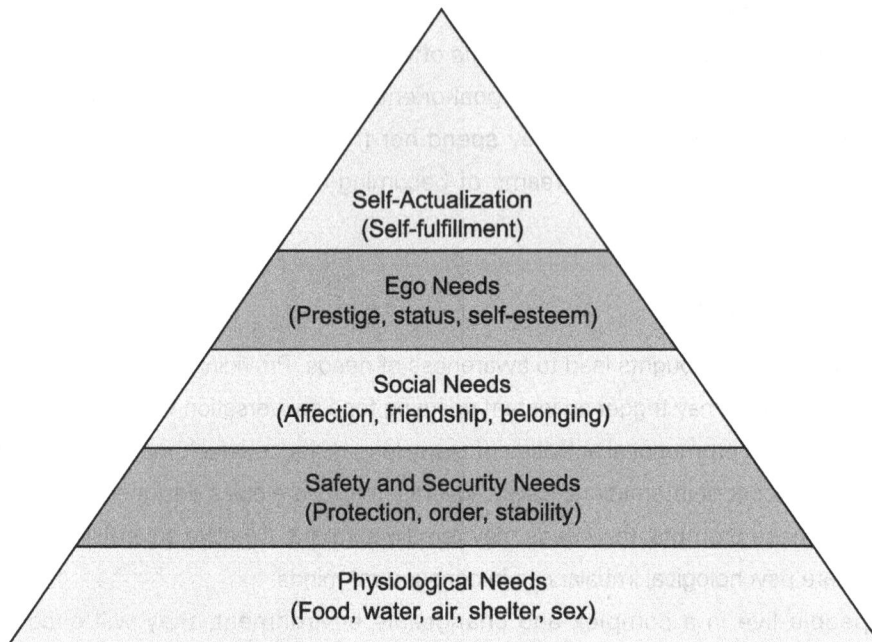

(*Consumer Behavior* written by Leon G. Schiffman & Leslie Lazar Kanuk)

1. Physiological needs

In the hierarchy of needs theory, physiological needs are the first and most primitive level of human needs. These needs, which are prerequisites to maintain biological life, including food, water, air, shelter, clothing and intercourse—all the biological needs, as a matter of fact, were previously listed as primary needs.

According to Maslow, when people are unsatisfied for a long time, physiological needs become dominant: "For an individual who is extremely dangerous and hungry, he has no other interest except food. He dreams of food, he remembers food, he thinks about food, he cares about food, he only feels food, and he only wants food." For many people in this country, biological needs can often be satisfied, and higher-level needs dominate. Melancholy is a common feeling in major cities. However, in underdeveloped countries, the lives of many homeless people almost entirely focus on fulfilling their biological needs, such as food, clothing, and shelter.

2. Safety needs

After satisfying the first-level needs, safety and security needs are the driving force of personal behavior. These needs not only involve personal safety, but also include order, stability, routine, familiarity, and control over an individual's life and environment. For example, health and medical care are significant safety concerns. Savings accounts, insurance policies, education and vocational training are all the means for individuals to fulfill security needs.

3. Social needs

The third level of Maslow's hierarchy includes needs such as love, affection, belonging, and acceptance. People strive for warm and comforting relationships with others and are motivated by love for their families. Due to the importance of social motivation in our society, advertisers in numerous product categories emphasize this appeal in their advertisements.

4. Egoistic needs

When social needs are more or less fulfilled, the fourth level of Maslow's hierarchy comes into play. This level is related to egoistic needs. These needs can be inward or outward, or both. Introverted ego needs reflect the needs of individuals for self-acceptance, self-esteem, success, independence and personal satisfaction of a well-done job. Extroverted ego needs include the needs for prestige, reputation, status, and recognition of others.

5. Need for self-actualization

According to Maslow, most people's ego needs cannot be completely satisfied, resulting in the move to the fifth level, the need for self-actualization. This need refers to the desire of an individual to recognize his or her potential and become everything he or she can be. In Maslow's words, "What a man can be, he must be." This need is reflected in various ways by different people. A young man may aspire to be an Olympic medal winner and work wholeheartedly for many years to become the best in his or her own game. An artist may be required to express himself on canvas. A research scientist may struggle to find a new drug that can eradicate cancer. Maslow pointed out that the need for self-actualization is not necessarily a creative impulse, but it is likely to be employed by people with a certain degree of creativity. Some of our largest companies encourage well-paid employees not just to look at their salaries, but to find satisfaction and self-realization in the workplace, and to view their work as a way to manifest their life achievements.

6.7.1 An evaluation of the need hierarchy and its marketing applications

Maslow's hierarchy of needs theory assumes a five-level hierarchy of dominant human needs. As lower-level needs are fulfilled, higher-level needs become the driving force behind human behavior. The theory actually points out that dissatisfaction, not satisfaction, motivates behavior.

The need hierarchy has been largely accepted in many social disciplines because it appears to reflect the hypothetical or inferential motives of many people in our society. The five levels of need are general enough to cover most individual needs. The main limitation of this theory is the fact that it cannot be tested empirically: it cannot accurately measure the degree to which one level of need must be satisfied before the next higher-level need can take effect. The need hierarchy appears to be closely related to contemporary culture.

Despite its limitations, the need hierarchy provides a very useful framework for marketers aiming to develop appropriate advertising appeals for their products. It can be fitted in two ways: First, it allows marketers to focus the appeal of advertising on a level of need that may be shared by most target audiences. Second, it helps product positioning or repositioning in that consumers can think of certain products to satisfy a particular kind of need.

Maslow's need hierarchy can easily adapt to market segmentation and the development of advertising attractions, because there are consumer products designed to satisfy each of the need levels and most needs are common to most consumers. For example, individuals purchase healthy foods, medicines and low-fat products to fulfill their physiological needs of hunger, and the egoistic needs of being admired. They purchase insurance, preventive medical services and home security systems to react to safety and security needs. Almost all personal care and beauty products, as well as most clothes can satisfy social needs. High-tech products (such as exquisite audio systems) and luxury products are purchased to satisfy the needs of ego and esteem. Postgraduate college education, hobby-related products, and adventure travel with exotic and physical challenges are sold as ways to attain self-realization.

Advertisers can also use the need hierarchy for positioning products and thus determine how prospective consumers should perceive the product. The key to positioning is to identify a niche, unsatisfied need, which is not being occupied by competing products or brands. The need hierarchy is a general tool for the development of positioning strategies, as different appeals for the same product can be relied on different needs presented in this framework.

6.7.2 A trio of needs

Some psychologists have faith in the existence of a trio of needs: the needs for power, for affiliation, and for achievement. These needs can each be included in Maslow's need hierarchy. Considered respectively, however, each is uniquely related to consumer motivation.

1. Power

The need for power is related to the individual's desire to control his environment. It includes the need to control other people and various objects. This need seems to be closely related to the ego need, because many individuals experience increased self-esteem when they exercise physical and mental power on objects or people.

2. Affiliation

Affiliation is a well-known and studied social motivation that has a profound impact on consumer behavior. The need for affiliation is very similar to Maslow's social need and shows that behavior is intensively affected by the desire for friendship, for acceptance, and for belonging. People with high affiliation needs have a tendency to rely on others in society. They often choose products that they think will be recognized by friends. Teenagers who hang out in comic fairs or technicians gather at computer exhibitions usually do this for the satisfaction of getting along with like-minded people.

3. Achievement

Individuals who have a strong need for accomplishment usually regard personal achievement as a goal. The achievement need is closely related to the self-esteem need and the self-realization need. People with a high need for achievement tend to be more assertive, willing to take planned risks, actively investigate their environment, and appraise feedback. The monetary reward provides a significant type of feedback as to individual performance. This kind of people inclines to situations where they can take personal accountability for formulating solutions. For many products and services targeting educated and wealthy consumers, high achievement is a handy promotional strategy.

All in all, individuals with specific, high psychological needs tend to pay special attention to the appeal of advertising for these needs. They also have a tendency to accept certain products. The motivation theory knowledge provides marketers with an essential foundation for market segmentation and promotion strategy development.

6.8 Freudian theory of motivation

Consider the following: Owners of sports cars give words to reasons for purchase as being able to improve safety during overtaking maneuvers. However, this may only be a good reason, and the underlying reason may be that sports cars help attract the opposite sex or is even a substitute mistress. This is not as implausible as it may sound and was actually the theme of a classical advertising for the MGB GT car in the early 1980s. The copy headline for that advertisement is expressed as follows: "Psychologists say a saloon car is a wife and a sports car is a mistress." The proposition of the MGB advertisement lies not only in consumer purchase benefits, but also in functions, and these benefits can sometimes be used to satisfy more deeply seated needs through the use of the above-mentioned slogan. In this case, the sports car was seen as a subconscious symbol.

Sigmund Freud's psychoanalytic theory reinforces this idea and distinguishes three basic structures of the mind: superego, ego and id.

Structure	Level
Superego	Conscious
Ego	Subconscious
Id	Unconscious

1. Id

The Id (identification) is an unconscious, instinctive source of individual's impulses: the source of spiritual energy. It is a beast seeking for instant hedonistic satisfaction, self-interest and short-term perspective. The Id tries to satisfy anything that provides pleasure without considering wide-ranging influences on others, so we say it this way, it is based on the principle of pleasure. Freud believed that sexual desire is the driving force of the id, but a more general explanation is that the id is the reservoir of basic instincts. These instincts may be related to sex or violence, or even past traumatic experiences which linger in the unconscious and exert influence on conscious and subconscious processes. This is a large degree of internal motivation here, based on deeply seated instinct drives.

Many people believe that subliminal advertising may affect consumers on the unconscious level. In the case where consumers are not aware of the influence attempt of such kind of advertising, it is considered to have an impact on behavior. Examples of subliminal advertisement include brief flashes, such as the insertion of "popcorn" or soft drinks in a movie. These flashes are just too short to be consciously perceived.

As we all know, although movies appear convincingly as movement, they are comprised of a series of still frames. The speed of images transmitted through the projector gives the impression of movement. The point is that our senses are not quick enough to distinguish each frame. The idea behind this kind of product placement was to use this knowledge and believed that the single-frame insertion will not be consciously noticed, but because it did physically appear on the screen for less than a second, there would be a chance that the receiver may subconsciously accept the information. Naturally, for the test products, soft drinks and popcorn, the sales during the commercial break were much higher than the sales of the control group of audiences where there was no insertion projection. This approach has been criticized by the media, and due to the general public concern, subliminal advertising is considered illegal in many countries or regions.

Subliminal images can also be inserted into pictures, in a disrupted or hidden manner. For example, the word "sex" is placed in the ice cubes in a glass of whisky. The suggestion is that these hidden flashes or pictures are being unconsciously observed and processed, and without any cognitive defense or screening of superego, conveyed to the mind of consumers. These subliminal messages can have a powerful influence on behavior without people perceiving that they are affected.

There is even a popular notion that we are unconsciously affected by pheromones, a sort of clandestine aroma that we all secrete, which has not yet been confirmed. The obvious application is in perfume formulation, which may promote greater sexual attraction between each other.

However, if subliminal advertising should work, it will raise many ethical questions about whether to allow this type of advertising. Nevertheless, there is still enough attention for the legislation to remain.

2. Superego

However, the superego represents the inner manifestation of the morals and values of those significant to us society and operates at the conscious level. In this way, the superego is more of an external motivation. It consciously controls our behavior by trying to make it conform to these internalized norms. It is our social conscience and can conflict with the id.

3. Ego

On the other hand, the ego reacts to the real world and plays an intermediary role between the id and reality. It does not operate at the conscious level, but neither is it merged into the unconscious; rather, it is a subconscious mediator between the other two aspects. Therefore, it controls our instinctive drives and tries to attain a realistic way to satisfy our impulses, or a socially recognized outlet that can completely address the desires the id drives.

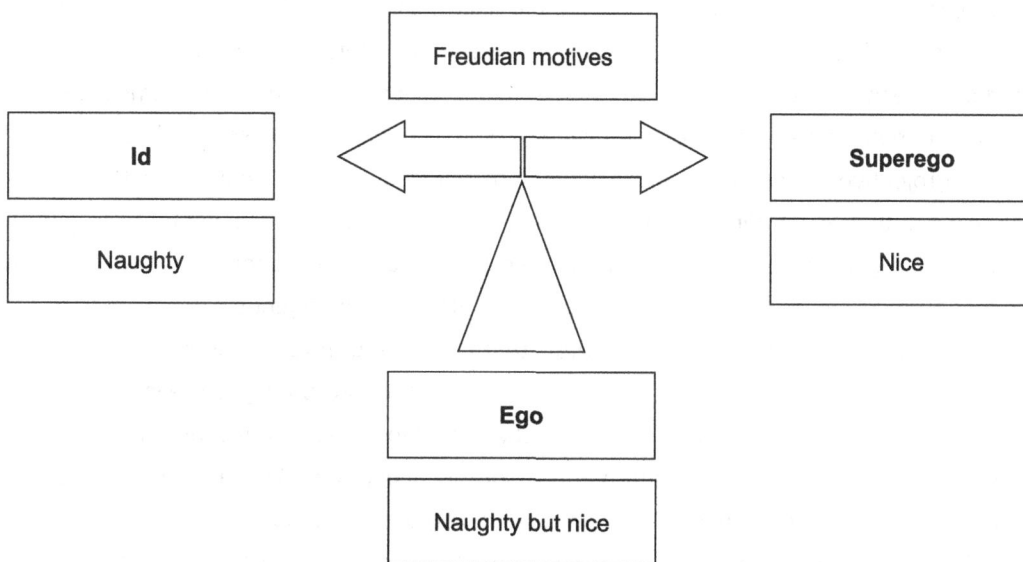

6.9 The measurement of motives

How to identify motivations? How to measure them? How do researchers know which motivations are related to certain kind of behavior? These are difficult questions to answer because motivations are hypothetical constructions, which means it's not possible to see or touch, process, smell or physically observe them. Therefore, no single measurement method can be regarded as a reliable indicator. Instead, researchers customarily rely on a combination of research techniques to try to determine the existence and strength of various motivations. By combining various research methods, including getting responses to questionnaires or survey data, as well as eliciting valuable answers from focus group discussions and in-depth interviews, consumer researchers can gain more effective insights into consumer motivations than they would by using any one of the techniques alone.

Under normal circumstances, interviewees may not be aware of their motives, or are unwilling to disclose them in direct questioning. In this case, researchers use qualitative research to explore consumers' unconscious or hidden motivations. Many qualitative methods are also called projective techniques because they require respondents to explain stimuli that have no clear meaning and assume that the subject will reveal or project their subconscious, underlying motivations into the abstruse stimuli. The findings of qualitative research methods rely heavily on the training and experience of analysts; these findings not only represent the data themselves, but also the meaning from the analyst's personal perspective. Although some marketers are worried that qualitative research will not produce unambiguous numbers that objectively prove the point under inspection, some other marketers still believe that qualitative research is more instructive than quantitative research.

6.10 Motivation research

It is apparent from the foregoing that the identification of consumers' motivations is a complex matter. The difficulties involved in ascertaining directly the exact motivational factors that influence purchase behavior led some marketers and consumer researchers to design techniques to reveal hidden motivations. Such techniques sometimes need to reveal the motives being suppressed, some of which are briefly discussed below.

(1) Projective Techniques: If individuals are relieved of direct responsibility for their expression, they will incline to answer more freely and truthfully. Projective tests aim to achieve this goal. These are called projective tests, because respondents are asked to project themselves into someone else's place or into some ambiguous situation.

(2) Third-Person Test: In third-person tests, the respondent is invited to respond through some third party. The reason for this is that there are both good reasons and real reasons for behavior. Good reasons are socially acceptable (to buy environmentally friendly products). Real reasons are sometimes not socially acceptable. While good reasons will probably be given in response to a direct questioning approach, such as "why did you buy this?", these answers may only be partially true. There may be a real reason for behavior that either the respondent is unwilling to admit or fails to recognize. An indirect question, for example, "what sort of people purchase this?" or "why do people buy these?" may be adequate to reveal real reasons for behavior.

(3) Word Association Test: This type of test is also known as free association and involves firing a series of words at respondents who must verbalize instantly the other words which come into their minds. The word association test can be employed to determine consumer attitudes towards products, stores, advertising themes, product features and brand names.

(4) Psychodrama: Here, the respondent is required to play a role and to do so, they are provided with a complete description of the situation. For example, the role-playing of respondents to describe two alternative painkillers with other respondents acting as the role of the pain. How the painkiller deals with the pain might lead to the copy strategy in direct response and other advertising campaigns.

(5) <u>Cartoon Test</u>: Informants are presented with a rough sketch showing two people chatting. One of them has just said something represented by words written into a "speech balloon" as in a comic strip. The other person's balloon is empty and the respondent is asked how this other person might reply. The idea is that the respondent's subjective feelings are projected through that reply.

Evaluation of Motivational Research

To this day, the development of early motivation research with its expanded qualitative direction, not only enfolds the aspects of Freudian origin, but also incorporates a wide range of qualitative methods and procedures, making it a well-established part in daily consumer research. Large and small businesses often use qualitative consumer research methods, including focus group meetings and in-depth interviews, as well as extensive lines of questioning and exploring routes to gain deep-seated insight into the reasons for consumer behavior. Since motivational research usually reveals unexpected consumer motivations related to product or brand use, one of its current strategic uses is to develop new ideas for promotional activities for the sake of uncovering consumers' conscious awareness by arousing unidentified needs.

Qualitative research also empowers marketers to explore consumer responses to ideas and advertising copy at an early stage, refraining from costly mistakes caused by placing invalid and untested ads. In addition, as with all qualitative research techniques, the results of motivational research provide understanding for consumer researchers, and these insights laid the foundation for structured, quantitative marketing research on a larger, more representative sample of consumers.

Summary

Motivation is the driving force within individuals that prompts them to take action. This driving force is generated by an uncomfortable state of tension, which exists due to unsatisfied needs. All individuals have needs, wants and desires. The individual's subconscious drive to reduce the tension caused by needs leads to behaviors that he or she anticipates will satisfy needs, resulting in a more comfortable internal state. Motivation can be either positive or negative.

An individual's innate needs are physiological in nature, which include all the factors required to maintain physical life. The acquired needs of an individual are primarily psychological, which include love, acceptance, respect and self-realization.

All behaviors are goal-oriented. Goals are the sought-after result of motivated behaviors. The form or direction that behavior assumes and the selection of goals are a result of thought processes and previous learning. There are two types of goals: generic goals and product-specific goals. A generic goal is one that may satisfy a certain need; a product-specific goal is a specifically branded or labeled product that the individual sees as a way to satisfy a need.

Product-specific requirements are sometimes known as wants. For any innate or acquired need, there are a lot of different and appropriate goals. The specific target selected leans on the personal experience, physical ability, general cultural norms and values, and the goal's accessibility in the natural and social environment. Needs and goals are interdependent and will change according to the individual's physical conditions, environment, interactions with other people, and experiences. As needs are fulfilled, new higher-order needs emerge that must be satisfied.

Failure to achieve a goal often leads to frustration. Individuals respond to frustration in two ways: "fight" or "flight". They might cope by looking for a way around the hindrance that disallows goal achievement or by taking up a substitute goal (fight); or they may assume a defense mechanism that empowers them to protect their self-esteem (flight). Defense mechanisms include aggression, regression, rationalization, withdrawal, projection, daydreaming, identification, and repression.

Motivation is not easy to infer from consumer behavior. People with different needs may seek satisfaction by selecting the same goals; people with the same needs may seek fulfillment through different goals. Although some psychologists have declared that individuals have various need priorities, others believe that most people experience the same basic needs, to which they assign similar priority rankings. Maslow's hierarchy of needs theory puts forward five levels of human needs: physiological needs, safety needs, social needs, egoistic needs, and self-actualization. Freudian theory of motivation distinguishes three basic structures of the mind: id, ego and superego. Other needs have been widely integrated into consumer advertising, including the needs for power, affiliation, and achievement.

Several self-reported and qualitative methods are adopted and employed for the identification and measurement of individual's motivations, and researchers combine these techniques to assess the existence or strength of consumer motivations. Motivation research and its current extended form (commonly referred to as "qualitative research") are aimed at in-depth study of consumers' conscious awareness level and to determine potential needs and motivations. In addition, quantitative research has proven to be valuable for marketers to verify the results obtained from qualitative research.

Exercises

(1) Briefly describe the motivation process based on needs, tension, and goals.
(2) Marketers create advertisement appeals by portraying an individual who solves a particular frustration with the use of the advertised product. Find one or more ads which utilize one aspect of the defense mechanisms (e.g. aggression, rationalization, withdrawal, projection, daydreaming, etc.) to help consumers address their psychological issues.
(3) Since a purchase decision may involve multiple motivations, consumers often find themselves in situations where positive and negative motivations conflict with each other. Identify and discuss the three general types of motivational conflict. In addition, please comment on how these conflicts help to produce the satisfaction of needs. Provide an example of how marketers adjust their marketing communications to suit consumer needs in each situation.
(4) List the primary needs demonstrated in Maslow's hierarchy of needs. Give an example of a product that is suitable for each form of need.

Case Analysis

Conduct a survey among your fellow students and find out their sporting habits and related purchase experiences, including preferred ways of working out, and the time and money spent on regular exercises. Combining the information provided below and the knowledge about motivation introduced in this chapter, formulate a comprehensive report on the ways of sports-related consumption of university students, including identification of potential business opportunities.

Fitness Craze Beefing Up Bicycling Boom As Urbanites Embrace Great Outdoors

Tan Lei, an architect in Beijing born in the 1980s, commutes daily by bicycle from Monday to Friday, and joins her friends in road cycling excursions on the weekends. Cycling has now become an integral part of her life. "I cycle for around 1 hour and 10 minutes to work every day, and the same duration back. When I get to my office, I take a shower and get refreshed for work. Cycling frees me from traffic jams and I can enjoy the view. On weekends, my friends and I usually cycle together," Tan said.

Travelers ride bikes alongside Qiandao Lake in Chun'an, Hangzhou, Zhejiang province, in May.

Tan is among millions of consumers in China who are embracing cycling as part of the rising awareness of healthcare and environmental protection, and thus helping spur the development of the country's sports industry. "My first bike, which was a folding bike, was bought for around 3,000 yuan ($463). Later on, I bought two more folding bikes, both costing me around 10,000 yuan, and a road bike, which cost me over 40,000 yuan. I also spend money on accessories, such as a spare chain, flywheel, helmet, glasses, cycling jersey, gloves and pedals. I don't spend too much on the accessories. One of my friends bought a limited edition of a cycling jersey series, which has seven sets of clothes he can wear from Monday to Sunday. Each set is priced over 1,000 yuan," Tan said.

Shenzhen, Guangdong province-based research firm OCN said that currently, there are over 100 million regular cyclists in China, among whom around 6 million are genuine bike enthusiasts. China has over 20,000 kilometers of cycling greenways, over 3,000 cycling clubs and more than 3,000 cycling-themed activities and races every year, which get millions of people involved in cycling. In 2020, the market size may have reached 160 billion yuan, and the compound annual growth rate in the coming five years will be around 10 percent, the firm said.

The cycling market has great room for development. According to data from the Chinese Cycling Association, the current annual average spending by China's cycling enthusiasts is 5,820 yuan, and over half of these consumers spend over 10,000 yuan per year. In 2019, the cycling population in both Beijing and Shanghai surged over 200 percent year-on-year. "Apart from building up people's bodies, cycling is expected to become a strong supporting subcategory within China's sports industry," said Shen

Jinkang, former president of the Chinese Cycling Association.

According to a report jointly released by Qinghai Lake International Cycling Race and Guangzhou, Guangdong province-based Magic Cycling Corp, in 2020, amid challenges brought by COVID-19, the global bicycle sales grew. The sales revenue of Brooklyn Bicycle surged by 600 percent year-on-year, while Brompton, the largest bike manufacturer in the United Kingdom, said that in April 2020, its online bike sales increased by fivefold year-on-year. Sigma Sports, a London-based retailer for high-end road bikes and triathlon equipment, saw its sales of entry-level bicycles skyrocket by 677 percent year-on-year in April 2020, and even bicycle-related accessory and tool kit sales grew by 255 percent year-on-year.

According to the report, in the first half of 2020, males dominated the Chinese cycling market, accounting for 95.28 percent of the total cycling population. Those aged between 31 and 40 were the major consumption group, taking up 29.26 percent of the total. In terms of people's cycling habits, 72 percent of surveyed consumers rode bikes at least once a week. People preferred to ride during mornings and evenings, with around 35 percent choosing to ride between 6 a.m. and 11 a.m. and another 35 percent riding from 7 p.m. to midnight.

An Guangyong, an expert at the Professional Committee of Credit Management of China Mergers and Acquisitions Association, said, "The pandemic caused people to stay away from enclosed transportation means such as buses and subways, and shift to safer means of transportation, such as bicycles. This brought opportunities to the cycling market. Correspondingly, the government should enhance awareness, such as publicizing the environmental protection role that cycling plays. Enterprises should explore more cycling scenarios, including traveling, contagion prevention and control, daily commuting and public welfare. They should also build up a cycling-related culture."

Lai Yang, a member of the expert committee of the China General Chamber of Commerce, said, "China's cycling consumption market is diversified. Some cycle for daily commutes, while others see cycling as a sport, fashionable and even a lifestyle. Enterprises should consider the needs of different consumer groups and work out specific business strategies."

CHAPTER SEVEN

Formation and Transformation of Attitudes

Learning objectives

After learning this chapter, you will be able to:

- understand what attitudes are, how they are formed, as well as their nature and characteristics;
- comprehend the composition and scope of selected modes of attitudes;
- apprehend how experience leads to the initial formation of consumption-related attitudes;
- identify the various ways in which a consumer's attitude is changed;
- recognize how a consumer's attitudes can lead to behavior and how behavior can lead to attitudes;
- master the effective ways of attitude measurement.

Lead-in Case

Fizz, Fortunes of Classic Soft Drinks Rising

Dai Jiangxiao took a huge gulp of her Asia Sarsae soda. With its unique flavor, the drink hit the spot.

Living in Guangzhou, capital of Guangdong province, Dai said she regarded Asia Sarsae, a sarsaparilla soft drink similar to root beer, as the taste of the city.

The iconic drink has a strong, minty flavor like Honghuayou (Red Flower Herbal Oil), a Chinese herbal remedy to relieve pain. While it has yet to rise to prominence throughout China, it has captured the hearts of many local residents.

The brown, carbonated drink, first rolled out in Guangzhou in 1946, using extracts from Ilex

asprella, a traditional Chinese medicine herb used to "clear inner heat". According to traditional Chinese medicine doctrine, "heat" trapped within the body can cause many ailments, especially for people who live in hot, humid places.

In the days when air conditioners were not widely affordable, residents in Guangdong had a habit of drinking chilled Asia Sarsae to refresh themselves on sweltering summer days.

"I still remember my friends and I swilling the soda with a straw from a white plastic bag in the 1980s," recalled He Wenfeng, CEO of Guangzhou Xph Asia Beverage, which produces the drink. "Glugging the drink was typical during the summers of my childhood."

However, Asia Sarsae soon fell out of favor as international beverage giants like Coca-Cola and Pepsi-Co entered the Chinese market in the 1990s. "Asia Sarsae nearly disappeared in the late 1990s and early 2000s," He said.

Asia Sarsae was not the only domestic drink brand losing its market share. Once served at state banquets, Beibingyang, a soft drink brand rooted in Beijing, was barely seen in the 1990s. Another Chinese cola brand, Tianfu, previously the country's top-selling soft drink in the 1980s, saw its market share plunge to only 1 percent in 2005.

But domestic drinks have made a comeback over the past decade after successful rebranding.

"The rise of Asia Sarsae was boosted by consumers' nostalgia for their childhood and a brand-new image of the old drink," He said. According to the CEO, 80 million bottles of Asia Sarsae were sold in 2019, and the sales volume surpassed 100 million bottles last year.

"The taste of Honghuayou is the soul of our drink," he said, adding that while keeping the taste unchanged, the company has improved the formula of the drink to make it healthier.

Asia Sarsae has rebranded itself to appeal to young consumers by offering diversified products, such as low-calorie soda and fruit-flavored soft drinks, and by participating in online shopping festivals.

The company has also expanded its cooperation with convenience stores and famous Cantonese restaurants like Tao Tao Ju to lure more young customers, he noted.

"I rushed to buy an Asia Sarsae when I rediscovered the drink on a shelf," said Dai, who is in her 40s. "The taste awakened my memories of school 20 years ago."

Other traditional Chinese soda brands have also staged comebacks over the past decade. Beibingyang achieved profitability only two months after it resumed production in 2011.

Hankow Er Chang, a new beverage brand born from an old-time classic in Wuhan, was catapulted into the limelight by marrying trendy cultural elements with eye-catching designs.

"The revival of domestic brands not only helps remind people of their childhood but also wins the hearts of the younger generation through continuous innovation," He said. "It is also an important channel for people, especially foreigners, to get a taste of the city."

7.1 Introduction

In view of consumers, every one of us has a large number of attitudes towards brands, products, services, e-mails, the Internet, advertisements, and so on. No matter where we are told whether we like a product (e.g., a scarf of a certain designer brand), a service (e.g., China Southern Airlines), a specific retailer (e.g., Suning), a particular direct marketer (e.g., Taobao), etc. or not, we often express our attitudes. What's more, it is very probable for consumers to form a positive or negative attitude towards the product, which you like or dislike, under conditions when advertisements are designed to show the specific aspects of the product. We can think about how our attitudes will be when we see a certain brand and the advertisement advocating it. In this chapter, we will take a close look at the events of attitudes towards marketing elements including brands, products and advertisements.

An appreciation related to prevailing consumer attitudes has huge strategic advantage in the context of consumer behavior. For example, with the rapid development in the promotions of natural-ingredient body wash all over the world, it tends to show the recently widely-spread attitude that "natural" things are nice and "synthetic" things are terrible. In fact, body wash is a combination of chemicals, some of which are safer and nicer than others only because of better ingredients. The perception among consumers about products being "natural" or not only depends on how and what the marketers claim it.

In order to get to know the center of what is developing an individual's behavior, researchers have been carrying out a number of attitude researches to answer a wide range of questions relevant to strategic marketing. For instance, researchers often conduct attitude researches to determine if target consumers will accept the proposed idea about a new product, to find out if they will react positively to the new designed theme, or to figure out why a company's claims haven't attracted consumers, or to collect comments on a proposed shift in the company's exterior design. For example, main shoe marketers such as New Balance or Sketcher often carry out surveys among consumers about which commercials of different kinds of functional athletic footwear that they prefer. Attitudes of consumers stating about different aspects of their shoes like size, comfort, fashion and other elements are tested; how consumers react to the newly designed patterns or functional features as well as the latest advertisements and other marketing information designed to develop is also analyzed; ways to switch consumer attitudes are tried out. Several marketing activities are relevant to the significant mission of influencing consumers' attitudes.

In this chapter, we will seek out the causes why some marketing activities had made so pervasive an influence on consumers' attitudes. And the properties that are essential to attitudes formation and transformation will also be discussed, along with some general limitations came across in attitude researches. Specific focus is devoted to the important themes of attitude formation, attitude change, and relevant strategic marketing events.

7.2 Basic concepts

7.2.1 Attitude

态度：一种后天形成的倾向，对某一客体一直喜欢或不喜欢的行事方式，形成对该事物的正面或负面的评价，并会长期持续一段时间。

Pepsi or Coca-Cola? This is such a hard question to answer. Pepsi and Coca-Cola are both carbonated soft drinks, but for some reasons like celebrity endorsement, taste, price, etc., some people prefer Pepsi to Coca-Cola while others Coca-Cola to Pepsi, or like or dislike both. Here, our "preferences" "likes" or "dislikes" about Pepsi and Coca-Cola is a kind of attitude.

Attitudes are what put us in the right position of behavior. We each have attitudes towards many things, such as our friends, our possessions, our families, government policies, or other people's behavior and so forth. Our divergent attitudes are (in part) what differentiate us as human beings. Since attitudes determine the direction of most consumption behaviors, they are of great significance to marketers, both in terms of finding out the nature of attitudes and effective ways to form and change them.

We do have a lot of attitudes and seldom do we question how we have established them. By asking a consumer some questions, a market researcher assesses the attitude that the consumer holds towards a brand by inference of the consumer's behavior. For instance, by asking a consumer questions regarding online shopping platforms, a researcher finds out that he/she constantly chooses Yili instead of Mengniu when buying something nutritional to drink for their breakfast, and often recommends the product to their friends or relatives, an inference might be drawn that the consumer holds a positive attitude towards this brand of Yili.

Besides, an attitude tends to last for long because it is a common concept that comes from temporary issues. For example, it is very normal for us to hear all kinds of noises in our daily life. Once you have heard an ordinary one, you might create a general opinion towards the characteristics of the noises in your mind, which eventually forms into attitudes towards all the other objects.

Therefore, in the context of consumer behavior, attitude is an acquired predisposition to behave in a constantly favorable or unfavorable way concerning a given object and is an evaluation of an object with some degree of positivity or negativity, which lasts for a long time.

Think about it:
When it comes to choosing drinks for breakfast, which one do you prefer, Yili or Mengniu? And why? What is your attitude towards each brand?

7.2.2 Attitude object

As far as the consumer-oriented definition of attitude has been concerned, the word "object" should have wide meanings including specific consumption or marketing-related concepts, for instance, products, brands, product uses, commercials, Internet sites, prices, etc. It is agreed that an attitude is learned and can be conceptualized as a compendious evaluation of an object. Attitudes regarding buying behavior are shaped on account of direct experience with the product, word-of-mouth knowledge acquired from others, or exposure to mass-media commercials, the Internet and such diverse forms of direct marketing as a retailer's catalogue.

> 态度对象：任何人持有态度的客体，可以是客观物体或抽象的想法。

Therefore, attitude research tends to be object-specific. Given this, an attitude object is anything to which one holds an attitude and can be either a physical object or an abstract idea. For instance, if we research carbonated soft drinks, the research "object" might include without limitations Pepsi, Coca-Cola, Spirit, Mirinda, 7-UP, Fanta and the like.

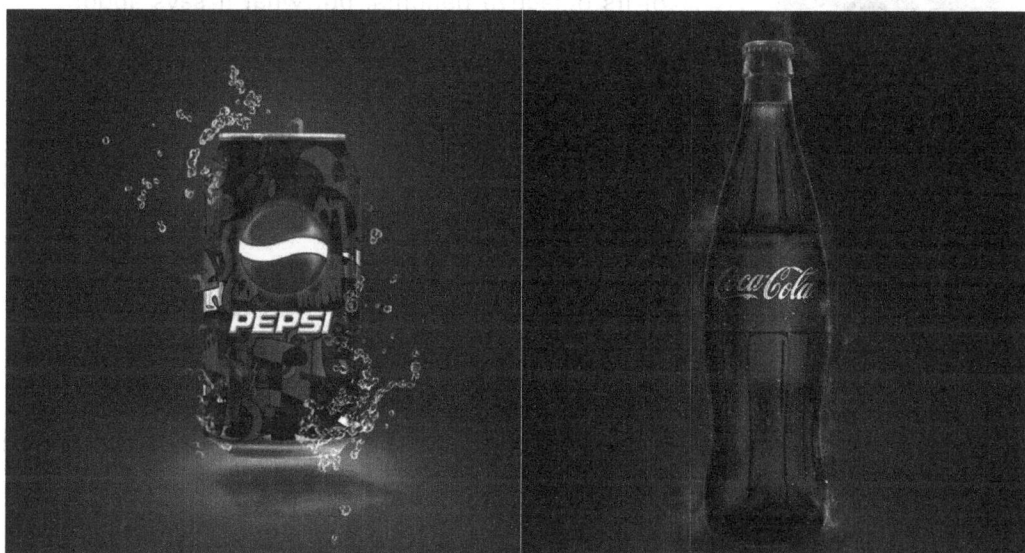

7.3 Functions of attitude

Functional Theory of Attitudes, proposed by the American psychologist, Daniel Katz, (1903—1998) talks about a pragmatic approach that focuses on how an attitude facilitates social behavior. According to Katz and his theory, attitudes are functional for a person and are decided by a person's motive, and a consumer can have the same attitude, but reasons can be diverse; the reason why attitudes exist is that they serve a certain function for the person, namely *utilitarian*, *value expressive*, *ego-defensive*, or *knowledge function*.

> 态度的功能：效用功能、价值表现功能、自我防御功能、知识功能。

1. The utilitarian function

The general rules of award and punishment are related to the Utilitarian Function. We develop attitudes on things if they are pleasurable or painful.

For example, a female consumer who always chooses Liby laundry detergent over other brands because she thinks it does an excellent job in keeping her clothes clean and fresh. Her attitude towards brands of laundry products is based on the practical functions the products serve. Advertisements that emphasize the existence of product benefits meeting customers' needs will appeal to those who hold attitudes resulting from the Utilitarian Function.

2. Value-expressive function

The consumer's central values or self-concept have an important effect on the Value-Expressive Function. In this situation, a person forms an attitude towards a brand or a product, not because of its objective benefits, but what it says about him. Take the selection of car brands for example. When a man is driving a Hongqi (meaning red flag), a Chinese car manufacturer, it actually reflects his status and patriotism. In conclusion, people tend to cultivate an attitude to show a particular identity.

3. Ego-defensive function

Ego-Defensive Function is built in the situation where consumers feel like protecting themselves from either external or internal threat insecurities such as spraying deodorant before going out, and carrying a small pack of mint drop in case there is bad breath in the mouth. They take these measures to prevent from embarrassing events like being discovered to give out unpleasant odor, and therefore protect their personal image.

4. Knowledge function

When a person is in an unclear situation or when he faces a new product, he might create attitudes that are related to learning about knowledge. For example, from product attributes or a probable source like *Consumer Reports*, consumers are able to learn about the goods from their detailed description.

Sometimes attitudes express kinds of common functions. As for marketing strategies, marketers know they can customize relevant advertisements if they are aware of the dominant function that constitutes target consumers' attitude.

In addition, degrees of commitment to the attitude objects seem not the same from consumers' demonstration. As for sport fans, they might need diehard fans, fair weather fans or social group attendees (going for party) for different purposes.

7.4 The ABC model of attitudes and the hierarchy of effects

7.4.1 The ABC model of attitudes

The ABC model of attitudes refers to the three parts most researchers agree an attitude has, including AFFECT(A), BEHAVIOR(B), and COGNITION(C) in which:

AFFECT (A) means how a consumer feels about an attitude object, that is, the way in which a consumer feels about an attitude object, or what a consumer thinks of the attitude object.

BEHAVIOR (B) refers to what the consumer intends to do, that is, the consumer's actions concerning an attitude object, or a consequence which doesn't always lead to an exact behavior.

COGNITION (C) is what the consumer believes to be true about the attitude object, that is, the beliefs a consumer has on the attitude object, or what a consumer is likely to believe about the attitude object.

> **态度的成分：**情感成分、行为成分、认知成分。
>
> **情感成分：**消费者对态度对象的感觉。
>
> **行为成分：**与态度对象有关的行为或行为倾向。
>
> **认知成分：**消费者对态度对象的认识、理解和评价。

7.4.2 The hierarchy of effects

The hierarchy of effects explains the relative impact of the three components: affect, behavior, and cognition. It is a fixed sequence of steps that occurs during attitude formation, which varies depending upon such factors as the consumer's level of involvement with the attitude object.

1. High involvement hierarchy

High Involvement Hierarchy is built when consumers come to know about more and more about a product, evaluating beliefs and forming a feeling. It is also called the Standard Learning Hierarchy because it is perceived as the "normal" or regular process to form an attitude. In this kind of situations, consumers buy products because of passion. This means that consumers pay extra attention to the high-quality advertisements of the products, which might contain plenty of information about these products. As for the people attracted to buy houses, their cognition about the houses comes first, and then the feeling about buying houses has been aroused, which results in the behavior of purchasing.

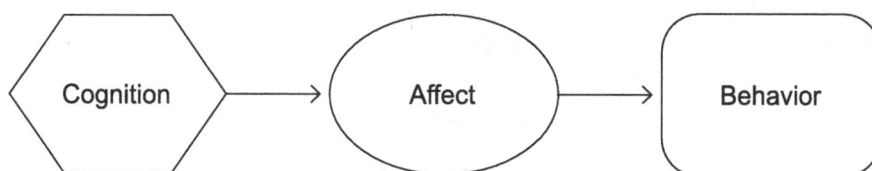

**Buying a Home
High Involvement
C-->A-->B**

Cognition (research, belief)
Affect (feeling)
Behaviour (buying)

2. Low involvement hierarchy

On the contrary, when the consumers are limited to the knowledge and have no preference on brands, they buy products for their inertia for the reason that they consider less when buying these goods with relatively low prices, such as candies, soft drinks and daily necessities, etc. In other words, they don't even bother to spend much time and effort studying information about low involvement products. There is almost little hesitation when the purchase behavior happens (do). Then the affection about the goods is built up while and after using them (feel). Gradually, experience and information regarding this category of products have been accumulated (think). Imagine yourself standing in front of a huge refrigerator full of soft drinks in a convenient store, trying to decide which bottle to choose to quench your thirst. Maybe you'd immediately pick up the one you always drink, and maybe this time you want to try something new. In this case, whichever seems appealing to you might trigger purchase. After trying out the new drink, maybe you'll feel good/bad about it. Such an experience becomes the memory which will aid your decision making next time.

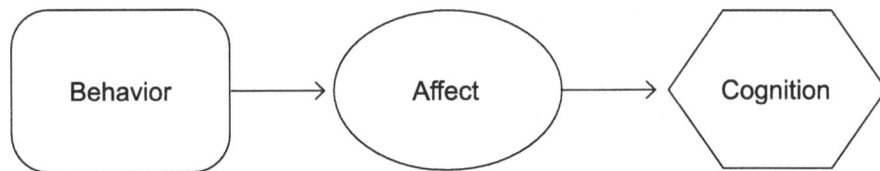

Behavior → Affect → Cognition

3. The experiential hierarchy

It refers to the situation when consumers don't know much about the product or the brand's attributes or benefits, but have an overall evaluation based on their own emotions or imaginations, then subsequently make purchases, and finally form some understanding about the brand or the product. A typical example of this type of attitude formation has something to do with celebrity endorsement. Most students have the experience of buying a product or choosing a particular brand because their idol is the spokesperson. This means you develop positive feelings for the brand first (feel), and then you buy the product in support of your idol (do). By using the product, you have acquired some knowledge about it (think), which will directly or indirectly influence your next purchase. In a broader sense, other intangible product attributes like package design, advertising, brand names and certain conditions (sound, scent and/or visual and/or haptic elements) of the surrounding in which the experience occurs would forge our attitudes towards the brands and/or products.

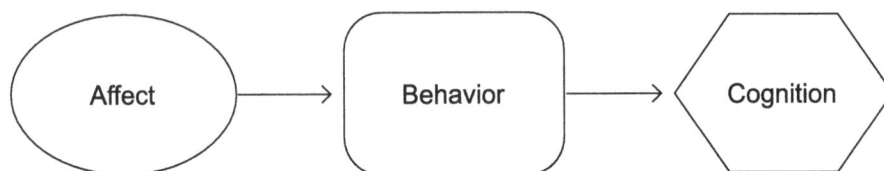

Affect → Behavior → Cognition

The Hierarchy of Effects sometimes leads to a rule which is in paradox: the less important the product is to consumers, the more important are the marketing stimuli such as a catchy jingle, or an interesting package, etc.

7.5 Attitude towards advertisements

The way a consumer chooses to respond in a comfortable way to a special advertising stimulation when a particular opportunity is exposed is called the attitude towards the advertisement. Not only does the consumer have an attitude to products but also to the advertisements for the reason that it can make the consumer form and even change the attitude towards the product.

Viewers' attitude towards the advertiser, how he/she evaluates the ad, how his/her mood is evoked and his/her level of arousal is raised can determine the their attitude towards advertisements, including how they react when seeing the ad appear in a certain time spot in their favorite program.

Advertisements have the ability to evoke feelings. When advertisements are made, different people seeing it are given different feelings by the advertisers (warm, negative, excited and so forth.). For example, most ads about baby care products create the atmosphere of warmth and harmony due to our fondness of puppies, kittens or babies. And what makes humans so willing to share their love with their babies, puppies and tiny animals? Let's see what the *Wall Street Journal* says about it: "Regarding of the fact that dog turns out to be short snouts, high foreheads, round faces and big eyes, which activates the dopamine reward center in the brain. In addition, many scientists think baby features evolved to 'release' caregiving behavior in adults. So why do we love piglets and puppies too? Because our brains aren't great at differentiating between our own cute babies and those of animals."

7.6 Forming attitudes

Attitudes are formed in a handful of different ways. From what we have learned in previous chapters, our attitudes may be formed resulting from classical conditioning or instrumental conditioning, or complicated cognitive processes.

7.6.1 The process of forming attitudes

Relying on the specific operation of hierarchy of effects, consumers form their attitudes towards the attitude object. A pleasant or memorable jingle, for example, will be paired with the brand name repeatedly. Transferring favorable feelings for the music to the brand is a typical process of *classical conditioning*. On the other hand, *instrumental conditioning* also helps attitudes reinforce, which makes you think your desire is exactly satisfied if the attitude object is exactly advertised. Additionally, during the process of complex *cognition*, consumers are able to learn to form an attitude. Friends or colleagues tend to wear products the celebrity has endorsed or used. Consumers think they'd fit in if they used things or achievements coming from people they are fond of or adore.

What's more, we create different types of attitudes when seeing different kinds of objects: the attitude object is strongly supported by brand loyal consumers who already hold a firm belief; while occasional users will give up the product if something special or fantastic shows up.

7.6.2 Levels of commitment to attitude

There are various levels for the consumers to commit to their attitude, which are related to the level of involvement with the attitude object. The following statements are the three levels of commitment.

Compliance (顺从)—Considered as the lowest level of involvement, an attitude is formed because of the rewards we gain or the punishment we don't want to face. This attitude is quite simple, and it is easily changed when consumers' behavior is not monitored any more or a new alternative shows up. You might eat bread because many ordinary stores are selling it, and going somewhere else for noodles will somehow be troublesome.

Identification (认同)—Identification exists under the condition that we create an attitude to agree with another individual's or team's expectations. Depending on the tendency of consumers, advertisers might simulate the behavior of desirable models and depict advertisements with the dire social consequences when consumers prefer to choose certain products rather than the expected ones.

Internalization (内化)—A part of internalization, regarded as a high level of involvement, consists of firmly consolidated attitudes coming from our value system. It might be quite difficult to change the attitude because they play a significant role in our daily life. What can happen when a marketer has trouble dealing with deep-seated attitudes can be reflected by the infamous Coke debacle of the 1980s, which is still considered as an example in marketing textbooks today. At that time, Coca-Cola made up its mind to change its flavor formula in order to satisfy the possible requirement of younger consumers that often have a preference on a sweeter taste, which can also show more special aspects of Pepsi. The company carried out strict random taste tests which showed individuals who were unaware of what brands they were drinking have a preference on the taste of the new recipe. Surprisingly, when New Coke was sent onto the shelves, the headstrong Coke fans strongly protested and the company suddenly faced a wide-ranging consumer rebellion. As for the company, the allegiance to Coke coming from the majority of loyal users matters obviously more than those who preferred a new formula. The brand had to deal with this social crisis and protect its previous properties rooted from intense persistence and nostalgia.

7.6.3 Principle of cognitive consistency

In our daily life we won't say things like "I like cats more than any other animals. They are the most terrible creatures on earth." or "My favourite singer is Jacob. His songs sound weird." It goes wrong because what we say and what we actually believe don't come together. According to the principle of *cognitive consistency*, consumers tend to chase for harmony among what they think, what they feel, what they behave, which means, they want to maintain harmony among these elements. Therefore, there is a chance that we might also change our thoughts, feelings, or behaviors to make them coherent with later experiences. A famous singer may do something terrible and live like an ignorant moron occasionally, but his fans maybe will understand him and choose to forgive him—or give him up. The consistency principle reminds us that we don't casually form our attitudes, and an essential factor influencing our thought is how they get along with other attitudes we have already held.

7.6.4 Theory of cognitive dissonance

According to the theory of cognitive dissonance, if a person is faced with inconsistencies among attitudes or behaviors, he/she will take some measures to deal with this dissonance. Maybe a change in his attitude or a modification in his behavior will be carried out to regain consistency. The theory plays an important branch for consumer behavior. Consumers usually meet with conditions where there are some contradictions between their attitudes toward a product or service and what they really feel like doing or buying.

7.6.5 Elaboration likelihood model (ELM)

After reviewing the attitude change related to particular strategies, the Elaboration Likelihood Model indicates a more general opinion that consumer attitudes could be changed by two clearly different "roads to persuasion": *a central route or a peripheral route*. The central route is mainly related to attitude change when consumers are willingly motivated or able to evaluate the attitude object. In other words, attitude change will happen when a consumer takes an active part in seeking out information about the attitude object. In addition, recent researches have found that an emotional center will occur during the cognitive process of the route. When consumers are buying a house, they pay extra attention to the major issues like what facilities are provided, what kind of structure it is, whether it is close to where transportation is convenient, etc.

On the contrary, if consumers are lack of motivation or don't feel like taking part in evaluation, attitude change is likely to happen through the peripheral route. In this situation, consumers focus less on the information which is relevant to the attitude object. For example, when you grab some quick snack, whatever is available nearby will influence your choice. However, even when the consumer is in the low-involvement situation, where both central and secondary motivations have the ability to arouse consumers' similar attitudes, central motivation eventually gets more continual power to make consumers create a change towards the attitude. That is to say, in the snacking scenario, if what's handy for you is not up to your appetite, you might choose not to eat any snacks, unless you are extremely hungry.

Dual Mediation Model (DMM) is a branch of the elaboration likelihood model, which connects brand cognition with the attitude. This model indicates the probability that a peripheral cue could affect the central route to persuasion. In this way, it demonstrates the inter relationship between central and peripheral routes. Besides, DMM is shown to explain the importance of advertisement in affecting consumers' behavior.

7.6.6 Self-perception theory

Self-perception Theory is an alternative explanation of dissonance effects. It shows that people buy things according to the beliefs in their mind (I must like ice cream); or the performances they operate (I keep buying ice cream), which includes self-observation and self-derivation. Self-Perception Theory is relevant to low involvement hierarchy which is stated above. For example, you might think about this: "I must have been into Wechat for a long time, as if I had spent half my lifetime on it."

The *foot-in-the-door technique* adopted by the salespeople when they drop in on consumers can be explained with the self-perception theory. Based on the observation that consumers are more likely to agree to a smaller request, the salesperson will propose a further request by asking them to spend a little more time listening to their introduction. In this way, consumers become willing to deal with or justify their previous decision.

7.6.7 Social judgment theory

Social Judgment Theory is a perspective that people receive and sum up new information about attitude objects according to what they have already learned or felt. They will regard the initial attitude acts as an instance, then standardize and categorize the new information they hear.

7.6.8 Latitudes of acceptance and rejection

There is an important aspect in the Social Judgment Theory. In terms of the information, people form levels of acceptance and refusal around their attitude standard. Ideas will be reconsidered or evaluated favorably in light of the latitude. However, if ideas fall outside of this zone, it gets easier for consumers to reject out of hand. Generally speaking, if consumers are highly involved with the attitude, they will have a relatively narrower latitude.

7.6.9 Balance theory

Balance Theory is a theory that considers relations among components a consumer may perceive as belonging together, and how they will react or justify the relation among the elements for the purpose that they will restore consistency or balance. In this way, a whole complete unit relation is formed.

The attitude structure is a triad consisting of:

(1) a person and his perceptions

(2) an attitude object

(3) some other person or object

① balanced   ② unbalanced   ③ balanced   ④ (un)balanced

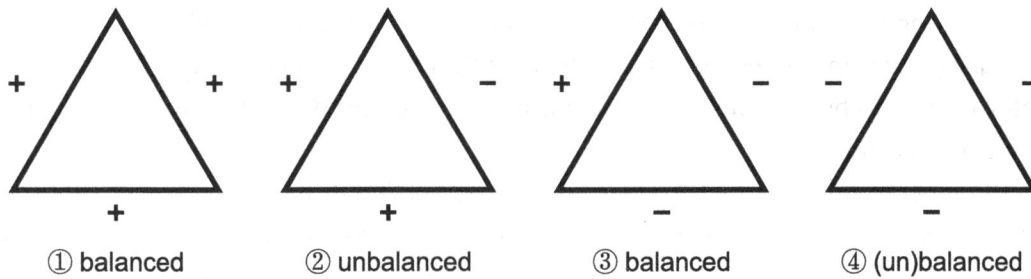

For example, Monica likes Jerry, when she knows Jerry likes to wear Nike sports shoes, even though she does not like Nike, she might try to find a way to balance her attitude and her feeling, which means she may grow to like Nike or reduce her affection for Jerry to achieve balance. In terms of marketing applications, the "balancing act" is in the center of celebrity endorsements, where marketers wish that the famous person's popularity will be transferred to the product. Besides, a celebrity is often invited to encourage charitable behaviors on a nonprofit organization.

7.7 Attitude models

7.7.1 Multi-attribute attitude models

If we need to know something about the reason why a consumer feels like that towards a product or what measures marketers can take to change a consumer's attitude, a simple reply doesn't seem to be enough. How we evaluate the product mainly depends on our beliefs about it. Therefore, we need a multi-attribute attitude model to understand the attitudes. The model assumes a consumer's attitude of attitude object depends on his beliefs about plenty of attributes of the object. The use of a multi-attribute model indicates that we can predict an attitude towards a brand or product if we identify a certain belief, combining them to attain a general idea of the consumer's general attitude.

There are three specific elements contained in the basic multi-attribute attitude model:

• Attributes—the characteristics of the attitude objects.

• Beliefs—cognition about a particular attitude object to see if a brand has a specific attribute.

• Importance weight—reflecting the priority of attributes—which vary across consumers.

7.7.2 The fishbein model

As the most influential multi-attribute attitude model, fishbein model focuses on measuring the following elements of attitude:

• Salient beliefs—What consumers believe about the attitude object during the process of evaluation.

• Object–attitude linkages—The probability that a special object has a significant influence.

• Evaluation of each of the important attributes.

This model assumes specification of how consumers consider related attributes, weighing and summarizing the result. After multiplying the consumer's level of each of the attributes for all brands, an attitude score is obtained by considering the importance rating for that attribute.

In order to improve predictability, an updated version of the fishbein multi-attitude theory, which is called the theory of reasoned action extended fishbein model comes up to focus on the situation considering elements such as the pressure coming from the society, the attitude towards the behavior when buying a product, instead of the ones towards the product itself. This theory pays extra attention to measuring the intention of the purchasing action, which means, how you feel about the purchase.

Limitations: This model pays attention to dealing with actual behavior instead of the outcome of behavior. However, some of the results are out of the researchers' control, which may require something else that is not possible to get. The assumption which states that the behavior of purchasing is intentional might be invalid, such as impulse, change in circumstance, novelty and repeated buying. Furthermore, it may not work across different cultures. Sometimes, measure of attitude doesn't correspond to behavior because the time frame is very important. Another aspect to be considered is that: consumers create stronger and more predictive attitudes when they come across direct, personal experience with an attitude object than those we form indirectly through advertising.

7.8 Attitude change and Interactive communications
7.8.1 Changing attitudes

Consumers' attitude originates from their requirement and what they believe. People select clear beliefs, which are most related to their personal needs, and develop attitudes towards products or services in light of their beliefs. For instance, beliefs related to superstition have been presented to influence attitudes towards novelty-seeking.

There are theoretical models that are functional for marketers in that it helps when designing tactics to change individual attitudes. There are a few ways which can shift attitudes and are shown as follows:

(1) Increase a new obvious belief. For instance, a restaurant may specify that it features an itinerant Gypsy violinist on Saturday evenings. This would become a new truth for a customer to take this restaurant into consideration, if he or she is looking for some exotic vibe in the dining experience.

(2) Switch the power of an obvious belief. If it is a negative belief, it can be deducted or acted down; if it's a positive one, it can be endowed with bigger significance. If a restaurant's customers hold a relatively low level of faith in the cleanliness of the cooks, but they highly value this attribute, then the restaurant needs to work on improving hygiene and promote this point particularly in its communication materials. The restaurant may, for instance, emphasize such measures like the health conditions of the chefs are verified, the dishes are meticulously made, and all the utensils are sanitized before arriving at the

table, to boost the confidence in its customers. In lots of Chinese restaurants, chopsticks are sent to the table in small paper sleeves: though the chopsticks have been employed several times, when they have been washed carefully and put on the sleeves, patrons would be comforted.

(3) <u>Switch the assessment of a belief that already exists</u>. An individual might present a low assessment of the prices in a restaurant. He or she may prefer restaurants with fancy elements in the atmosphere to the ones providing a cheap meal. In this situation, the restaurant may add the assessment of this attribute in a way of stressing that the low prices indicate that the customer is able to come to the restaurant more often, they can also treat friends to a meal without "going backrupt".

(4) <u>Change an existing belief into a more salient one</u>. A restaurant customer may not perceive the kindness coming from the waitress as a salient attribute. In this way, the restaurant might stress that it makes a huge difference to the satisfaction of the night if the waiters or waitresses are in a good mood and provide attentive services.

When the three elements of attitude (cognition, affect and conation) are in a balanced situation, it is very hard to switch the attitude for the reason that the attitude has already become stable. For instance, on one hand, when someone is getting too much weight, and believes that this is not a good thing, which results in having a diet, the attitude is stablized and would be hard to switch. On the other hand, if the same individual that becomes overweight, believes that it is harmful but just never takes measures to reduce weight, it is relatively simple to persuade the individual to treat themselves to some snacks or other things. In the latter scenario, the attitude is not coherent because of the conation which doesn't work as an equivalent way with the affect and cognition. Switching a person's beliefs could be an efficient method to change the consumers' attitudes.

7.8.2 Elements of communication

In general, marketers depend on the communication models to study how consumers change their attitude. The communication model indicates the components that need to be controlled through which marketers can have a communication with their customers. One of these components is *source*, from which the communication originates. Another is called the *message*. Many things like information and ideas could be transmitted in this way, and the form of the message (visual, audio, etc.) has an important influence on how we understand it. We need to encode the message and then transfer it through media such as television, radio, newspaper, magazines, daily conversation, etc. One or more consumers given the message will decode it according to their own experiences; and then respond to it in their own ways. Eventually, the source receives feedback, which enables the marketers to judge on the receivers' reactions to evaluate the effectiveness of the message and improve details about it accordingly.

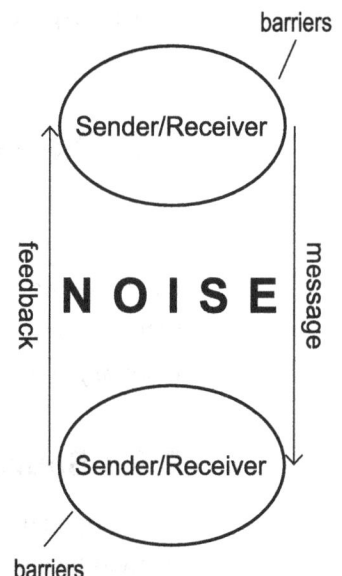

7.8.3 The uses and gratifications theory and interactive communications

The previous simple communication model is limited for the reason that the consumer is not a passive entity, but a receiver when facing with attitudes. According to the Uses and Gratifications Theory, users dealing with uploaded contents are able to affect the communication model immediately. This theory holds a perspective that different kinds of media are used by the consumer to satisfy over sternly informational needs. Because consumers are active and they will pay extra attention to drawing on mass media which are the resources, to meet their needs.

In the past, the advertising model tends to push a message; today, the model emphasizes focus on pulling something fantastic. Nowadays, the consumer is able to derive a message and pull what first gains his attention.

Now what competes with media is entertainment, not only their diversion, but also information, which means, there is an unclear line between marketing and entertainment, escapism, etc.

7.8.4 Levels of interactive response

Except for pure buying behavior, response is widely aware, with its feature identification, its ability to remind people of buying, and develop a long-term relation. At the time a consumer produces a message for a product which can be widely spread, he or she has already been involved with the brand.

First-Order Response: It is the first order to yield a product which offers a direct response. In addition, revenue and sales data could be the source of the feedback.

Second-Order Response: It is the second order to yield a product which delivers a marketing message that is related to what the customer gives back to the marketers. It requests for information, and needs to join the mailing list, including referral to other relevant aspect.

7.9 The source

In terms of communication effectiveness, who or what the source is exerts a significant impact on the level of persuasiveness. In other words, whether we find something convincing or not may depend on who tells it to us, even if the content is written or spoken with the same wording. The criteria to choose a suitable source for communication are *credibility* and *attractiveness*.

7.9.1 Source credibility

It is persuasive if credibility related to a communicative source's skills, objectivity or trustworthiness that has been perceived, especially when consumers get in touch with a new or unknown product. Learning how to build credibility is an important aspect, where the source's qualifications have direct connections with the product. Having a professional celebrity to endorse a brand or a product can enhance its competitiveness if other aspects show no major differences from their counterparts in the market.

With the development of e-commerce and social media, not only experts and celebrities can be the authoritative source, users who have bought and used products can also leave comments on these platforms and offer great referential value to other consumers. Such experience is perceived as useful and believable since it's obtained through actual product usage.

初次评价:　安装师傅专业态度好，沙发也颜色好看很舒服
2020.11.15

收货90天后追加：沙发皮质特别好，颜色这个蓝色好喜欢，坐着相当舒服，座位下面还能装东西

颜色分类：莫兰迪蓝
【RBI2K单人+右三人+左贵妃】
适用人数：组合

兰***基（匿名）

An anonymous user's comment on Taobao.com
It's especially helpful when it comes to products like furniture because consumers can see what the product actually looks like and the authentic experience when using it.

Another type of influencers in-between is the minor celebrities on social media platforms like Red and Tik Tok, who have a considerable amount of followers. They either proactively seek out or receive from marketers novel and popular products to try out and demonstrate the details along the way with verbal or written introductions, pictures, video and/or livestreaming. This type of sharing has its own merit that the risk of buying and using an unknown product is reduced. Consumers can take a closer look at the product in a way that mass communication wouldn't walk them through.

7.9.2 Source attractiveness

Appearance, charisma, social status, and the range of their similarity to the audience can all be a part of the source's perceived social value. It is celebrity endorsement that plays an essential role among sources because stars or famous people have cultural influences, and their particular status or class helps evoke a general personality and match the characteristics to the product.

But it is also very important to choose a proper public figure, because the person will create an invisible relationship with the marketers, which means that the star can have an influence on the company's value according to what he/she has done or said to the society. Think about the good-looking idols that were later reported serious scandals that showed they are immoral or even criminal. Under such circumstances, brands need to clarify their positions to show a clear attitude. If, however, brands support values that are against the mainstream opinion, a publicity crisis might be unavoidable.

7.10 The message

In the communication model, the key aspect lies in the *message*—its main content and the way it's delivered. Since consumers are bombarded with an enormous amount of commercials every day, it's critical for marketers to emphasize a unique, memorable and convincing attribute or benefit of the product.

7.10.1 Message formulation

In order to increase memorability of the messages, marketers need to formulate the message in an innovative way. Therefore, they pay attention to observe a special attribute called USP (Unique Selling Proposition) to consider impressive benefits and/or features that aim exactly at target consumers' needs. The expression of the message could be verbal as well as visual. Questions like whether it is full of vividness, whether there needs to be repetition, whether it should draw a conclusion or leave it up to the audience are carefully considered. In addition, they study through indirect comparison or demonstration to see and analyse tangible results.

One-sided vs. two-sided arguments: Sometimes marketing messages are considered as a persuasive debate. The majority of messages reflect only one side, to be clearer, the positive or supportive side. Others hold a two-sided message where both positive and negative arguments are presented, but this kind of message is not widely used. Two-sided argument could be a better choice when the audience is well educated, but not loyal. It'll seem like they have reach the expected conclusion by themselves, which seems more convincing.

Drawing conclusions: Think about whether the message should tell you what to think, or leave you alone and conclude by yourself. Consumers concluding on their own tend to build up a stronger attitude, but it's not guaranteed that such conclusions are what the marketers expect. If it is difficult for consumers to follow an argument, drawing a conclusion in the advertisement could be a safer way.

7.10.2 Comparative advertising

Comparative advertising is mainly about a message that makes comparisons among several noticeable brands and evaluates them according to one or more specific attributes.

This strategy can have repercussions, especially when the promoter describes the match in a terrible or negative way. Though several comparative ads lead to attitude changes, they might also be weak in believability and arouse source derogation (i.e., the consumer might have some doubt about the credibility of a prejudiced expression). Frankly speaking, in certain cultures (such as Asia), it is not easy for the comparative advertising to be seen for the reason that people find it offensive to face with such an aggressive approach.

7.11 Types of message appeals

A persuasive message is able to attract your attention or make you feel scared, make you laugh or cry, or leave you looking forward to learning more. In this part, we will review the main substitutes available to communicants.

7.11.1 Emotional vs. rational appeals

There are two ways for commercial communications to appeal to consumers: aiming at the head or the heart. Which one is more effective? It comes down to whether marketers want to establish a certain brand image or showcase a competitive edge of a product. It also depends on what type of product it is and what kind of relationship consumers have with it. For example, facts and figures regarding how fast and innovative of the latest model of laptops can be quite attractive for programmers. On the other hand, telling a touching story in a shampoo commercial aims right at the soft spot in the hearts of its target consumers.

China Mobile: From parents to friends, all you need is going on a trip.
The commercial depicts the generation gap and the physical distance between parents and children, which can be shortened by mobile service. Young consumers who are working and living away from hometown resonate with this sentiment.

It's difficult to measure the accurate influences of emotional versus rational appeals. Though doing some recalls to the ad content turns out to be a better choice for "thinking" ads than for "feeling" ads, traditional methods of measuring advertising efficiency (e.g., day-after recall) might not be enough to evaluate increasing effects of emotional ads. These unlimited ways evaluate cognitive replies, which might punish feeling ads for the reason that the reactions are sometimes difficult to express.

7.11.2 Sex appeals

Maybe it is not surprising that in printed advertisements female nudity creates negative feelings and strain among women consumers, while men's reactions turn out to be more positive—though women who behave relatively more generous attitudes towards gender tend to be tolerant. In a case of reversion, one study reported that males seem to hate to see nude males in advertisements, while women responded well to males who are half undressed, but not totally naked. Females also respond more actively to gender themes when they show up in a certain context, which comes from a committed relationship, instead of lust which is without reason.

Therefore, does sex have an influence on appeals? Though the sexual content indeed seems to drive attention to an advertisement, the use of it might actually be contrary. In a certain study, a dominant 61 percent of the respondents said that erotic imagery coming from a product's advertisement makes them have less motivation to buy it. To our surprise, a stimulant photo can be quite effective. It has the ability to draw so much attention as to prevent the processing and review of the advertisement's contents. Gender appeals turn out to be useless when marketers regard them only as a "trick" to gain attention. However, they seem to work if the product is born to be relevant to gender. A research company tried to explore how males and females look at the ads related to sexual themes and what kind of effect that they decide to see might have some influence on the ads' efficiency. A proportion of the research utilized particular software to study the visual behavior of respondents when they saw the tested print advertisements. The advertisement instance was made up of two print ads coming from America, one sexual and the other nonsexual, from each of five product types. Looking at a sexual ad, males were likely to neglect the text when they focused instead on the woman in it, while the female participants had a tendency to observe the advertisement's text elements firstly. Men participants stated that they preferred the sexual advertisements, as well as the products advertised in them. At the same time, they might even tend to purchase those products. On the contrary, females think less highly of the sexual ads than the nonsexual ones among all kinds of criteria.

7.11.3 Humor appeals

Researchers and marketers find out that humorous advertisements have the ability to gain attention. One of the studies discovered that liquor consumers recognize and remember humorous advertisements better than regular ads. But do funny ads really have an influence on whether consumers can recall the ads or the products and on their attitudes toward either or both of them? The result is mixed. To some extent, humor can change the audience's opinion because it's a source of *distraction*. This is because the interesting elements in the ads prevent *counterarguing* (with which a consumer comes up with reasons why he or she disagrees with the message). Therefore, it's more probable that the message can be accepted easily because the consumer does not focus on figuring out arguments against the product.

7.11.4 Fear appeals

Fear appeals address the negative results that can show up if the consumer doesn't change his behavior or attitude. It is very common to see fear appeals in advertising, but they are more common in social marketing contexts where organizations inspire people to change to healthier lifestyles. For example, they can stop smoking, use contraception, or depend on a selected driver (other than a random driver). Besides America, a number of countries are searching for new strict criteria for cigarette advertising and packaging. The criteria consist of a range of horrible images to show up on the package of cigarette directly (as well as in cigarette ads) to present people who have already gone through the damages of cigarettes.

This strategy might frighten away willing smokers effectively, but generally fear appeals work more. The majority of research studying this theme implies that these negative messages become most efficient when the marketer makes use of merely a moderate threat and when the advertisement shows the way to solve the problem. Otherwise, consumers will ignore the advertisement for the reason that there is nothing they can do to get rid of or solve the threat.

7.11.5 Creative ways of expression

Just like telling a story, the content of a message can be expressed in various ways to achieve optimal results. The following are the typical forms adopted in advertising.

Metaphors: When two dissimilar objects are placed into a tight relation like "A is B", while a similar expression compares two objects, "A is like B." A and B, although dissimilar, both have certain quality that the metaphor emphasizes. The marketer is allowed to apply useful images to daily events by the metaphors. As it can be seen in the ad below, the manufacturer intends to compare the experience of using the air-conditioner to living in a forest, which applies a meaningful image to an everyday event.

Resonance: Advertisers often make use of resonance as another kind of literary device. It can use a relevant photo to present and mix a play in words. While metaphor changes one meaning into another by linking two things which seem somehow similar, resonance uses a component that has more than one meaning. For example, there is a pun where two words sound similar but express different meanings. A newly launched high-end ice cream brand called Chicecream features the classic Chinese pattern as its signature shape. Its Chinese name Zhongxuegao has the pronunciation of the characters like China and ice cream, which is self-evident where it comes from. There are also interesting tastes highlighting Chinese characteristics.

Another brand using pun in its slogan is a car manufacturer, Geely, which sounds auspicious in Chinese. So its slogan is "A joyful life has Geely as a companion", which means driving the car can bring you good luck.

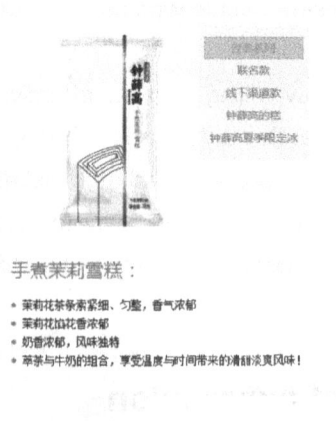

Drama: A story or drama draws viewers' attention and tends to raise their emotional resonance. For example, in the 1990s, HGC Telecom began to run lengthy TV commercials in a series, which featured the romantic stories of super star Leon Lai and his fictional girlfriend May, who developed their relationship in different scenarios using mobile phone services.

The commercials were so successful that they won most of the major advertising awards and have become collective memory for the young people at the time. There were multiple reasons why the series had such a huge impact:

• *Plot*: Unlike other commercials that were quick and direct, the series tells the stories just like movies. It kept the audience interested to find out what would happen to the hero and the heroine.

• *Product placement*: Instead of showing product benefits right away like any other commercials, this series incorporated functions of the mobile services into the plots. In this way, the audience can understand how the intangible services can make a difference in their lives, which was really effective.

• *Relatability*: The first of the bunch told a story about Leon and one of his fans May, and how they got to know each other. The idol was then so popular that every girl who had a crush on him can relate to the situation.

• *Background music*: Each commercial of the series infused one of Leon's catchy canto pop songs that not only helped develop the right mood for the story, but also left a positive impression on the audience.

7.12 Attitude measurement

It is clearly interesting for the marketers to measure attitudes, because attitudes play so major a part in consumers' purchasing behavior. It is obviously significant for merchants to understand what the consumers' attitudes towards the product or service are. However, it is not easy to quantify an attitude for the reason that it consists of elements of both cognition and effect. There are two contrary models for attitude measurement: the Rosenberg Model and the Fishbein Model.

The rosenberg model states that a consumer's attitude towards a product or service stands for the level and direction of the attitudinal effect resulted from the product. Simply put, an attitude is made up of a large number of feelings and a direction, and has two major elements.

(1) <u>Perceptible instrumentality</u>: This is the internal ability of the object to obtain the value in question, that is, the usage of the object.

(2) <u>Value significance</u>: This is the amount of contentment the individual originates from the achievement of a specific value. More easily, this is the significance of attaining the conclusion that the individual is wishing to achieve in a way of purchasing and making use of the object of the attitude.

Perceptible instrumentality states the level to which the person believes that the product or service will have an effect as it should. Value significance is the level to which getting along with the job well is significant to the individual.

In general, perceptible instrumentality and value significance are really autonomous, and taken separately from each other they don't predict replies well, but taken together they are helpful predictors of behavior which is explanatory of attitude.

The Fisbbein model holds a distinct opinion on the problem by concentrating on the individual rather than on the product. For Fishbein, attitudes can be forecasted from beliefs and assessment. Belief is the potential which the products stand for a specific attribute; assessment is whether that attribute draws attention or not. This is not congenial with the value significance concept in the Rosenberg model.

In the model, the individual's belief in the object's capabilities takes the place of the perceptible instrumentality aspect. For instance, it might be helpful for a car to develop a huge boot (the Rosenberg model) while whether a specific car's boot is numerous or not is a relevant term and depends on the individual's belief (the Fishbein model). What's more, the belief that a car's boot is big doesn't den if it's ly show that the expected owner will be fond of that attribute (the Fishbein model). This might reply on how significant the attitude is to the individual (the Rosenberg model).

Comparing and mixing the two models up, three obvious aspects of the significance of attitude appear as follow:

① Perceived instrumentality

② Evaluative aspect (affect)

③ Value importance

Rosenberg		Fishbein model
Perceived instrumentality: how well does the product create value?	Strength of attitude	Belief that the object has a particular characteristic.
Value importance: how important is the value to me?		Evaluation that the characteristic is desirable.

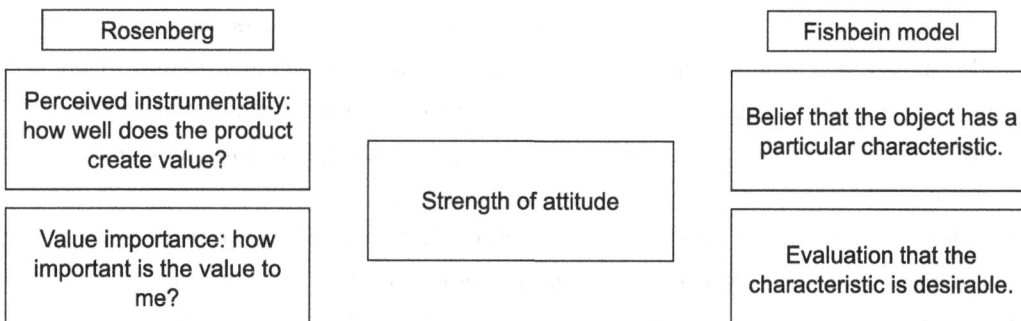

Figure 7-1 Strength of attitude

These are illustrated in Figure 7-1 as above. Examples of these aspects are as follows:

(1) I believe the Ford Mondeo is the most comfortable car in its class.

(2) I like comfort.

(3) Comfort is very important to me.

Note that the second two are not identical. Someone probably likes something without it being very important to him or her.

Summary

In this chapter, we have studied attitudes and the ways in which attitudes are formed and sustained. We have also looked at ways of changing attitudes and some of the theories of attitude measurement. Attitude is the starting point of all behaviors: people's attitudes will affect their decision-making, create their motivations, and both generate and are created by their consumption experiences. Marketers are always concerned with how to establish favorable attitudes towards products and companies, and most marketing communications are aimed at the cultivation of those favorable attitudes.

As for people making research about consumers, it is very important to learn about the function of attitude. An attitude is a tendency to assess an object in a positive or negative way. The attitude towards products or services might be formed by consumers, which will make them decide whether to buy or not. The attitude tends to be complex than it appears for the first time. An attitude consists of three elements: affect, beliefs and behavioral intentions.

An attitude can be formed in different ways. Generally, attitude researchers suggested that we create attitudes in a stable order, that is, the consumer first forms his cognition about an attitude object, then he assesses it, and he takes some action. Besides, the consumer's attitudes can be relevant not only to his level of involvement but also to other hierarchies of effects. It is very important to learn about the function of attitude towards the attitude object if we need attitude formation. In order to remain consistent, the consumer is often motivated to alter one or more components. As for the consumer, he will take some measures to alter some portion of an attitude so that they become consistent. Among these theories, the cognitive dissonance theory, the balance theory and the self-perception theory play important roles in balancing the elements.

Attitude models recognize relevant elements and mix them up to predict a consumer's general attitude towards a product or service. Multi-attribute attitude models stress the importance of the complication of attitudes. In other words, the consumer recognizes and combines specific beliefs and evaluations to predict an attitude. Researchers merge different factors such as subjective criteria and features of attitude scales into steps to develop predictability.

The communication model assesses some significant elements for marketers when they take steps to change the consumer's attitudes towards a product or service. An attempt to change the consumer's attitude is called persuasion. When marketers want to deliver meaning, they will analyse the elements in the communication model including a message, a source, a medium, a recipient and feedback.

Not what marketers once believed, the consumer processing a message is active in receiving information. The conventional opinions of communications look on the people who perceive as a less active component in the process. Brand development which is relevant to interactive communications underlines the requirement to take the active parts a consumer play into consideration when he gains information about the product and establish a relationship with the marketer. It is stated from the advocates of permission marketing that sending messages to consumer turns out to be more effective when they develop an interest in understanding a product, rather than try to influence the consumer with these solicitations.

The effectiveness of a message source could be influenced by some factors. The attractiveness and credibility of a source play important roles in determining the efficiency. Though celebrities are able to behave in this way, their credibility is sometimes not as effective as the company hopes. Marketing messages which are related to the consumer's perception such as buzz, which is accurate and generated from the consumer, prove to be more efficient than those considered as hype, which is inaccurate and generated from company.

How a marketer makes structures for his message results in how persuasive the message will be. The effectiveness of the message is determined largely by several components such as conveyance of the message with words or pictures; application of a rational and emotional appeal; how frequent the repetition is; appeals related to fear, sex, humor and so on. Messages to be advertised combine components from art or literature such as resonance, metaphors, dramas, etc. The effectiveness of the source or the message is determined mainly by audience characteristics. The consumer's level of involvement with the communication leads to influencing the effect of the source and the message. The elaboration likelihood model (ELM) indicates that it is more likely for source effects to attract a less-involved consumer, while a more-involved consumer prefers to deal with elements of the actual message.

Exercises

(1) Describe the functional theory of attitudes and its elements (functions).

(2) Attitude researchers have held out the concept of a hierarchy of effects to demonstrate methods to study attitudes and how they form. Introduce and simply describe all the three hierarchies which were delivered in this chapter. Be clear about your description.

(3) A consumer's level of involvement for the attitude object influences the range of attitude he behaves. Define the power of commitment relevant to the following aspects and present an example:
- Compliance
- Identification
- Internalization

(4) Compare the usages of the emotional appeals of sex, humor, and fear in advertisements. What are the advantages and disadvantages of each appeal?

(5) What is the Elaboration-Likelihood Model of persuasion? Depict and summarize its features. What are the implications of the ELM for marketing promotions?

(6) Why should marketers know about consumers' cognitive consistency and cognitive dissonance? How can dissonance be decreased? Make use of the post purchase behavior coming from a customer as an example.

Case Analysis

In the past, digital products of foreign brands used to be favored by Chinese consumers. But nowadays, devices like smart phones, home appliances and drones that are made in China are enjoying increasing popularity. Have a group discussion with your fellow students by addressing the following questions:

(1) In your opinion, what are the characteristics of local trendy brands?

(2) Can you think of one Chinese brand that can represent Chinese characteristics? Please elaborate.

(3) What is the essence of "Made in China"?

Summarize your opinions in the discussion, incorporate the knowledge of this chapter, analyse the reasons why locally produced products have been widely accepted by Chinese consumers, present a report on this topic.

"Made in China" Brand Comes of Age

Feng Jidong can still vividly remember one summer night nearly a decade ago when he and four college roommates, their eyes glued to computers, waited with bated breath for an online presale to kick off.

As the clock struck 10 p.m., up to 100,000 of the latest models of the once little-known domestic smartphone maker Xiaomi had been sold out in the blink of an eye. One lucky dog among them managed to bag one. Poor guys like Feng still struggled to refresh the landing page until the presale was all over almost as soon as it began.

"At that time, it was a rare experience indeed to scramble for domestic products," Feng recalled. "There was always a rush for iPhones, European luxury bags and even Japanese rice cookers and toilet seats. But when it comes to homegrown brands, most consumers simply didn't believe they were well worth the time and trouble."

In the past 10 years, however, Feng has witnessed the boom times for indigenous products. Not only have historical or time-honored brands, whose popularity slowly waned in the '90s as more customers were attracted to foreign goods, been revived to become cool again, new domestic brands are also very much part of the wave.

The 30-year-old native of Yunnan province had helped his cousin snap up the refined edition of the classic Warrior sneakers — a 94-year-old Shanghai-based sporting footwear label deemed as "must-haves" for gym classes at school in the old days. Feng also joined the Singles' Day shopping spree to scramble for the special edition of Song Dynasty (960—1279) ceramics-inspired lipsticks, released by the emerging Chinese mainland beauty brand Huaxizi, for his girlfriend. Despite coming away with nothing in the presale 10 years ago, he has become an ardent supporter of Xiaomi, Huawei, Vivo and their domestic peers.

Although some may argue that the renewed interest in homegrown brands is the result of well-crafted "hungry marketing" and whimsical branding, it can't be denied that once a badge of honor, foreign products may no longer be the alpha and omega for consumers feeling cool.

Today's new generation of consumers want items that reflect their own culture rather than just foreign heritage and exclusivity that have been so popular to date, which makes guochao, which literally means "national hip" or "Chinese retro", a trend to take seriously.

"Nowadays, the 'Made in China' label no longer inherently means cheap, inferior and unfashionable," said Zhou Zhendong, professor at the School of Journalism and Communication of Xiamen University. "But unlike campaigns spearheaded by a small number of designers and creators in the previous years to promote the so-called China chic element, which were arguably too cultured to be appreciated by the masses, the ongoing guochao trend goes beyond a basic 'proudly Made in China' concept and proves to be a real market force to be reckoned with."

More than 80 percent of ready-to-buy items in Taobao consumers' online shopping carts were domestic products, according to a report unveiled by China's biggest e-commerce company Alibaba Group in May. Over half of guochao fans were found to be consumers born after 1995 and 60 percent of them come from third- and higher-tier cities.

Hu Yu, executive dean of the Institute for Cultural Creativity at Tsinghua University, highlighted three major factors behind the rise of guochao. "The first one is ethnic cultures and the second, homegrown brands. The third and most important one, is the power of youth."

The dizzying growth of the world's second-largest economy has given birth to a new breed of super consumers, who've now gone beyond mimicking the patterns of the more sophisticated Western shoppers to being trendsetters and innovators. Deemed one of the most remarkable footnotes to the nation's growth story, Generation Z come of age with a sense of national pride and self-esteem, and are known to be enamored of brands carrying serious cultural connotation.

CHAPTER EIGHT
Personality and Lifestyle

Learning objectives

After learning this chapter, you will be able to:

- acquire the definition of personality and understand major theories regarding personality;
- build up the concept of brand personality and get to know its significance to establishing brand image and the different means to communicate brand personality to promote products;
- gain insights into consumers' lifestyles along with its relationships with purchase decision-making;
- comprehend the notion of psychographics and its roles in segmentation;
- grasp ways of measuring lifestyles (AIOs and VALTS) and how psychographic data is used in developing marketing strategies.

Lead-in Case

Fragrance Sector Poised for More Expansion

Increasingly market-savvy consumers bolster potential; gifting of perfume, cologne during COVID a popular phenomenon

The fragrance market in China is poised for growth to meet demand of the nation's increasingly sophisticated beauty consumers, and online sales are expected to become more important, industry insiders said. In the next five years, the fragrance market in China is expected to grow at a compound annual growth rate of 17 percent, hitting sales revenues of 15.4 billion yuan ($2.4 billion) in 2025, according to the market research firm Mintel.

Scent Library holds an exhibit in a shopping mall in Beijing in June, 2021.

China has some 20 million consumers who have the habit of using perfume regularly, according to a report by market consultancy iResearch. "Chinese consumers pay lots of attention to discretionary categories such as fragrances, which are positioned to *offer more emotional benefits and help express their individuality*," said Alice Li, beauty and personal care associate director of Mintel.

"The majority of users have started wearing fragrances as part of their routine. Encouraging more frequent use may be a challenge. Therefore, brands should focus on driving ownership of multiple fragrances and encouraging consumers to switch scents or layer different scents in order to increase usage," Li said.

Perfume and aromatherapy form a subcategory of consumer goods with top sales on Tmall. This year, aromatherapy products such as candles or decorations for the home, aromatherapy items for cars and salon fragrances made by smaller studios or salons have seen growth rates of more than 100 percent year-on-year.

New product launches of unisex fragrances have been growing quickly in China, fueled by gender neutrality as a beauty trend. Botanical and herbal fragrances have become the top sellers in that category. Women's frequency of using fragrances has remained somewhat flat, but more men have become occasional users. Buying fragrances for personal use has declined with the pandemic, but giving fragrances as gifts has increased.

While leading international companies account for a bigger market share, they have been facing an increasing competition from niche fragrance brands that have entered the China market in the past few years as well as the emergence of local players. Chinese fragrance brands usually have different competitive strategies as they target younger consumers. Some top domestic fragrance brands include Scent Library, Uttori,

Reclassified and Young Beast.

"We would like to do business based on different kinds of scents, and focus not only on perfume. *We hope to create more scents that cater to the preferences of Chinese consumers, help scents become part of their lifestyle, and thus leverage the olfactory economy*," said Huo Xuefei, senior manager of branding at Scent Library.

"We launch perfumes in different scents to tell stories, and we are quite happy that many consumers understand the stories behind our products. For instance, a consumer said after he smelled one type of scents, he could sense the smell of camphor and think of his grandparents and old times," Huo said. Camphor has been traditionally used for its medicinal qualities.

Scent Library has agreements with a few major global essence-making companies. It often provides some abstract concepts to international suppliers in such categories as rain, snow, different colors and food. The company acknowledged that it is sometimes somewhat difficult to turn abstract concepts into specific products. Still, in 2017, the company launched a perfume named LBK water, which is short for Liang Bai Kai, meaning cooled boiled water, and the product became one of its bestsellers. In 2018, its monthly sales volume reached 400,000 bottles. The perfume contains the smell of a water blend and freesia blossoms with aldehyde intensifiers. Scent Library said the perfume conjures a water-moistening feeling and a pleasant scent.

Domestic perfume brands boast significant growth potential, given that Chinese consumers consider natural elements, scent durability and the type of scent as priorities when choosing perfumes. High-end brand images have become a secondary consideration. Domestic perfume brands can utilize consumer preference for the Chinese style and traditional culture to tell their own brand stories. "In the past year, an increasing number of traditional Chinese-style scents, such as tea and osmanthus, have become more popular. Also, more consumers have shifted their habits to buying perfume online, and domestic brands, especially startup companies, can leverage their strengths in social media marketing and attract more consumers online, given that sales are not limited to an offline shopping experience anymore," Li of Mintel said.

"Still, the high-end domestic market for perfume is dominated by foreign brands, and most domestic brands are competing with each other in a lower price range targeting younger consumers. That group pays less attention to brand histories and pursues more emotional resonance with the brands," she said.

Introduction

The olfactory business has a lot to do with the two major topics in this chapter: personality and lifestyle—wearing perfumes is a way to express one's individuality, part of which is comprised of the person's personality; using aromatherapy or extensively including scents in the atmosphere we live in is part of a sophisticated lifestyle. Personality characteristics have long been used as an appealing point for marketers and advertisers to attract consumers. We all remember some perfume commercials that show us an imaginative world to express our moods, some are soft and gentle, some sporty and dynamic, and some romantic and dreamlike... Consumers of diversified personalities are drawn to the different types of feelings created by the various combinations of fragrances. The same perfume can even smell differently if it's worn by different persons, that's how individuality works! In other words, fragrances as part of a personal style can be used to build up and accentuate one's own image. This is probably why some consumers consider not wearing perfumes is like going naked. What's more, the growing demands for aromatic products like scented candles, air freshener spray, and diffuser sets in various shapes suggest that consumers' continuously upgrading living standards have led to a modern lifestyle that regards nice smells as part of a superior environment.

This chapter consists of two essential factors that are considerably influential to consumer behavior: personality and lifestyle. The two domains of knowledge, along with sensation and perception, motivation and attitudes are the indispensable inner aspects that have a lot to do with how consumers make purchase decisions. The first half of this chapter sets out to introduce the definition of personality and its related key theories, as well as the application of the knowledge in this field to consumer research and marketing activities. Additionally, brand personality will also be examined and discussed. The second half of this chapter concerns what lifestyle is and ways of measuring and describing the lifestyles of different segments of consumers, and how lifestyles play a part in consumers' purchase decision-making.

8.1 Personality

In order to define what personality is, you might need to consider the following questions: If you were to describe the personality of someone you know, what words would you use? What about the words your friends would use to describe your personality? By finding answers to these two questions, you might have a vague idea about what personality is: it's about the way one person reacts to the things happening around, it's that unique something inside you that sets you apart from other people, and it seems to be persistent and consistent.

There are different ways to approach the study of personality: either emphasizing how heredity and childhood experiences worked together to affect the development of personality; or focusing on the combined influences of the society and the surroundings, and on the fact that personalities are shaped as time goes by. Personality can be viewed as an organic whole or its specific traits can be studied separately. Therefore, the definition of personality can be summarized as *the internal psychological features that define and embody the ways a person reacts to the surrounding environment*. This means that personality refers to the essential qualities that distinguish one individual from another, which are deeply rooted and are highly probable to sway how consumers choose different products: consumers of varied personalities respond differently to marketing campaigns; the time, the place and the way they consume products and/or services can also differ. As a result, the logic of market segmentation strategies can be based on the recognition of certain personality features related to consumption behavior.

In practice, personality, in addition to lifestyle and social class, is a significant variable when conducting psychographic segmentation. This is because a personality with rich taste and preference will be equipped with the purchasing power to lead a corresponding lifestyle. If someone's favored fashion style is to dress lavishly, this personality trait will require the corresponding buying power to maintain. Brands often utilize this kind of market strategy, as different brands target different personalities. For instance, Harley Davidson Motor Bikes aims at personalities that are masculine, adventurous and love to lead a rough lifestyle.

8.2 Personality related theories

Three major theories related to personality will be introduced in this part: (1) Sigmund Freud's Theory of Personality; (2) neo-Freudian theories; (3) trait theory. These theories are widely used in the study of the relationship between consumer behavior and personality.

1. Sigmund Freud's theory of personality

Psychoanalytic Theory of Personality was developed by the Austrian psychologist Sigmund Freud, which laid the foundation to modern psychology. The prerequisite of this theory is that the underlying needs or urges, sexual and other physiological drives in particular, form the core of human motivation and personality. This theory was established based on the early childhood experiences recalled by Freud's patients, whose dreams and the intrinsic quality of their psychological and physical adjustment problems were also analyzed.

弗洛伊德个性理论的三个方面：本我、超我和自我。

According to the findings of his studies, Freud proposed that three interacting elements constitute the human personality, namely, the **id**, the **superego** and the **ego**.

● The *id* is like the storage of primal and immediate impulses—the biological needs like hunger, thirst and sex that human beings look to gratify at once, not thinking about the consequences and the means of satisfaction. It follows the pleasure principle, which means our primitive desire to amplify pleasure and ignore pain leads our actions.

● The *superego* is the opposite of the id. In essence the superego can be regarded as a person's conscience, which is like a person's inner interpretation of moral and ethical codes of social conduct. It works to keep the id from selfishly gratifying the basic needs.

● Lastly, the *ego* is like a mediator between the id and the superego. It virtually works to balance the struggle between the devil and the angel. It follows the reality principle by neutralizing the two opposing powers. In other words, it seeks to satisfy the impulsive needs of the id in ways that are socially acceptable. Altogether, the interactions of the three elements result in the psychological makeup of an individual, especially one's personality.

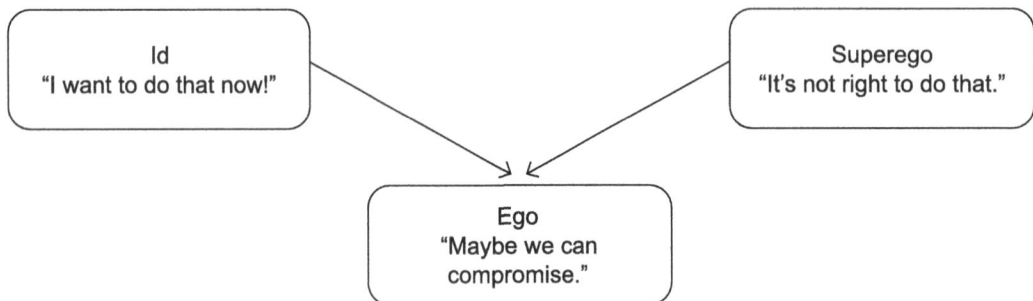

Figure 8-1 An illustration of the interactions of the three elements of the Freudian Theory

2. Neo-Freudian theories

Being known as the father of the modern personality theory, Freud had many followers who are psychiatrists and psychologists labeled as Neo-Freudians. They agreed with Freud's underlying beliefs and notions of psychoanalysis (the tripartite structure of personality) and the important function of unconsciousness when driving human sentiments, cognitions, ideas and actions. However, Freud's theory failed to take social and cultural influences into consideration when it comes to the formation of personality. Rather than believing that personality is instinctual and sexual in nature, these Neo-Freudian theorists argued that it's shaped by social and cultural aspects. They proposed that social relationships play a critical role in forming and developing personality.

Four neo-Freudians are worthy of mentioning: Alfred Adler, Eric Erikson, Karen Horney, and Carl Jung.

Alfred Adler considered that Freud's theories placed too much significance on the motivating function of sex on human behavior. The role of the unconscious is put aside, while interpersonal and social influences have been emphasized. The term "individual psychology" is knows as Adler's approach to highlight the inner push that every person would compensate when they feel inferior. Adler described the emotions and doubts that a person has when not being able to live up to expectations of the people around and the society as a whole as inferiority complex. According to his work, individuals would work hard to achieve superiority by getting over the feeling of inferiority. Under such circumstances, they would react connectedly and cooperatively when feeling motivated and acknowledged; they would compete, withdraw or give up when frustrated.

Erikson proposed a psychosocial theory of development, arguing that an individual's personality evolves throughout the whole life, distinct from Freud's opinion that personality remains unchanged since early life. Instead of emphasizing the importance of sex like Freud, Erikson focused on the social relationships that are fundamental to the different phases during the development of personality. Each of the eight phases identified by Erikson embodies a conflict or developmental task. Whether each task can be completed successfully determines the possibility of building up a healthy personality and a sense of competence.

Carl Jung disagreed with Freud's emphasis on the sexual influences on personality, despite being considered as Freud's successor. He was convinced that people's nature nowadays has been shaped by older generations' accumulated experiences. The term "collective unconscious" was coined to describe the storage of memories serving as inheritance from our ancestors. Archetypes derived from these common memories are created to represent ideas and behavior patterns identified universally. Figure 8-2 below illustrates the 12 typical archetypes developed by Carl Jung: Ruler, Creator/Artist, Sage, Innocent, Explorer, Rebel, Hero, Wizard, Jester, Everyman, Lover, and Caregiver.

These archetypes are considered as personality types or the "role" that consumers identify with, accurately representing their motivations and aspirations. The implication for marketers is that they need to figure out what role the target consumers might try to fulfill by using the products or services. Most people are trying to be something—a caregiver, a ruler or an explorer. If marketers can play into those desires with specific strategies, they can connect with the target audience on a much deeper level.

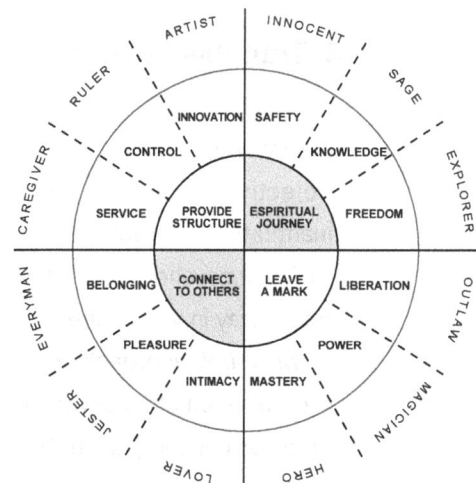

Figure 8-2 The 12 archetypes

How child-parent relationships affect personality is the research focus of Karen Horney, particularly one person's yearning to overcome feeling anxious. Accordingly three personality types have been identified: the compliant type, the aggressive type and the detached type. This model of three types of personality facilitates to demonstrate how people perceive their surroundings and how they tend to behave towards events.

(1) The compliant personality type: This group is keen on feeling being loved, accepted, liked, approved and appreciated. In their social atmosphere, these people can acutely detect other people's needs, spontaneously trying to reach other people's expectations. If they cannot share their experience with others, it's considered to be meaningless.

(2) The aggressive personality type: People of this type regard every other individual as hostile. They would only care about their own benefits. What matters to this type is to be dominant when dealing with others. They aspire to be superior, successful, reputable and famous. The strongest, the craftiest and the most needed are what these people want to be perceived. Therefore, specific skills and abilities would be developed for them to build up their personal image.

(3) The detached personality type: Individuals of this type keep a distance from other people. They emotionally alienate themselves from others. Socializing, social norms and undertaking social obligations for the long haul are among the things they don't like. This type of persons tend to keep their private life secretive, not sharing any type of personal experiences. The important values for them are not being stressful, and not being attached with anyone else.

An early study in the framework of consumer behavior used Horney's theory to determine the linkage between the three personality types and their consumption preferences. To be more specific, participants who are highly compliant tend to prefer products with brand names; the ones identified as aggressive would favor brands with masculine appeal; detached consumers are found to be heavy tea drinkers (as opposed to the mainstream beverage—coffee) just to show their unwillingness to conform. The implication of studies like this for marketers is that corresponding strategies could be applied to consumers of varied personality types.

3. Trait theory—how personality is measured and tested

The common research approach for Freudian and neo-Freudian theories is basically qualitative (personal observation, experiences brought up by the subject, dream diagnosis, projective skills, etc.) Toward another direction, the trait theory is approached in a quantitative or empirical way. Such orientations aim at measuring personality in terms of particular psychological features named traits. A *trait* means a distinctive and relatively long-lasting way in which one person can be distinguished from others.

Multi-trait approach: In order to have a general understanding of a person's personality, a combination of its several traits would be examined in a multi-trait personality test. One of the most popularly used theories in this field is the Five-Factor Model. The five major traits identified are openness, conscientiousness, extraversion, agreeableness, and neuroticism. The table below shows the meaning of each trait and manifestations of the different levels of each trait.

Table 8-1 The five-factor model

Factor	Meaning	Those who score high on this trait...	Those who score low on this trait...
Openness	being open to experiencing new or different things.	tend to be intellectually curious, willing to try new things, and more creative or unconventional	usually opposed to change and struggle with abstract thought
Conscientiousness	behaving in an organized or thoughtful way	self-disciplined, strive for achievement, and follow a plan or schedule	approach tasks in a more unstructured way and procrastinate more often
Extraversion	seeking stimulation when being with others	don't mind being the center of attention and tend to be very social and energetic	prefer to be alone and may be anxious in social situations
Agreeableness	being compassionate and cooperative towards others	tend to get along well with people and are more sympathetic and caring	less empathetic and seem uninterested in others
Neuroticism	emotional sensitivity — especially to environmental or situational factors	easily stressed and sometimes come off as worry-warts	tend to be more emotionally grounded and laid-back

Understanding consumer personality traits can help identify and draw conclusions about consumer behavior, including preferences, habits, and motivations. Targeting consumers by personality is a proven approach to persuasion. One research tests the difference between targeting viewers with ads based on whether they are extroverted or introverted: results show that when targeting viewers based on this, conversion rates double.

In conclusion, personality is instrumental to how we behave. By learning more about the personality trait theory in consumer behavior, we can become more effective in marketing messaging and targeting.

Single-trait approach: In consumer behavior studies, single-trait personality tests are often adopted and developed to measure just one trait, like self-confidence. Some of the major traits being measured in specifically devised personality tests include consumer innovativeness (the degree of a person's acceptance to novel experiences), consumer materialism (how important "worldly possessions" mean to a consumer) and consumer ethnocentrism (the possibility of a consumer to embrace or repel products made in a foreign country). Each of these traits is considered to have special relevance to the understanding of a specific set of consumption-related behaviors.

1) Consumer Innovativeness

Consumer innovativeness, meaning their wiliness to try new things is an important personality trait for marketers who look for pioneers to be the first batch of consumers to take a chance and try out innovations. The consumer's tendency to adopt new products, ideas, goods or services has substantial meaning to marketers because the launch of new products and services is a crucial source of expending the size of a business and obtaining profits for a company. Firms rely on innovators to adopt new products and spread the word and lead the trend. From a macroeconomic point of view, essential resources assigned to producing new products would be wasted if they are not accepted by consumers.

Innovativeness can represent: (1) the level of a consumer who could be among the firsts to adopt innovation in contrast with other members of the society they belong to; (2) how receptive a person can be to new ideas and how decisive to adopt these ideas without considering other people's experiences. Innovativeness can be perceived as a potential feature being realized when consumers prefer novelty and uncommon experiences. Consumers with innovativeness are motivated to seek new challenges intellectually or emotionally. Two types of innovativeness, cognitive and sensorial, are identified. Cognitive innovativeness refers to the consumer's tendency to think, to rationalize, and to solve problems or other mental exercises. Sensorial innovativeness refers to the consumer's preferences for experiences that may stimulate their senses. Subsequently, two types of innovators can be found: cognitive innovators and sensorial innovators. The table below shows their main characteristics:

Table 8-2 Features of cognitive innovators and sensorial innovators

Cognitive innovator	Sensorial innovator
drawn by the functional and practical characteristics of the new products, which may solve their consumption problems	drawn by the product's hedonistic function
prefer processing the information verbally, establishing ratios between causes and effects	prefer visual processing over a verbal processing
with low tolerance towards risk, the hedonistic risk has a negative impact on adopting the innovation	tolerant towards risk, the hedonistic risk does not interfere with adopting the innovation
being used to evaluate the products utterly, the financial risk, functional risk and complexity degree do not influence adopting decisions	satisfy their needs without a rational evaluation

According to Hirschman (1981), two dimensions of innovation determine the level of innovativeness: symbolic dimension and technological dimension. The symbolic innovation means the social meanings that are non-existent before. The technological innovation possesses tangible features that are not discovered. To classify the dimensions of innovation, products can be divided into four categories.

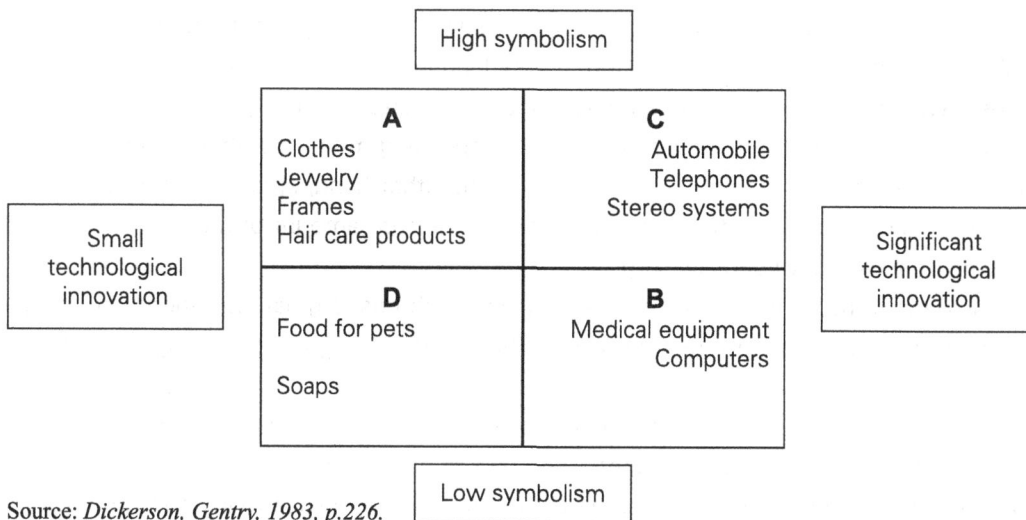

Source: *Dickerson, Gentry, 1983, p.226.*

Figure 8-3 Classification of innovation by Elisabeth Hirschman (1981)

As it can be seen in this figure, the technological innovation is high in financial cost, but low in social cost. If a consumer desires to build up a new personal image among his social circle, this person is seen as gaining the relative advantage of symbolic innovation. The technological innovation is mostly discontinuous, so the likelihood of meeting consumers' customs and experiences is quite low. This is why it's not as easy to be understood as symbolic innovation. On the other hand, the symbolic innovation is generally a continuous innovation. With a low cost, symbolic innovation is more accessible to consumers. Its social function makes it more noticeable to consumers.

Consumers with innovativeness generally have the following features: They are opinion leaders who are tolerant toward risks; they are oriented from inside and independent from the norms of the belonging group; they prefer getting informed by mass media and are less interested in noncommercial sources such as oral communication or interpersonal relationships of the belonging group; they are cosmopolites who are open to new ideas and changes; they have a higher socio-economic standard (high income, higher education).

2) Consumer materialism

As one of the personality-like traits, materialism differentiates consumers into two groups: the ones who consider their identities and their lives are strongly related to possessions; and the ones who regard possessions as less important. Materialistic people are proved to have the following characteristics: (1) Obtaining and flaunting assets seem to be of utter importance to them; (2) Self-centered and selfish; (3) Lifestyles that are abundant in possessions are what they've been looking for; (4) Large amounts of possessions cannot provide them with more gratification.

This aspect has to do with consumers' willingness to spend money to buy things. There are two extremes when it comes to this regard: *tightwads* and *spendthrifts*. The former segment usually has lower spending power than what they imagine because they anticipate it would be painful when paying for the purchases; while the latter ends up paying more than they assume beforehand because they have no trouble spending money. The following scenario can help visualize these two types of consumers: When going to a shopping mall with a good friend for a shopping spree, they see there is a "one-day-only sale" in this large department store. Everything in the store is labeled 10%—60% off. These two types would react differently: Tightwads realize they can get great discounts of many items they desire, however, the agony of spending more than they should prevents him from excessive consumption behavior. On the other hand, spendthrifts cannot resist the temptation of special offers and eventually pay a large amount of money even though they don't necessarily need anything.

Nowadays the consumption culture prevails which poses great challenges for college students to buy things in a rational way. While students enjoy consuming with credits and all kinds of consumer loans, parents have shown their worries about their children's irrational behavior because it is the parents who will pay the bills. Once in a while we are told stories about college students who had to quit school and take a temporary job because they could not pay them credit card bills. This is because many college students have just gained independent paying rights, who do not possess rational consciousness for money management and economical consumption. When they have high credit limits in hand, irrational consumption will hardly be avoided. Therefore, it is of great importance that students pause and reflect on whether the purchase is actually indispensable when faced with abundant and appealing options no matter shopping online or in physical stores, so as to avoid putting yourself in a difficult position where expenses exceed your affordability.

> **消费者民族主义：** 体现个体对于购买国外产品持有偏见的倾向程度。

3) Consumer ethnocentrism

Consumer ethnocentrism *embodies how different individuals can be in terms of their tendency to hold prejudice against the behavior of buying foreign products.* Consumers who are highly ethnocentric tend to embrace their own national culture, more traditional and more likely to choose domestic products over foreign ones. They feel it's not appropriate or even wrong to prefer imported products because such behavior would negatively influence domestic economy and the nation as a whole. Whereas consumers who are less ethnocentric would be more open to other cultures, less conservative and more likely to buy foreign products. They seem to objectively assess foreign-made products based on their external features. To determine the level of consumers' likeliness to welcome and accept commodities manufactured by or in other countries, the *consumer ethnocentrism scale* has been developed and tested.

If marketers emphasize a nationalistic motif in their campaigns, they might succeed in aiming at ethnocentric consumers in a national market. The reason is that this type of consumers is presupposed to favor domestic products. When formulating the 4Ps of the marketing mix, marketers should employ appropriate strategies according to consumers' perceptions of the products made in the country in which their products originate: Suppose the potential customers perceive the image of such products as positive, marketers should emphasize the product is made in that country, price it as premium, choose exclusive locations to distribute it and stress the country image and national sponsorship when promoting it. In contrast, when the potential customers view the image of such products as negative, marketers should emphasize the product's brand name instead of its native country, use low prices to attract consumers who are value conscious, establish supply chain partners, highlight the brand image and that it is manufacturer-sponsored when promoting it. Furthermore, research among Chinese consumers discovered that people who are highly ethnocentric had low favorability and purchase intentions towards symbols and texts that are shown in another foreign language along with Chinese.

Think About It

As the domestic auto industry develops, more and more consumers choose Chinese brands of vehicles over foreign ones, which was unimaginable 20 years ago. Read the following excerpt of business news, analyze and explain consumers' mindset using the knowledge related to consumer ethnocentrism.

Chinese Brands Grab Half of Domestic Auto Market Share

Chinese-branded vehicles have taken more than half of the domestic automobile market share, and 40 percent passenger vehicle market shares. Chinese-branded vehicles are benefiting from the country's huge automobile market, he said. Wang Xiaoqiu, president of SAIC Motor, said the Chinese vehicle sector is rebounding rapidly thanks to the support of the government. Wang added that the rebuilding of the company's brand was directed by younger consumers and the upgrading trend of consumption. He also noted that cooperation among Chinese brands is vital in tackling core technologies in key areas such as internet-connected vehicles.

The global automobile market has seen sales slump amid the coronavirus pandemic, while the Chinese market has rebounded since May, 2020, indicating the market resilience and positive effects of policies. The next five years will be the key period for the upgrading and transformation of China's auto industry. Industry players should seize the opportunities and expand their footprints in both domestic and overseas markets.

> **品牌个性:** 指消费者对品牌联想到的像个性一样的各种特点。

Brand personality

When it comes to personality, not only human beings are endowed with it, brands are also formed to possess humanlike characteristics such as personality. As part of the brand image, brand personality is created by marketers to build up emotional connections with target consumers. Brand personality refers to the varied personality-like features consumers associate with a brand. It can be concluded from researches among consumers that they can naturally describe brands with human qualities, which would arouse consumers' expectations for the brand. Brand personalities are essential to cultivating brand loyalty since it can create the foundation for a relationship with the brand in the long run. Attributing personalities to a brand facilitates differentiation from competitors, which can enhance consumers' brand preference and purchase intentions.

Among the four elements in the marketing mix, promotion is the most influential one when it comes to establishing a brand personality. An extensive and massive research summarizes the five fundamental dimensions of brand personality stimuli: *sincerity, excitement, competence, sophistication,* and *ruggedness*, each of which encompasses specific characteristics that represent the nature of a brand's personality. These dimensions along with the aspects constitute the framework of the brand personalities that consumers pursue. Marketers might adopt such directions when trying to build up and shape the personality of a brand.

BRAND PERSONALITY FRAMEWORK

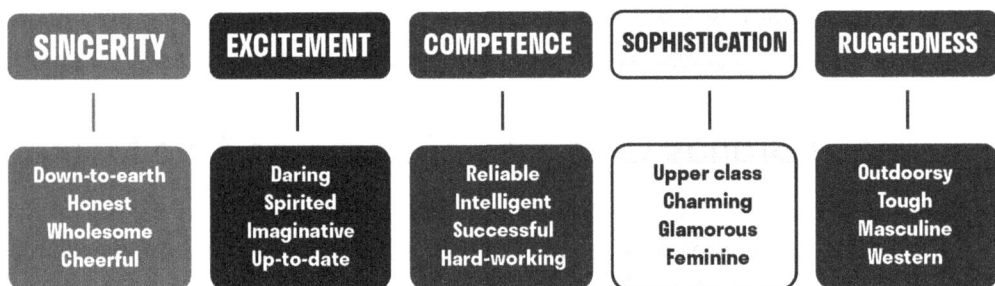

SINCERITY	EXCITEMENT	COMPETENCE	SOPHISTICATION	RUGGEDNESS
Down-to-earth Honest Wholesome Cheerful	Daring Spirited Imaginative Up-to-date	Reliable Intelligent Successful Hard-working	Upper class Charming Glamorous Feminine	Outdoorsy Tough Masculine Western

Figure 8-4 A brand personality framework

It is of vital importance that a brand's personality is able to have an impact on its relationship with customers. The critical insight of a study points out that it's likely that sometimes consumers foster a relationship with a brand that is to some extent similar with the relationships they have with other people, such as friends, family, colleagues, neighbors, etc. For instance, consumers might be engaged in a "friendship" with brands which are perceived as "sincere"; a "temporary fling" might happen with "exciting" brands, which would gradually fade.

A study focusing on brand personality and its outcomes in the Chinese automobile industry concluded that both purchasers and non-purchasers have consistent perceptions of the same brand's personality in terms of the dimensions of responsibility, activity, aggressiveness, simplicity, and emotionality. It also found that brand personality is essential to the improvement of perceived quality and the establishment of brand trust among consumers.

Lifestyle

To put it simply, lifestyle is the way a person lives. It is how a person put his or her self-concept into practice. Lifestyle is formed as a result of the combination of what this person has gone through in the past, his or her inherent features and life status at the moment. For example, the lifestyles of a single young woman and a mother of two can be tremendously different, even though they might be at the same age.

A lifestyle determines a person's consumption routine that represents his or her decisions on the ways of spending their time and money. In the old days when economy was underdeveloped, people's social status, hometown and family background limited a person's choices for consumption. Nowadays, the modern consumer environment provides us with various options of products, services and activities, enabling us to choose within budget according to our tastes and interests.

The chart below illustrates the relationship between lifestyle and the consumption process.

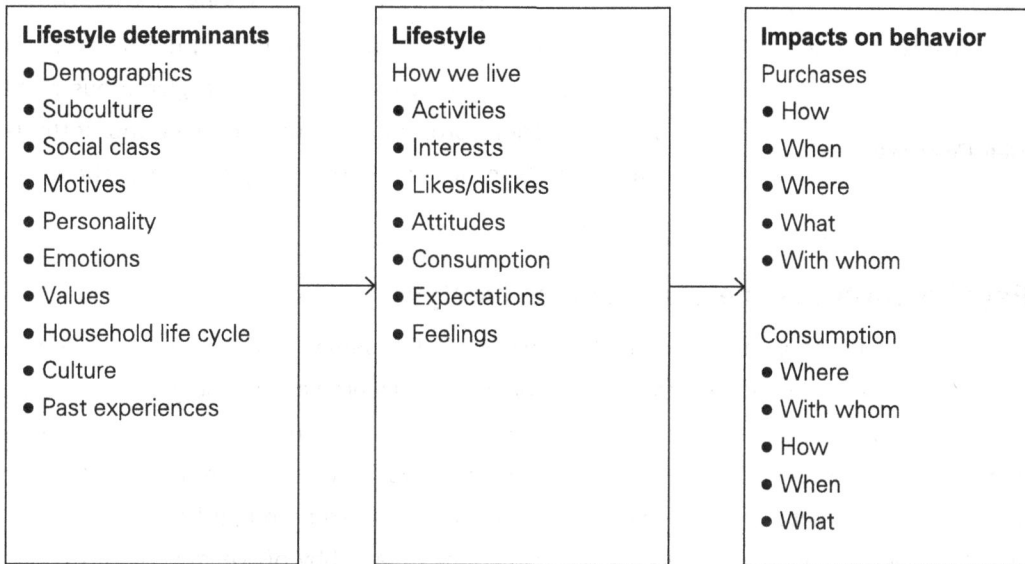

Lifestyle determinants	Lifestyle	Impacts on behavior
• Demographics • Subculture • Social class • Motives • Personality • Emotions • Values • Household life cycle • Culture • Past experiences	How we live • Activities • Interests • Likes/dislikes • Attitudes • Consumption • Expectations • Feelings	Purchases • How • When • Where • What • With whom Consumption • Where • With whom • How • When • What

Figure 8-5 Lifestyle and consumption process

To have a better understanding of how our lifestyles impose an impact on our consumption patterns, one can simply recall the differences in how people live pre- and post-pandemic: Before COVID-19, travelling in a foreign country can be achieved easily (as long as your time and budget allow), whereas now one has to think about the unavoidable process of quarantine and the period and cost derived. Traveling practically means to leave home and go to a place you are not familiar with. In order to still have this experience, a new way of spending vacation emerged in Hong Kong, China—Staycation, which means to stay in the city where you usually live, but book a hotel room to enjoy your leisure time. Since the outbreak of the pandemic, people have also been more conscious about personal hygiene than before, thus the sales volumes of all kinds of disinfectants surge. Working from home and distant education have become the new normal—online meetings and classes used to be perceived as informal and even unacceptable for most formal organizations. Such changes undoubtedly affect our ways of living, which eventually results in differences in our purchase and consumption habits.

Consumers' lifestyles have been taken into account by marketers in terms of the amount of time we have to focus on the things we are fond of and the ways we'd like to spend our leisure time. Lifestyle marketing aims to enable consumers to enjoy life by pursuing the ways they opt for. It involves dividing the market into different segments

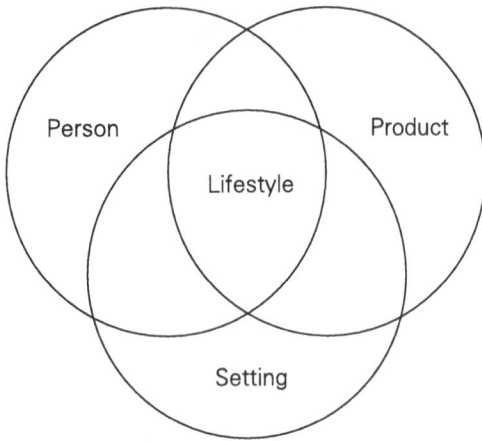

Figure 8-6 Consumption style

based on lifestyle dimensions, positioning the product in a way that appeals to the activities, interests and opinions of the targeted market and carrying out specific promotional campaigns which utilize lifestyle appeals to consolidate the market value of the offered product. It is crucial for this strategy to be successful that it pays attention to the segment who would apply different products to suitable social settings. Advertisers have been trying hard to incorporate a product into a social situation, for example, highlighting sports clothes and/or shoes in a basketball match, zooming in a new flavored sauce in a family barbecue, or a new type of cocktail in a glamorous night club, etc. Therefore, consumers, products and settings altogether form a consumption style, as it's shown in Figure 8-6.

Psychographics—measurement of lifestyle

Every consumer has to make purchase decisions frequently. It's quite common to see two people having similar backgrounds like age, gender, income and residential area choose to allocate their time and money in significantly different ways. Just think about your dorm-mates or the fellow students sitting next to you—all of you have the aforementioned similar demographic characteristics, but your ways of living vary: some might be fond of active entertainment like hip hop dancing; some might pick up a hobby of wearing and collecting Hanfu; some would rather immerse themselves in calligraphy, paintings, etc.

As we have learned in previous chapters, demographics and psychographics are two essential dimensions when marketers try to identify targeted consumers. Demographics are observable variables that help marketers "locate" their target market; while psychographic variables provide them with more insight about the segment. Psychographics refers to the application of psychological, sociological and anthropological aspects to find out the ways the market is divided according to the tendencies of different groups and the reasons behind to decide on a product, person, ideology and/or to have an attitude or choose a certain medium.

How is a psychographic analysis conducted?

Based on the different degrees of specificity, lifestyle measurements are established to two extremes: At one end, a population's lifestyle patterns are studied in a general sense. Approaches like this do not lay particular emphasis on any one product or activity, which makes it possible to be applied to the development of marketing strategies specific for various products and brands. In later sections of this chapter, general methods like AIOs and VALs would be introduced to create a full picture. At the other end, lifestyle studies can be done with very specific focuses. Researchers could look into lifestyles of individuals or households that are highly related to any product or service.

In its common practice, a psychographic study has a list of statements formulated to obtain a consumer's relevant aspects like personality, motivations, interests, attitudes, beliefs and values. The respondent is supposed to give a score to show how much they agree with each statement, like "5 points" means "strongly agree", "3 points" means "neutral", and "2 points" means "somewhat disagree". Then a total score could be calculated and the corresponding type could be identified.

When the study becomes oriented towards a particular product, the consumers have to respond to statements which are selected for the purpose, i.e. on products, brands, services, competitive situations, etc. Specifically, these studies can be categorized into the following forms:

• A *lifestyle profile* divides a product's users and nonusers based on their purchase preference and product usage.

• A *product-specific profile* distinguishes a group of target consumers and sketches a profile of them along product-relevant dimensions.

• A *general lifestyle segmentation study* is carried out among a large number of respondents as research samples, which divides them into homogenous groups according to the level of similarities of their overall preferences.

• A *product-specific segmentation study* focuses on a product category and design questions around it. For a research on dermatology medicine, a researcher might reorganize the wording of a statement "I worry too much" as "I get skin allergies if I worry too much." This kind of questioning enables the researcher to spot users of competing brands in a more refined way.

The list below is an example of a psychographic research focusing on the category of skin care products. One can have a general idea about what questions would be asked in this kind of studies.

Table 8-3 Psychographic statements

Based on how much you agree with each statement, please give a score from 1 to 5.

(1) I know some things I do are bad for my wellness — late nights, smoking, or drinking. I don't know when I'll see the impact of my lifestyle on my appearance but I want to do what I can to compensate and prevent effects without giving up my fun.

(2) I often go out after work, and I want to look my best. I'd like to change my clothes and redo my beauty [personal care] routine, but I can't carry everything with me.

(3) I want to look effortlessly beautiful [handsome] and know it takes a lot of steps and commitment. But I really don't have the time, especially in the morning. I wish there was a way to make by beauty [personal care] routine faster and easier without feeling guilty or lazy.

(4) I have favorite beauty [personal care] products from different brands, but I worry if they are all working together well. Sometimes I buy makeup that doesn't work well with my moisturizer. I wonder if that is also true with cleansers, serums, shampoos, conditioners, but maybe

Continued

the mis-fit isn't as obvious. Could I be getting better results if my products worked well together?

(5) I love the idea of creating my own beauty [personal care] products just for me, but I don't have the knowledge or materials to make products from scratch.

(6) I prefer to shop online but want to see and feel the products before buying.

(7) Skin care is boring. Personal care is boring.

(8) There is too much information and solutions when I search online how to solve a beauty problem I have. I do not know whom/what I should trust.

(9) My beauty [personal care] regimen is important to look my best. But I wish someone could help me process all the information out there and tell me what is best to use for MY needs and when.

(10) Most beauty [personal care] products today work on the surface, but I believe that solving the root cause starts from the inside.

(11) I want to be able to check beauty care [personal care] product safety and ingredients but it takes so much time. I'm overwhelmed and don't know whom to trust.

(12) Ingredients with long names are scary and chemicals are harmful, how do I know which products to trust?

(13) I want to prevent my beauty [personal care] problems because once I see the problem, it's too late to do anything by stopping it from becoming worse.

(14) I know Traditional Chinese Medicine works, but it takes longer than western medicine. I wish I could get natural beauty products that use the best of science to make natural products that are very efficacious.

(15) I know things like doing proper skin care, sleeping enough, and eating right help me look my best, but there isn't enough time in the day to do everything that is right, and then I feel guilty, adding to my stress. Please make it fun and easy for me to stay on track and give me little nudges of help when I don't.

(16) I need to look good all day and sometimes into the night. I need products to help me stay fresh and beautiful [handsome] on the go.

(17) I want to know the bare minimum I need to do to maximize my skin care efforts and results.

(18) Finding the right beauty [personal care] products for my needs takes a lot of time and money. I like to learn about new products from people who say they have the same problems as I do and I want help to be connected to these people.

(19) I am overwhelmed by the business of my life. My beauty [personal] care products are a moment of indulgence when I get home, but I wish I could take with me for a pick-me-up when I'm on the go.

(20) My old beauty [personal care] routines and habits aren't working as well as they used to. I need help to find new products and habits that work for me in this stage of my life.

Continued

# of the question	Strongly disagree (1 point)	Disagree (2 points)	Neutral (3 points)	Agree (4 points)	Strongly agree (5 points)
1					
2					
3					
...					
19					
20					

AIOs

AIO is the abbreviation of activities, interests and opinions. The combination of these three variables is used to put consumers into different groups in psychographic researches. During a typical AIO survey, the respondent is asked a few questions to indicate their degree of agreement or disagreement with a number of statements pertaining to this person's lifestyle, entertainment preferences, fashion choices, and so on.

Activities: Activities focus on an individual's daily routine and hobbies. A person who rides a bicycle to work and plays sports on the weekends likely has different purchasing patterns than an employee who drives a car to work and watches a lot of movies. Club memberships, entertainment choices, vacation destinations, and social events can give marketers clues about a consumer's activities.

Interests: A person's interests reveal concepts and ideals that drive their passions. A mother of two children may list family, baking, crafts, and toys as interests on a survey. Interests may also include hobbies, affiliations, and pastimes. A consumer may have varied interests, such as stamp collecting, model-plane building, gardening, and fishing. By identifying the interests of a target consumer, companies can better identify how to appeal to them.

Opinions: Everyone has opinions, which reflect their feelings and thoughts, and consumers are no different. Marketers would like to know people's comments on movies, public figures, politicians, actors, and television shows. Marketing agencies also need to collect and analyze consumers' opinions about brands, products, and business outlets.

AIO aims to create a psychographic profile of a consumer, with the goal of targeting advertising to various types of people. Combined with demographic dates, AIO data is especially valuable. Collecting data from a great number of respondents, marketers establishes profiles of customers who have similar activities and product usage habits. The table below shows typical AIO dimensions used frequently.

Table 8-4 AIO dimensions

Activities	Interests	Opinions	Demographics
Work	Family	Themselves	Age
Hobbies	Home	Social issues	Education
Social events	Job	Politics	Income
Vacation	Community	Business	Occupation
Entertainment	Recreation	Economics	Family size
Club membership	Fashion	Education	Dwelling
Community	Food	Products	Geography
Shopping	Media	Future	City size
Sports	Achievements	Culture	Stage in lite cycle

Marketers are familiar with the 80/20 rule: 80% of sales rely on 20% of consumers. The implication for psychographic analysis is that only one or several lifestyle segments contribute significantly to the large proportion of sales. Thus, such analysis should start with identifying the lifestyle segments that encompass the majority of customers for a certain product. The heavy users of most products could be discovered through psychographic techniques. The ways these users relate the product to the brand and the product benefits they perceive can be better obtained.

The findings of psychographic studies can be used in the following ways: identify the target market, look at the market from a new perspective, determine and/or adjust product positioning, communicate product attributes in a more effective way, discover new product opportunities and develop product strategies.

The VALS system—China VALS

Until now the most widely applied psychographic research among marketing managers is the VALS program developed by a global research and consulting services firm Strategic Business Insights. VALS is used most frequently for strategic planning, consumer insights and communication. In other words, marketers use this tool to discover the exact consumer target for strategic marketing actions and then use the descriptions of a certain segment to direct business decision-making about delivering messages to the target consumers, optimizing product design, managing portfolio, and so forth. VALS is concerned with different segments' purchase patterns associated with long-lasting psychological characteristics. Consumers selected as samples are categorized based on their primary motivations and the natural and social resources they are able to have access to. The key prerequisite for VALS to work is that: in order to build shape and infuse substance and satisfaction to their lives, consumers choose and purchase products and services, and/or try to find experiences that gratify featured motives.

Adopting this framework, China VALS divides Chinese citizens into nine segments: Accomplisheds, Pacesetters, Preservers, Sustainers, Traditional Achievers, Trendy Achievers, Experiencers, Adapters, and Provincials. Such segmentation is carried out on the basis of primary motivations: Tradition, Achievement, and Self-Expression. The survey was done in 2013 among a number of 3,300 respondents, between the ages of 15 and 64, the result of which is projected to 516 million people. The sample frame consists of 62 areas that cover major geographic regions, cities of different tiers (one to four), and villages in China.

China VALS Framework

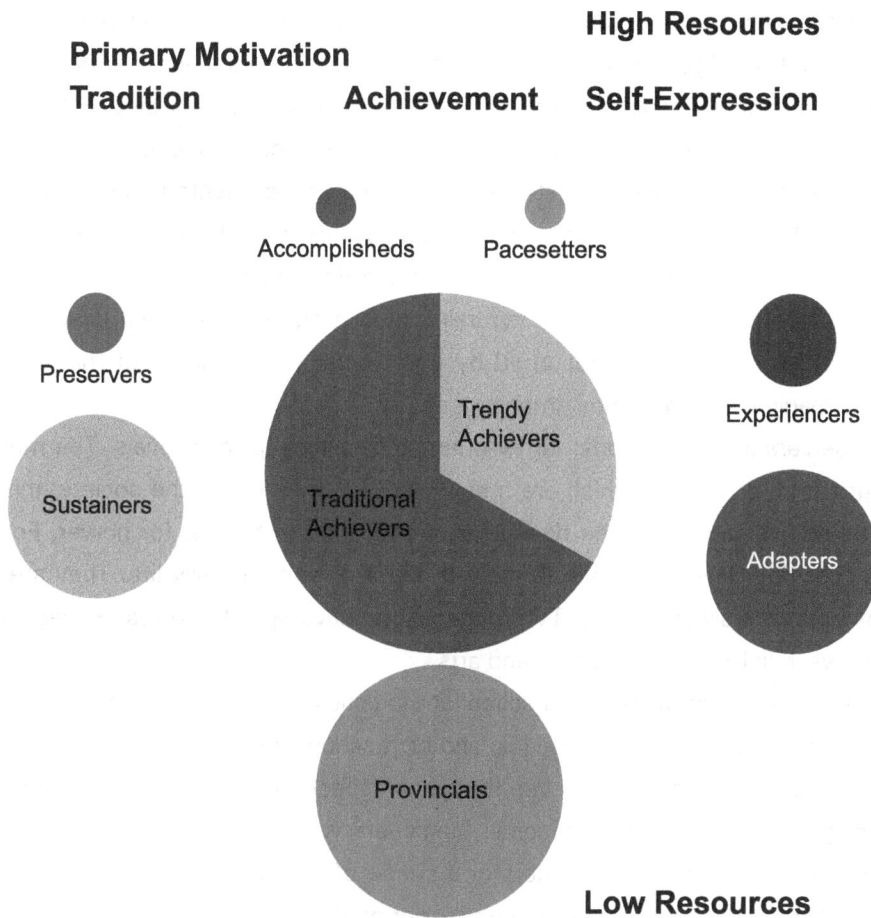

Figure 8-7 China VALS framework

The three primary motivations identified among Chinese consumers are Tradition, Achievement, and Self-Expression, which can most strongly contrast individuals:

● People motivated by *tradition* tend to live up to the standards in a traditional society, which have withstood the test of time. Their choices are made according to principles instead of status. As a type, they function to correct their own behaviors and others', such as seeking justice in wrongdoings.

● People motivated by *achievement* mainly pursue profits and an upper hand for themselves. Their choices are made according to power, status and reputation. As a type they possess a transaction function. Cultural values are adopted to facilitate their own aspirations, rather than consolidating values. They devote their energy in setting goals.

- People motivated by *self-expression* try to get rid of the restrictions from tradition and/or achievement. As a type, their function is to ease or modify social norms. Their choices are made based on newness, emotional and sensational stimulus and personal exploration.

The characteristics of each segment identified by VALS are as follows:

- *Accomplisheds* are perceptive, highly competent, and trustable. The median age of this group is 39, 59% of which are men, with 86% married. While seeking strategic advantages to elevate their social status, they do not wish to draw attention to themselves. This group read and digest more global, national, and local news than other groups do, and are most interested in finance and economics. They take actions to maintain their physical health, yet are more likely than other groups to consume beer and wine.

- *Pacesetters* are aspirational, status-seeking and future-oriented. The median age of this group is 28, 66% of which are women, with 54% married. They want to be approved by peers and to be perceived as having a role or social position. Fame might even be what they want. This group uses social networking most frequently. A great deal of material goods and experiences are consumed by this group. It is their belief that cultivating children's imagination is of utmost importance.

- *Preservers* are harmonious, family-oriented traditional professionals. The media age of this group is 43, 68% of which are men, with 91% married. In the society, this group offset the tide of careerism, the desire for wealth and the hunger for power. For them, being successful means having stability and peace of mind in daily life. They are incline to choose print media and watch TV programs that have specific topics like legal issues, health, news, folk landscape, theater, and arts.

- *Sustainers* are introverted, old school and practical. The median age of this group is 49, 77% of which graduated from middle and high school, with 89% married. They adhere to a conservative way of life, and even though in aspects of their daily life, they may look like other groups that are not traditional. Sustainers would likely return to village life for the reason that it offers a well understood sense of purpose. Most of them work in a factory, and are most likely to cook and go to wet markets. They tend to have a practice to commemorate their ancestors, while having low access to Internet.

- *Traditional achievers* are ambitious, while constantly pursuing approval from others. The median age of this group is 38, 55% of which graduated from high school and more, with 76% married. They want to keep up with upwardly mobile Chinese but are not sure about how and whether to do so. They are adaptive to both traditional and trendy attitudes, rather than aligning with any one-fold perspective. They are concerned about personal spirits and assets, and are insecure about personal safety and employment problems. While being interested in home improvement, they shop more frequently than other groups at the jewelry market. This segment has the highest percentage of population.

- *Trendy achievers* is a sub-group of the achievers, so they share similar characteristics with traditional achievers. But they have the greatest desire to be seen as successful and worthy of admiration. The median age of this group is 30, 40% of whom graduated from technical college or above, with 62% married. They are the most likely to want other people to know if they buy something expensive. It's more likely for them to own a variety of high-tech goods such as MP3 players, video game consoles, and desktop computers.

• *Experiencers* are creative, experimental and interested. The median age of this group is 21.5, the youngest among all groups. Only 20% of them are married, the lowest of all groups. Motivated by self-expression, with access to high resources, they seek personal advancement and look for innovative ways to move ahead in a career or an area of interest. They are the most ready and open to experiment with Western things like art or business. Conflicts between traditional and trendy ways of living do not resonate among them.

• *Adapters* are faithful and informal trend-followers. The median age of this group is 28, 61% of whom are women, and 47% graduated from technical/vocational institutes or above. They are similar to Experiencers but do not have the explicit drive for personal advancement or exploration. They are more likely than other groups to work in wholesale or retail trades. While they are more likely than average to take vacations, they are also the ones who are more likely to take skills-building classes.

• *Provincials* are rural and simple. The median age of this group is 43, 73% of whom graduated from middle school or less, with 76% married. Most Provincials grew up, and continue to live, in rural village areas. They are not media centric and have a relatively low information-seeking profile. Provincials are more likely than others to say that having children and being financially responsible are important attributes for success.

Summary

Personality can be summarized as the internal psychological features that define and embody the ways a person reacts to the surrounding environment. Three major theories related to personality are: (1) Sigmund Freud's Theory of Personality; (2) neo-Freudian theories; (3) the trait theory.

The prerequisite of Freud's personality theory is that the underlying needs or urges, sexual and other physiological drives in particular, form the core of human motivation and personality. Freud proposed that three interacting elements constitute the human personality, namely, the id, the superego, and the ego. The id is like the storage of primal and immediate impulses. The superego is a person's conscience, the internalized codes of conduct. The ego is like a mediator between the id and the superego.

Rather than believing that personality is instinctual and sexual in nature, these Neo-Freudian theorists argued that it's shaped by social and cultural aspects. They proposed that social relationships play a critical role in forming and developing personality.

The common research approach for Freudian and neo-Freudian theories is basically qualitative, whereas the trait theory is approached in a quantitative or empirical way. One of the most popularly used theories in the multi-trait approach is the Five-Factor Model. The five major traits identified are openness, conscientiousness, extraversion, agreeableness, and neuroticism.

Single-trait personality tests are often adopted and developed to measure one single trait that is considered to have special relevance to the understanding of a specific set of consumption-related behaviors. Some of the major traits being measured are consumer innovativeness, consumer materialism and consumer ethnocentrism.

Brand personality refers to the varied personality-like features consumers associate with a brand.

A lifestyle determines a person's consumption routines that represent his or her decisions on the ways of spending their time and money. Lifestyle marketing aims to enable consumers to enjoy life by pursuing the ways they opt for. It involves dividing the market into different segments based on lifestyle dimensions, positioning the product in a way that appeals to the activities, interests and opinions of the targeted market, and carrying out specific promotional campaigns which utilize lifestyle appeals to consolidate the market value of the offered product.

Psychographics refers to the application of psychological, sociological and anthropological aspects to find out the ways the market is divided according to the tendencies of different groups and the reasons behind to decide on a product, person, ideology and/or to have an attitude or choose certain medium. AIOs and VALs are the two major ways to measure purchase- and consumption-related lifestyles.

Exercises

(1) Retell the concepts of id, ego, and superego in your own words. Describe how they function according to the Freudian theory.

(2) Establish a list of key words to describe brand personality for three different brands within the same product category. Ask a small number of consumers to give a score to each brand on ten different personality dimensions. What differences can you find? Do these "personalities" relate to the advertising and packaging strategies used to differentiate these products?

(3) List three products that seem to have personalities, preferably the ones you are familiar with. Describe the perceived personalities. What types of people would buy these products? Is there a connection between the purchaser's personality and that of the brand or product?

(4) Extreme sports. Shooting short videos and uploading them to Tik Tok. Playing video games. Veganism. Can you foresee and estimate what will be popular in the near future? Identify a lifestyle trend that is just emerging in your university. Describe this trend in detail and give reasons to your prediction. What specific styles and/or products are parts of this trend?

(5) Collect a selection of recent advertisements that attempt to relate consumption of a product to a specific lifestyle. In class, give a presentation and demonstrate what you have found. Discuss how the goal of linking product consumption to a lifestyle is usually achieved.

(6) Student groups should identify three examples of lifestyle marketing on the Internet. Members of the group would demonstrate these examples in class. Show how the social media platform uses lifestyles to the organization's advantage.

Case Analysis

Read the following news and find out more about the development of the pet product industry in China. Using the theories about lifestyle learned in this chapter, incorporating personal experiences of yourself and the people you know, analyze how pet economy (raising pets at home, going to pet cafes, etc.) affects people's consumption pattern. Give a presentation to share your findings.

Holidays Provide Opportunities for Pet Hotels

Before the recent five-day May Day holiday, pet owners who planned to travel outside the city became more and more concerned about who could take care of their animals.

In Changchun, Jilin province, more people turned to pet boarding services as they made their advance plans.

"We are always busy during the holidays," said the owner of one pet supply shop in the city. "About a year ago, I noticed that during the holidays, there would be more pets needing to be looked after when their owners were away, so I started to provide pet boarding services in my shop."

To ensure the safety of pets, the shop only provides the service to its VIP guests "because we are familiar with their pets' health and temper conditions", the owner said. "Guests need to pay 28 yuan ($4) to 35 yuan per day for each pet, including three meals and some grooming services."

A female resident surnamed Wang found out about the service when she purchased pet food in the shop.

"I keep four cats and three dogs at home and I cannot imagine the mess if we leave for several days," she said. "It is really a good service that allows me to make a travel plan for the National Day holiday."

Some cat owners can also find boarding services in a cat-themed cafe in a shopping mall. Each cat gets its own house and all the cats can move freely in the cafe. Pet owners are charged 50 yuan per day for each cat.

CHAPTER NINE
Decision-Making Process

Learning objectives

After learning this chapter, you will be able to:

- describe the five steps in consumers' decision-making process;
- understand various types of information search;
- identify different decision rules when consumers evaluate alternatives;
- list post-purchase outcomes;
- formulate strategies to avoid post-purchase dissonance.

Lead-in Case

How Short Video Platforms Are Shaping Gen Z Consumer Behaviors

Short-video apps have the world's young consumers hooked with their compelling and easily digestible feeds of fleeting content. Leading the pack in this burgeoning sector are ByteDance platforms Douyin and TikTok, which in a few short years have come to dominate the pop culture conversation as much as the attention of digital natives.

Since launching in 2017, TikTok has amassed more than 1 billion users in over 150 countries, with 90 percent of its users accessing it daily. China alone is responsible for around 86 percent of TikTok's revenue. Gen Z-ers and millennials, those consumers-to-watch, make up a bulk of the apps' demographic: Parklu reports that 85 percent of Douyin users are aged below 24.

In 2020, Douyin and TikTok have only swelled in popularity as they've kept users entertained and scrolling during COVID-related lockdowns. According to SensorTower, they are now the top grossing apps worldwide. But just as consumers have guaranteed the apps' successes, Douyin and TikTok have naturally come to shape the tastes and habits of its audience.

Personalized marketing over blanket advertising

Blair Zhang, China Analyst at global market research company Mintel, tells Jing Culture & Commerce that apps like Douyin are demonstrating that consumers are more receptive to personalized marketing. "Consumers nowadays need brands to have enthusiasm to be close to them," says Zhang. "Video content that can better resonate to attract consumers wins more screen time."

Thus, ultra-aspirational or generic advertising is no longer relevant; familiarity and individualized marketing, which translate into authenticity and trustworthiness for the brand, are in. Douyin's first partnership with a luxury brand is a prime example in this manner of strategic marketing: in 2017, in collaboration with Michael Kors, it asked users to create and post their own homemade catwalk videos with the unique hashtag #城市T台 不服来斗# (Combat me on the city's fashion stage). Since then, Douyin has not lacked for such online campaigns that effectively convert consumers into active marketers and participants in the brands that matter to them personally.

Don't make ads; tell stories

TikTok's June 2020 campaign "Don't Make Ads, Make TikToks"' highlighted how advertisers can gain traction on short video platforms through creative and concise marketing, as opposed to maximalist, lengthy advertisements. As TikTok and Douyin have become the primary advertising outlets for many brands, the apps have further encouraged advertisers to emphasize their brand personalities through down-to-earth humor, inclusivity, and storytelling.

According to a recent Nielsen study commissioned by TikTok, 43 percent of TikTok users feel that advertising "blends in" with other content on the platform, while signaling their readiness to engage with fun, authentic, and inspiring branded content. Moreover, these young consumers want to laugh with the brand they are buying from. As Zhang notes, "One of the most important characteristics of Douyin is to encourage personality. All users can easily express their own views, so an era of individuality has arrived."

Introduction

The development of E-commerce and new platform of social media have reshaped the global marketing environment, which affects the ways consumers form their needs, search information, make decisions on their choices and how they buy and dispose products. The online campaigns of Douyin and Tiktok improve consumers' participation, and make an influence on what types of information consumers will collect when they are trying to meet their needs by purchasing products. Ads on these social media platforms tell consumers which brands they should choose, and how they should use those products.

In this chapter, we are going to explore the process that consumers go through when they buy products and services. All the consumers are regarded as problem solvers, who will undergo five steps in the process of finding solutions in the form of purchases.

9.1 Introduction to the consumer decision-making process

The consumer decision-making process model represents the steps that consumers go through before, during and after making a purchase. A consumer realizes that he/she wants to make a purchase, and he/she will undergo several steps to accomplish it. The five steps are: need recognition,

消费者决策过程:
表示消费者在进行购买前、过程中和购买后经历的各个阶段。

information search, evaluation of alternatives, purchase, and post purchase behavior. Figure 9-1 illustrates this process.

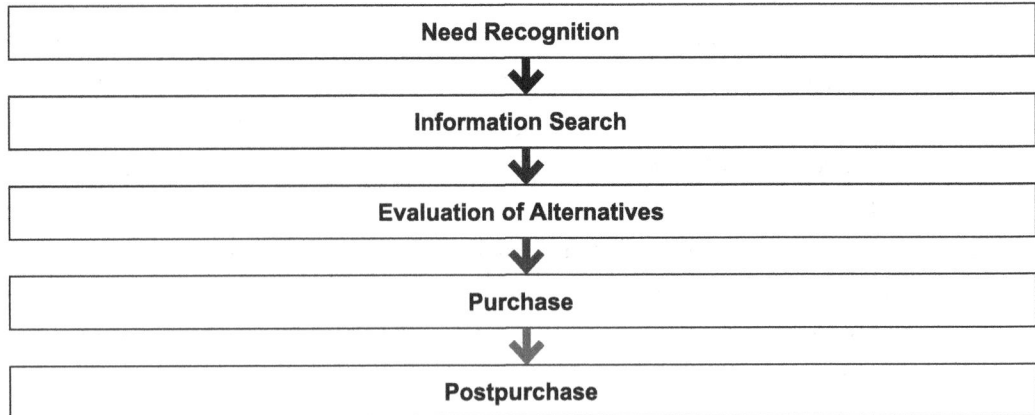

Need Recognition
↓
Information Search
↓
Evaluation of Alternatives
↓
Purchase
↓
Postpurchase

Figure 9-1 Consumer Decision-making Process Model

9.2 Types of consumer decision-making

Figure 9-1 presents the overview of consumer decision-making process, reflecting the general scenario a consumer experiences when he/she makes decisions. However, in order to understand more about this process, it should be clarified that not all consumer decision-making processes require the same amount of efforts to put in. Some purchase seems to be more important to certain consumers, which leads them to spend more time and effort to make decisions. Therefore, based on the level of effort consumers make, the decision-making process can be classified into three types: extensive problem solving, limited problem solving and routine response behavior.

扩展式问题解决：
当消费者没有或只有很少的关于产品的信息和经验时，需要付出较大的努力去解决问题，他们便会寻求扩展式问题解决方案。

有限型问题解决：
当消费者已经有了关于某产品的信息和经验，但尚未完全建立强烈的品牌偏好，从而进行的决策。

1. Extensive problem solving

When consumers have no or little information/experience about the products, they usually go for extensive problem solving when a completely new need is discovered, which requires significant efforts to be satisfied. In most cases of extensive problem solving, the products are featured with high risk and high involvement to the consumers. For example, when it's your first time to purchase a car, it's more likely for you to collect a great deal of information about car brands and models. In other words, you'll embark on an extensive search of car-related information, to set criteria to distinguish among alternatives.

2. Limited problem solving

In another case called limited problem solving, consumers have had some previous experience and information about the products, but have not fully established their strong preference to select from the alternatives. At this level, consumers conduct a little search for additional information and spend less time than extensive problem solving, and always use some previously established principles to choose the products. Purchasing T-shirts is an example of limited problem solving. You have already obtained information about the T-shirt brands, so your decision-making relies on your past experience.

3. Routine response behavior

Routine response behavior involves the regular purchase of low cost products that requires little decision-making effort. In this case, consumers have established clear preference and a specific set of criteria to assess the alternatives. Under this circumstance, consumers make little, even no conscious effort. For instance, you plan to invite your best friend over this weekend and you send her a message via WeChat without considering any other apps. WeChat has already been a routine choice for communication, so it is a routine response behavior based on your habit.

No matter which type of decision-making it is, a purchase decision actually consists of a series of steps, as mentioned above. The steps will be explored in the rest of this chapter.

例行性反应行为：表示仅需很少决策投入的定期购买低成本产品的行为。

9.3 Need recognition

Need recognition is the first step of the consumer decision-making process, which reveals the difference between our current state of affairs and the ideal state we desire. The greater the difference between those two states, the more intense the level of need recognition there will be. Figure 9-2 below demonstrates the relationship between the current state and the ideal state of a consumer, and the related implication for marketers. For instance, you are quite satisfied with the current smartphone which was bought last year, because the screen is large enough, the pictures taken are quite sharp and beautiful, the response speed of the operating system is quick enough, etc. After using it for maybe two or three years, the system starts to slow down, and the cameras fail to deliver clear images at the night scenes. So there's a decline in the phone's performance which results in a gap between what you believe is ideal and the current state. This is when you realize there's a need to switch to a new smartphone (need recognition). Another scenario is that your phone performs just as usual, and you see no reason to replace it until the brand you are aware of has recently launched a new model of smartphone which has a lovely appearance and can take pictures in a much complimenting way, along with other attractive new features. That is to say, there's an increase or update in the ideal state, and what you are currently having suddenly becomes obsolete or outdated. (opportunity recognition)

需求识别：消费者意识到当前状态与所期望的理想状态之间的差异。

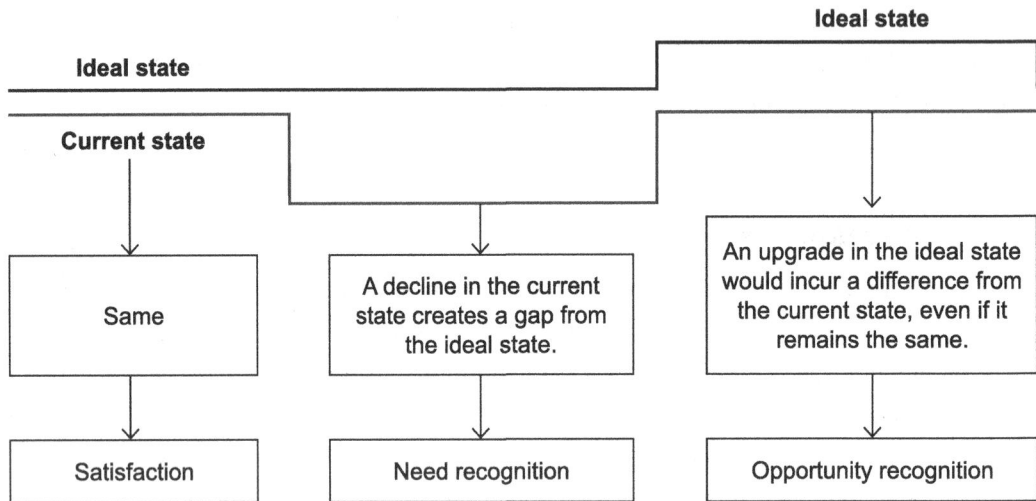

Figure 9-2 Discrepancy between consumers' ideal state and the current state

9.4 Information search

信息搜索：消费者从长期记忆、和／或外部环境中搜索信息，从而做出购买决策。

Suppose you feel hungry and you want to have a bowl of noodles; or you found it's time to buy some new winter outfits; or you realized a book to improve your English level is a necessity... Once you recognize a problem, you need to find a way to solve it. Information search is the second step in the consumer decision-making process, by which we search appropriate information from our long-term memory or/and the environment, to make reasonable decisions. Therefore, there are two types of information search: internal search of information and external search of information.

9.4.1 Internal search of information

内部信息搜索：从消费者过去的经验，即长期记忆中搜索信息的过程。

Information collection from past experience, or rather, from the storage in consumers' long-term memory, is regarded as internal search of information. For example, every time you plan to buy a new pair of running shoes, Li-Ning will be the first brand in your mind. This is how you search information based on your past experience, since you have owned several pairs of running shoes under the same brand and you are quite satisfied with the quality.

9.4.2 External search of information

外部信息搜索：消费者从外部环境中搜索信息的过程。

On the other hand, if the collected information from past experience and memory cannot provide solutions yet, or the consumer doesn't have prior experience, the consumer will search information from the external environment to make the purchase decision. The information might be from their families and friends, or from commercial sources. For instance, you would like to buy a new smart television for your apartment, but you have never bought one before. Afterwards, you decided to ask some of your friends for advices, or just check the television recommendations and rankings on IT portal websites.

ZOL.com provides a way to collect information about products (smart television in this case), which refers to external search of information.

It is worth emphasizing that a lot of consumers make decisions based on the combination of internal search and external search. But consumers always take internal information search prior to seeking external sources. In other words, we always search from our past experience and memories before asking others. The larger amount of the relevant past experience, the less external information the consumer needs to solve problems.

9.5 Evaluation of alternatives

Once consumers recognize their needs, and collect enough information about the products which can meet their needs, they will realize that there are several possible choices available. Evaluation of alternatives means using specific criteria to judge among a selected set of options to decide which one is suitable for the consumer. As mentioned above, you are eager to purchase a new television, and you have asked your friends and your parents for advices. Also, you have done searching information about different brands and features about the smart televisions in physical stores and online shops. Not surprisingly, you will be exposed to lots of choices of smart televisions, which denotes the initiation of alternative evaluation.

While consumers are making choices, psychologically, they organize and classify all the choices to help them get through the decision-making process. Under such circumstance, alternatives fall into three different sets. All possible choices for a product category are categorized in **universal sets.** For example, while you are choosing a smart television, the universal set includes all the possible brands of smart TVs. But obviously you are not going

选项评价： 对有限几个选项使用特定的评判标准来决定哪个更适合。

普遍阈： 包含某一产品品类所有可能的品牌选项合集。

回溯阈： 消费者能随时从回忆中调取的某些品牌的选项合集。

激活阈： 包含消费者为了解决某一特定问题将要评价及考虑的品牌。

to choose from all the brands available. It draws forth another term: retrieval sets. **A retrieval set** refers to the brands that the consumer can readily bring forth from memory. If you are able to recall five brands of smart televisions, let's say Huawei, Haier, Sony, TCL and Samsung. They are in your retrieval sets that you know and can recall. Finally, being able to recall doesn't mean you would definitely make a choice on those brands. It indicates the more significant set in marketing—evoked sets.

9.5.1 Evoked sets

An evoked set includes all the brands that a consumer is aware of, and thinks well of, when considering a purchase. It is also called the consideration set. As a brand, being in a target consumer's evoked set is crucial to marketers, because without it, the purchase will not happen. Only if your brand is in consumers' evoked set, they would probably actually consider purchasing it when they are making decisions. Suppose a consumer would only consider three brands of smart televisions, Huawei, Haier, and TCL, perhaps it's because he/she only considers domestic brands for the reason of his/her patriotism. As a result, the three brands are in the certain consumer's evoked set. In other words, even though the consumer is capable of recalling five brands of televisions, they will only choose from their evoke set. Figure 9-3 shows the options identified and considered while purchasing a television.

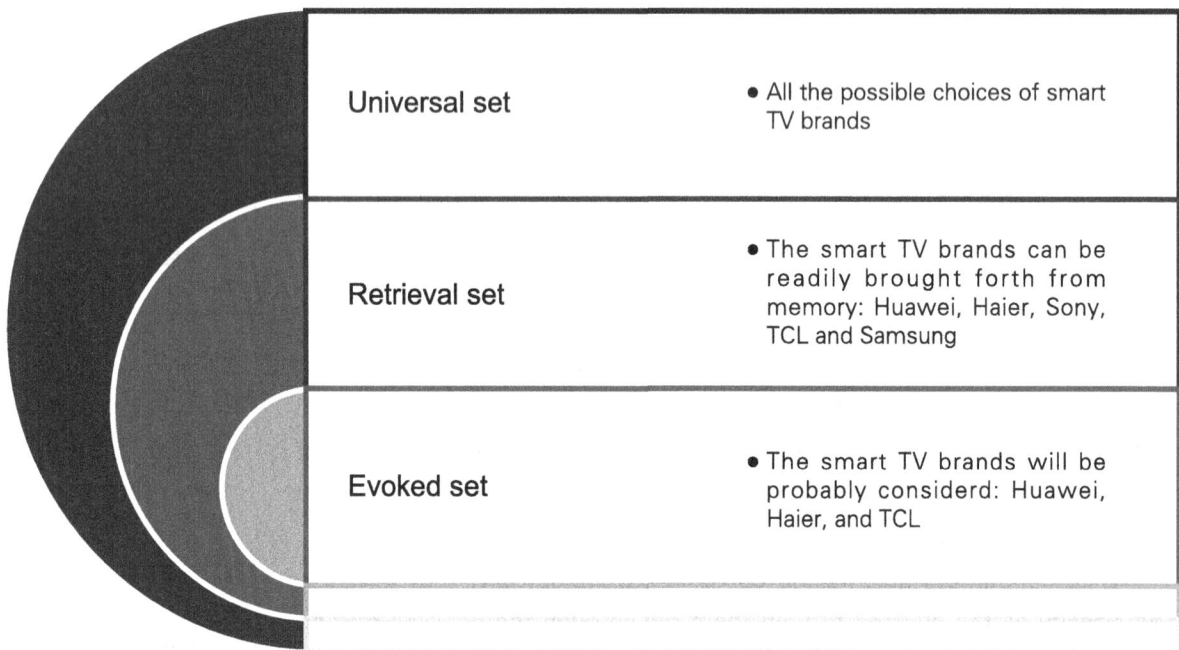

Universal set	• All the possible choices of smart TV brands
Retrieval set	• The smart TV brands can be readily brought forth from memory: Huawei, Haier, Sony, TCL and Samsung
Evoked set	• The smart TV brands will be probably considerd: Huawei, Haier, and TCL

Figure 9-3 Options identified and considered while purchasing a smart television

9.5.2 Evaluative criteria

When you are selecting a smart television, you focus on the three brands and completely ignore other brands. In this case, you have narrowed down the alternatives once you only consider the brands in your evoked set. And now the issue is raised: which specific brand are you going to choose?

Evaluative criteria consist of a set of prominent or significant attributes, or a combination of facts and values, to aid consumers in order to judge the worth of a particular product. To consumers who are experiencing the decision-making process, evaluative criteria of the products are always benefits the product should provide. For example, when you are selecting a smart television, the price, size, storage, and customer service are the attributes for considerations.

In addition, not all the types of decision-making process involve the same level of evaluation of alternatives. The routine response behavior requires no evaluation of any alternatives. In this case, you are able to make the decision without assessing any attributes. Limited problem solving involves considering one or two attributes while comparing among a few brands. Extensive problem solving requires more criteria evaluation among an extensive set of brands.

It is not enough to merely consider evaluative criteria when we choose among alternatives, the importance weight also plays a role. Figure 9-4 illustrates the process that consumers evaluate products among alternatives and make decisions.

> **评价标准：** 由一系列显著或重要的属性，或某些事实与价值的结合组成，消费者依靠评价标准来判断某一特定产品的价值。

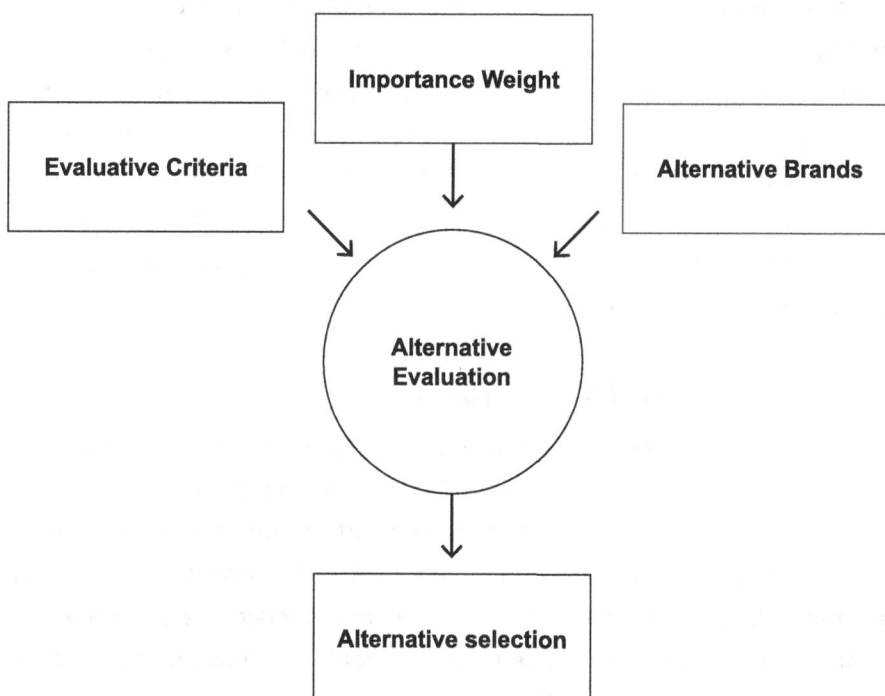

Figure 9-4 Alternative evaluation and selection

It is significantly essential for marketers to understand how important each criterion to consumers. Once again, let's take the example of purchasing a smart television. As shown in Table 9-1, four evaluative criteria and the importance weight of each are listed.

Table 9-1 Evaluative criteria and their importance weights when purchasing a smart TV

Evaluative Criteria	Price	Size	Storage	Customer Service
Importance Weight	40%	10%	30%	20%
Huawei	10	8	7	8
Haier	8	9	8	7
TCL	6	10	4	9

To this consumer, price is the priority when selecting a digital camera, followed by the attribute storage, customer service and the least important one, size. The next step for this consumer is to evaluate the three brands, Huawei, Haier and TCL by rating each attribute. The price of Huawei got the highest score among the three brands, while TCL provides the best possible size. In the same way, the consumer rates the other two evaluative criteria — storage and customer service based on his/her own perception. This is how a consumer assigns the important weight to each criterion and rates it, leading him/her to make decisions.

9.5.3 Consumer decision rules

消费者决策规则:
消费者为更方便进行备选方案选择而使用的程序。

Consumer decision rules are the procedures used by consumers to facilitate alternative selection. In order to make decisions promptly, consumers use a set of rules consciously or subconsciously to select from the alternatives. These rules reduce the burden of making complicated decisions by providing guidelines or routines that are meaningful and useful to the consumer. There are different forms of consumer decision rules, which are categorized into two types: *compensatory decision rules* and *noncompensatory decision rules*.

1. Compensatory decision rules

补偿式决策规则:
消费者将选择在有关评价标准的判断上总体表现最好的品牌, 即考虑所有合适的评价标准, 并认为好的属性可以抵消不好的属性。

In some cases, a consumer arrives at a choice by considering all of the appropriate attributes of a product and by mentally trading off the alternative's perceived disadvantages on one or more attributes with its perceived advantages on other attributes. Let's turn back to the scenario of purchasing a smart television. All the four evaluative criteria (price, size, storage, and customer service) are considered, but you don't just focus on one specific attribute (price for instance). Instead, you trade off one characteristic against another to make your final purchase decision. The formula below states the brand with the highest sum of rating scores will be chosen, which can be illustrated as:

$$R_b = \sum_{i=1}^{n} W_i B_{ib}$$

Where

R_b =Overall rating of brand B

W_i =Importance weight of evaluative criterion i

B_{ib} =Evaluation of brand B on evaluative criterion i

n =Number of evaluative criteria

To be more specific, table 9.2 reveals how compensatory decision rules work when purchasing a smart TV.

Table 9-2 Compensatory decision rules for purchasing a smart TV

Evaluative Criteria	Price	Size	Storage	Customer Service	Overall Rating
Importance Weight	40%	10%	30%	20%	100%
Huawei	10	8	7	6	8.1
Haier	8	9	7	7	7.6
TCL	6	10	4	9	6.4

Although this consumer believes the size of the TCL smart TV outperforms the other two brands, and it provides the best customer service among the three, it is still given the lowest overall score (R_{TCL}=6×40%+10×10%+4×30%+9×20%=6.4). In contrast, Huawei seems to produce the smallest device and provide the worst customer service compared to Haier and TCL, but the advantage of it (i.e. price) plays the most important role to the perception of choosing a smart TV for this consumer. In other words, the positive attributes compensate the negative ones. Therefore, the final purchasing decision made by this consumer after comparing the three alternatives will be the brand with the highest overall score (R_{Huawei}=10×40%+8×10%+7×30%+6×20%=8.1), which is Huawei.

2. Non-compensatory decision rules

In contrast, sometimes consumers employ non-compensatory decision rules when making purchasing decisions. They find positive performance on one evaluative criterion does not offset or compensate for negative performance on another evaluative criterion of the brand. That is to say, a consumer chooses a brand on account of some certain attributes, regardless of the performance of other attributes. For instance, you believe that a good brand is supported by the way it handles with customers. While you are making decisions of buying a smart television, you are going to choose the one that you suppose provides the best customer service, rather than how much it costs, or how big it is. A reasonable price or a big size of a smart TV

非补偿式决策规则:

表示消费者选择一个品牌是基于某些特定属性，而不考虑其他属性。

doesn't compensate the negative customer service. Although TCL is more expensive and provides the lowest storage among the three alternatives, it still will be his/her choice (refer again to Table 9.2).

When consumers are less familiar with a certain product category, or they are reluctant to go through a complicated decision-making process, they are more likely to use noncompensatory decision rules. Precisely, noncompensatory decision rules can be summarized in four types.

1) The conjunctive rules

The conjunctive rules suggest that consumers establish a minimum, separate acceptable level for each considered criterion and accept an alternative only if it equals or exceeds the minimum cutoff level of all the criteria. Referring to Table 9-3, you have given the performance level on each evaluative criterion for the three considered brands of smart TVs as mentioned above.

> **连接式决策规则：**
> 消费者对每一评价标准设置最低的可接受水平，选择所有等于或超过每个标准的最低可接受水平的备选方案。

Table 9-3 Consumers' given performance level of each brand of smart TVs

Brands / Evaluative Criteria	Huawei	Haier	TCL
Price	10	8	6
Size	8	9	10
Storage	7	7	4
Customer Service	6	7	9

As far as it's concerned, there are, cognitively, several established minimum standards of a smart TV that you would like to purchase. In general, on the basis of the conjunctive rules, you will eliminate the brands of smart TVs which fall below any of your perception to the minimum standards, also called cutoff points. As shown in Table 9-4, you suppose the price of a smart TV brand to be chosen should at least reach 7; the same is true for size. You assign 5 to storage, and 6 to customer service respectively. At this moment, you have found two brands are eliminated from further consideration, which are TCL (the price and storage) and Huawei (the size and customer service), since they don't meet the minimum scores that you established for purchasing a smart TV. Therefore, your final decision is Haier. If there is more than one brand left, other decision rules will be employed to make a further decision.

Table 9-4 The minimum standards of a smart TV

Evaluative Criteria	Minimum standards
Price	7
Size	7
Storage	5
Customer Service	7

2) The disjunctive rules

The disjunctive rule is the mirror image of the conjunctive rule, that is, a consumer establishes a separate minimally acceptable cutoff point for each attribute (in most cases a relatively higher level than by the conjunctive rule). All the brands that exceed the cutoff point for any specific evaluative criterion will be accepted. Let's assume that you are selecting a smart TV from the alternatives by using the disjunctive rule, the perceived cutoff points for the attributes are presented in Table 9-5.

析取式决策规则：

消费者对每一评价标准设置最低的可接受水平（通常比较高），任一品牌只要有一个属性超过了该水平都会被接受。

Table 9-5 The minimally acceptable cutoff points of a smart TV

Evaluative Criteria	Minimum standards
Price	9
Size	9
Storage	8
Customer Service	8

You would realize that Huawei (the price), and TCL (the size and customer service) would fall into your further considerations. You might purchase either of them, or select one between them by using another decision rules, or by adding new evaluative criteria to make a decision.

3) The elimination-by-aspects rules

When a consumer is exposed to several alternatives, he/she first identifies the most important attribute of brands when evaluating alternatives. As the decision rules introduced above, a cutoff point for each attribute should be assigned. When an option doesn't meet one of the cutoff points for the criteria, it will be eliminated from consideration. Evaluations of different attributes are applied until a single "best" option is left. Assume that you have established the cutoff points and the rank order for each evaluative criterion (See Table 9-6).

排除式决策规则：

消费者根据重要程度对评价标准进行排序，并对每一评价标准设置临界点，按顺序依次排除所有没有超过临界点的备选方案。

Table 9-6 The cutoff point and rank order for attributes of a smart TV

Evaluative Criteria	Cutoff point	Rank order
Price	7	1
Size	7	2
Storage	6	3
Customer Service	7	4

According to Table 9-6, if you use elimination-by-aspects rules to make decisions when purchasing a smart TV, the price is regarded as the most important feature. In the first step, TCL is eliminated since it is only given 6 of the price performance level, lower than cutoff point 7. As for the two brands left, Huawei and Haier meet the cutoff points for the size and storage. Then Huawei is eliminated in terms of customer service. At last, Haier would be chosen.

4) The lexicographic rules

编纂式决策规则: 消费者根据重要程度对评价标准进行排序，并选择在最重要属性中表现最好的品牌。

If a consumer chooses a brand to purchase among the alternatives, based on a simple priority ranking of the attributes available, he/she is taking the lexicographic rules, which means an alternative is better than another alternative if and only if it is better than the other alternative in the most significant attribute on which the two alternatives differ. Still, let's take a look at the scenario of buying a smart TV. You have ranked the criteria based on the importance of each, referring to Table 9.6, in which case, you regard the price as the foremost attribute. According to Table 9.3, Huawei is given 10 points as far as you are concerned, exceeding other brands, so Huawei would be your choice. Assume you graded 9 on the price for Huawei, which is exactly the same as Haier, and then you would be in a dilemma of choosing from Huawei or Haier. What will be the next step? Size is the second important criterion to you, so you will check which brand between the two gets a higher score on size. The answer is Haier.

比较广告: 指直接将自有产品与竞争对手产品进行比较的广告。

In the light of the lexicographic decision rule, marketers found that it is very important to inform their target consumers that their brands are outperforming the competitors on the most important evaluative criterion. Only if the relative advantages are established in terms of the most significant attributes, the brands will be chosen. It inspires the design of **comparative advertising**, in which brands are compared to one another. For example, Burger King introduced Whopper, a competing product to McDonalds' Big Mac. The comparative advertisement below illustrates how Burger King emphasizes the advantage of size over McDonalds', assuming their target audiences take size as the most important evaluative criterion when making purchase decisions.

Burger King implies that Whopper excels Big Mac in terms of size in its comparative advertisement.

To summarize, when you are evaluating the alternatives among the three smart TV brands, Huawei, Haier and TCL, by applying different decision rules, you'd come up with various results (See Table 9-7).

Table 9-7 Decision rules and the brand chosen

Decision Rules		Brand Chosen
Compensatory Decision Rule		Huawei
Noncompensatory Decision Rule	The Conjunctive Rule	Haier
	The Disjunctive Rule	Huawei/ TCL
	The Elimination-by-aspects Rule	Haier
	The Lexicographic Rule	Huawei/ Haier

9.5.4 Technological assistance in consumer decision-making

It is believed that individuals are only equipped with limited information-processing capacity. While they are searching information, evaluating and comparing the alternatives, it is difficult for them to make decisions with limited knowledge and capability. The current technological development, especially the Internet, impacts the way consumers make decisions. In the case of choosing a new smart TV for your apartment, you find it hard to make the final decision all by yourself since there are so many attributes for you to consider and there are a great number of brands available. WeChat, Douyin, Weibo and other social media platforms allow you to mutually communicate your dilemma to your families, friends, and even opinion leaders in the product category. In order to aid consumers to make decisions in a faster way, E-commerce platforms like Taobao.com provide consumers opportunities to share links of the product to others, or participate in Taobao Livestreaming（淘宝直播）to obtain more external information.

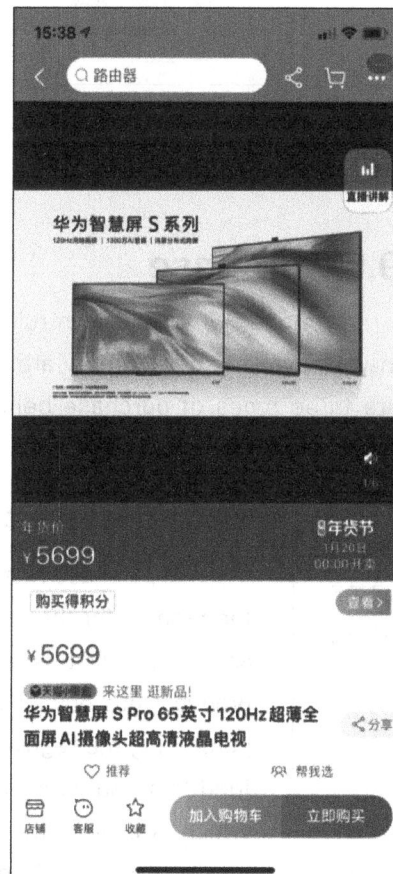

Taobao.com provides online video-streaming of the featured products, to reach and engage with their consumers, consolidating brand awareness. Consumers can also share links of products with others by clicking on the button on the right bottom.

Evaluating and comparing products on attributes could also be a difficulty for consumers, on account of vast quantities of information available. JD.com provides an effective tool of merchandise comparison, which assists consumers to compare the products in terms of various attributes, simplifying alternative evaluation and facilitating decision making.

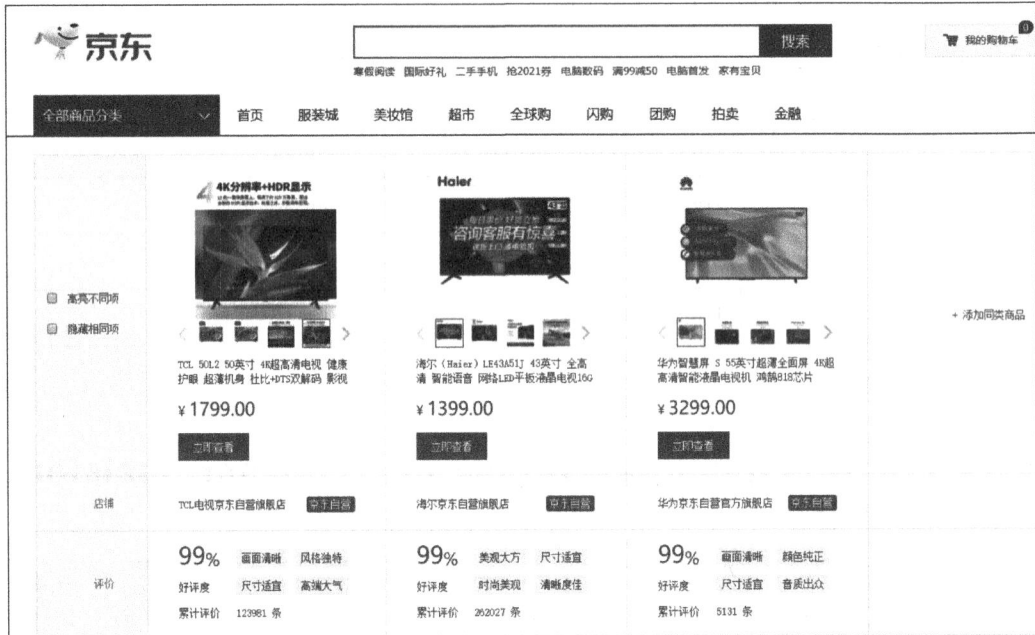

Consumers are able to compare smart TVs on brand, weight, customer service, interactive device, and other specifications on JD.com.

9.6 Purchase

No matter which decision rules you choose, you have evaluated all the alternatives in your evoked set, and now are ready to perform the actual purchase behavior. There are three types of purchase behavior: trial purchase, repeat purchase and long-term commitment purchase.

9.6.1 Trial purchase

试购： 指的是消费者第一次购买某产品，通常购买少量的产品作为"尝试"的购买行为。

Trial purchase refers to the purchase behavior that a consumer purchases the product for the first time, usually buying a smaller amount of the product as a "trial". In this case, the consumer tends to be less familiar with the product, thus buy less to reduce risks, aiming to evaluate the product before purchasing the regular quantity. For example, you plan to buy a brand of dog food that you've never tried before. Instead of buying a 10kg pack directly, which is exactly the regular pack size you buy routinely, you purchase a smaller sack — 1.5 kg — of it, to evaluate the quality of it, in case your dog refuses to eat it. As such, marketers encourage consumers to try their newly introduced products by providing free samples, sample packs, coupons along with other promotional tactics.

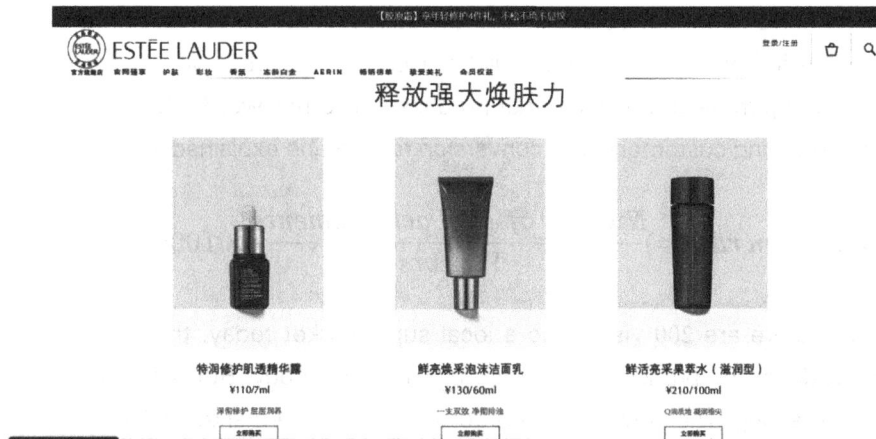

Estée Lauder encourages consumers to purchase sample products with a smaller size at the trial center of its official website.

9.6.2 Repeat purchase

If a consumer has been satisfied with a brand and has established clear brand preference, he/she will purchase the same brand to replace the previous purchased products. Compared to trial purchase, a larger quantity of the products would be bought. For instance, you have bought a 15ml of the Estée Lauder moisturizing essence, and you are pleased with it. Hence you decide to buy it again, and this time, you are more likely to purchase a bigger size of it, like the 50ml bottle. Repeat purchase is a crucial term to marketers, since consumers only purchase the products repeatedly if the product has met their expectation. Also, brand loyalty can be measured through repeat purchases of the brand.

> **重复购买：** 如果消费者对某一品牌产生满意度，并建立了明确的品牌偏好，该消费者就会再次购买同一品牌。

9.6.3 Long-term commitment purchase

If a consumer is satisfied with a certain brand, he/she will agree to purchase the products over a period of time. You have repurchased the bigger size of Estée Lauder moisturizing essence, and you decided to make it a routinely regular skincare purchase. Over the next 5 years, once you are about to run out of a bottle of the essence, you cannot wait to purchase another one.

> **长期购买：** 消费者对某一品牌产生满意度并在一段时间内持续购买该产品。

9.6.4 Conversion rate

In addition, marketers realize that consumers don't always purchase the products they have already decided to buy after alternative evaluations. Before going into the store or making a deal on an ecommerce platform, maybe the consumer has a particular "candidate" in mind, as the result obtained from the previous process. However, this doesn't guarantee the purchase of the supposed product. Sometimes a consumer just changes his/her mind one second before he/she is about to pay for it. In other cases consumers find

> **转换率：** 表示将访问者转换成实际购买者的比率。

their selected alternative might not be available in the stores, or for other reasons, they are not able to purchase it. The conversion rate will be used to measure how well marketers convert the intended purchase into an actual purchase, in other words, how well they convert visitors into paying customers. The conversion rate can be explained as:

$$Conversion\ rate = \frac{Number\ of\ goal\ achievements}{Visitors} \times 100\%$$

Assuming that there are 200 visitors to a local supermarket today, they looked for, picked up and put down the products they were considering to buy. But only 100 visitors actually bought something. The conversion rate for this local supermarket today would be 50% (100/200=0.5). A high conversion rate is indicative of successful marketing. Abandoned carts, stock-out, too long the waiting time, the disappointing shopping environment and a lot of other factors reduce the conversion rate. The factors influencing purchase and helping to increase the conversion rate will be explored in the next chapter.

9.7 Postpurchase

The consumer decision-making process doesn't terminate in the stage of purchase. Marketers are especially enthusiastic about the final step — post-purchase, since only the actual purchasers, rather than potential customers are engaged in this step. There are several elements involved in consumer postpurchase behavior (see Figure 9-5).

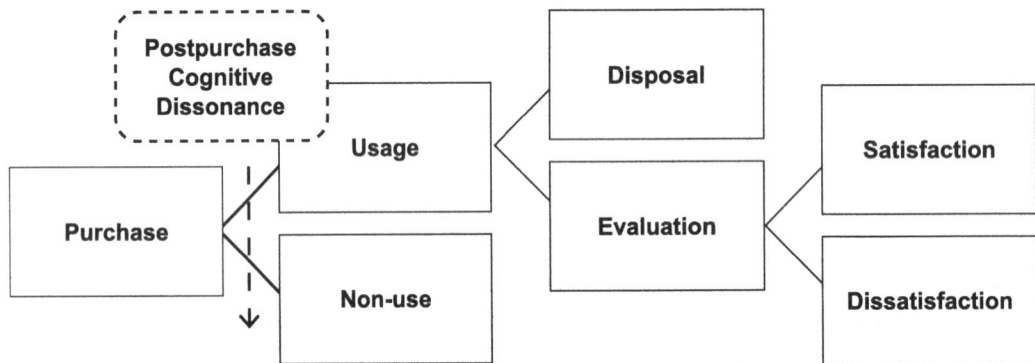

Figure 9-5 The consumer postpurchase behavior process

Once a consumer has purchased a product, he/she might use it or not. During and after the process of usage, the product will be evaluated by the consumer, which could either be satisfied or unsatisfied. Satisfaction contributes to repeat purchase, increase usage and recommendation to others and enhanced loyalty; whereas dissatisfaction leads to complaints, negative word of mouth and other adverse consequences. Also, the way consumers dispose the package or the product itself should be considered.

购后认知失调: 表示在购买行为发生后,由信念和行为之间的不一致导致的一种心理上的不适感。

9.7.1 Post-purchase cognitive dissonance

During the process of postpurchase behavior, especially before using, a phenomenon known as postpurchase cognitive dissonance might occur. Postpurchase cognitive dissonance is a mentally uncomfortable state generated by an inconsistency between beliefs and behaviors after a purchased behavior engaged, resulting in the buyer's remorse. In other words, you regret buying a product, which makes you feel very uneasy. For instance, you have bought an expensive smart phone, and then you are haunted by a thought: is it really better than the other less expensive one presented in the store — the one you hesitated but didn't buy? That is your belief. At this moment, you might realize that psychologically, an inconsistency between your belief and your behavior occurs. That is how postpurchase cognitive dissonance is generated.

Obviously, not all purchase behaviors lead to postpurchase cognitive dissonance. The likelihood of generating postpurchase cognitive dissonance is affected by several factors, they are:

• *The level of product involvement*: Product involvement is the degree to which a consumer searches for, attends to, and thinks about a product's information before purchasing the product. The higher level of product involvement, the more likely postpurchase cognitive dissonance occurs. Suppose you are in the scenario of purchasing an expensive car, rather than a bottle of mineral water. This infrequent purchase is very important and expensive for you. In order to make the right decision, it costs you half a year to collect information and compare among the alternatives. After purchasing, there is a high possibility that post-purchase cognitive dissonance would occur because you've invested time, attention and effort to try to make the right decision. Along the process, high expectation has been established.

• *The level of difficulty of selecting from among the alternatives*: If the category of products that you are considering to purchase presents a number of choices to you, and there is no distinct difference between all the alternatives, you'll find it difficult to make a final decision. The higher level of difficulty of selecting from among the alternatives, the more likely you will experience postpurchase cognitive dissonance. For instance, there are plenty of car brands available for you to choose from, and it is hard for you to evaluate which one is superior to the other. You tend to regret after purchasing one of them since you will always tell yourself that it might not be the best one.

• *The product doesn't work as intended*: Post-purchase cognitive dissonance barely occurs on the condition that the product could just live up to your expectations. For example, you have purchased a brand new car. You are pleased with the performance, maintenance and functionality of it, which is exactly what you expected, and it seems less likely for you to regret your previous purchase behavior. On the contrary, if the car performs poorly, with the occurrence of several malfunctions, post-purchase cognitive dissonance would arise without any surprise.

• *Personal anxiety aptitude*: Even though two consumers went through the exact same purchase experience, they might present various levels of post-purchase cognitive dissonance. Some consumers tend to feel more anxiety than others, who are more likely to experience post-purchase cognitive dissonance.

In the scenario of purchasing a car, you have spent half a year to obtain knowledge about cars and compare the brands. You went to several 4S stores to take it for a test drive, and finally, bought a Toyota Camry. It costs you an entire year's salary with a three-year mortgage. However, after driving it home your father told you that he didn't like it, and reminded you there were tons of other options available. He even blamed you for purchasing it without consulting him. Now looking at this newly purchased car, you seem to be less impressed by it. "Is it really the best option?" "Did I make the decision too hastily?" You asked yourself. With the addition of being a naturally anxious person, you feel unsettled and regretful. In order to decrease the level of postpurchase cognitive dissonance that you are experiencing, what should you do?

● *Return the car or switch to another model*: Generally, post-purchase cognitive dissonance results in returning the merchandise to exchange items because of purchase regrets, if it is possible.

● *Reduce the significance of the car*: You might find it useful to tell yourself that it is only a vehicle, which is not a big deal.

● *Focus on the positive aspects, or seek more positive aspects of the car*: For the purpose of comforting yourself, you could console yourself by recalling the favorable features of the product: at least it is less expensive than the other models that I considered, or, there are many positive comments about this car online, which are convincing evidence of the quality of the car.

● *Pay attention to the negative aspects of other alternative cars*: You could check negative comments about the other brands that you have considered, telling yourself that the other brands are worse! You didn't make the worst decision.

9.7.2 Post-purchase satisfaction/ dissatisfaction

購后满意度：消费者在购买和使用某一产品后，会形成对该产品的整体感受，即购后满意／不满意。

After purchasing and using a certain product, a consumer would form overall feelings towards this product, which are referred to as postpurchase satisfaction/ dissatisfaction. A satisfied consumer would possess a higher level of customer loyalty and tends to recommend the product to others.

Apparently, the level of postpurchase satisfaction is highly relevant to the performance of the product itself. You are more likely to be satisfied if you found that a jar of cold cream that makes you look younger, a holiday destination that makes you pleasant and a smartphone that is more functional. But in fact, factors leading to postpurchase satisfaction are more than that. Let's suggest a possible scenario: you have bought and consumed the latest Vivo smartphone, which is brand new, multifunctional, and reasonably priced. Nonetheless, you are not satisfied with it yet. How come? You asked yourself. It turns out that you expected more than what it actually provided. Therefore, marketers realized that postpurchase satisfaction is also related to the individual's expectation, which can be explained by expectancy disconfirmation model.

期望不一致模型：显示不一致（期望和感知性能之间的区别）对消费者满意度的影响。

The expectancy disconfirmation model (EDM) refers to that disconfirmation (the distinction between expectations and perceived performance) affects consumers' satisfaction.

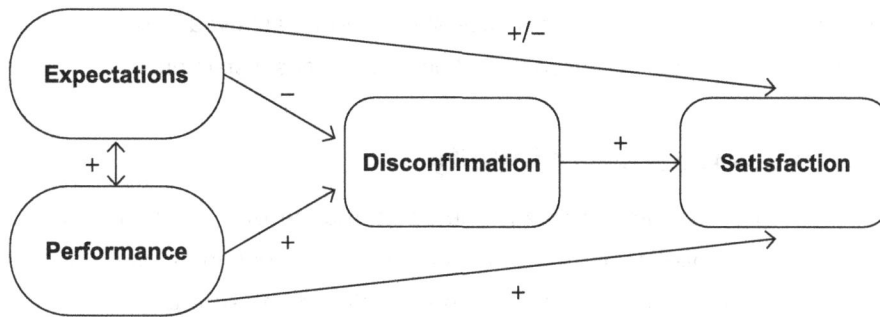

Figure 9-6 The expectancy disconfirmation model (EDM)

According to the expectancy disconfirmation model, there are three relationships among the factors — consumers' expectations to a certain product, perceived performance of the focal product, and disconfirmation between them and consumers' satisfaction. The first relationship is a fairly intuitive effect that indicates perceived performance of a product will directly affect a consumer's satisfaction. The better performance of the product possesses, the higher satisfaction the consumer presents. The second relationship is a direct effect of expectations on satisfaction. Prior experiments show either a positive or negative effect of consumers' expectations on satisfaction. The next relationship, also the core link of this model, is about disconfirmation. With the same level of expectation, it is believed that higher performance will increase chances of positive disconfirmation. On the contrary, with the same level of performance, higher expectations decrease the chance of positive disconfirmation, but increase the chance of negative disconfirmation. Subsequently, positive disconfirmation leads to higher satisfaction and negative disconfirmation leads to lower satisfaction. In other words, performance exceeding expectations will lead to higher satisfaction.

In contrast, higher expectations, which are more likely to exceed consumers' perceived performance, will lead to negative disconfirmation and lower satisfaction. Let's take a look at the scenario of purchasing a Xiaomi smartphone. Before you actually perform your purchase behavior, you have done a lot of things to collect information, in order to study the brand and the smartphone model, including browsing the official website, checking user's comments, analyzing the advertisements, and asking advices from KOLs. All those approaches establish an extremely high level of expectation. You expected this smartphone to be your best owned phone ever, which might help you become more sociable, knowledgeable and humorous. Now you have bought it and it sure works well — the only issue is — you asked more from it. In this case, your high expectation of the smartphone exceeds its actual performance that you perceived, resulting in a lower level of satisfaction. Conversely, we assume that you did nothing before buying the smartphone, since it is just an impulsive purchase — you saw it accidentally online, on sale on the "Double Eleven" shopping festival and decided to buy immediately. After receiving the package of the smartphone, you took a picture with it. Surprisingly, it seems better than your old phone, even better than your current digital camera. Additionally, you found it very user-friendly and light, and providing a lot of other great features than you expected. You decided to recommend it to your parents, your friends and post a positive comment online. More importantly, Xiaomi is now in your shopping list of electric products. This case shows how perceived performance exceeds expectation, generating positive disconfirmation and higher satisfaction.

9.7.3 Customer loyalty

If a consumer realizes the performance of a product he/she bought exceeds his/her perceived expectation, this consumer might purchase the product repeatedly, so customer loyalty might emerge. Customer loyalty is positively related to customer satisfaction as pleased customers would consistently favor the brands that meet their needs over time. A loyal customer doesn't only purchase a certain brand, and he /she excludes other brands in his/her evoked set. If you are a loyal customer to Oppo, which means you will never consider any other brands if you are considering buying electronic products. Consequently, if a consumer is loyal to a certain brand, it is less likely for him/her to search information externally, more likely to repeat purchase and build positive word-of-mouth. It indicates that loyal customers are significantly essential to any business, seeing they are more profitable than occasional buyers. This would be explained by the **80/20 rule**: 80 percent of a specific company's profits derive from 20 percent of its customers. In order to improve customer loyalty, **CRM (customer relationship management)** programs are launched, showing how companies use databases to collect data on customers to build stronger marketing programs. By implementing CRM programs, companies are more capable of identifying and targeting the right customers with the best value to build long-term relationships. CRM programs are widely employed in various business fields, and here, let us take a look at the execution of China Southern Airlines.

顾客忠诚度： 忠诚顾客不仅会只购买特定品牌，并且会在其激活阈中排除其他品牌。

80/20 法则： 一个公司 80% 的利润来自其 20% 的顾客。

客户关系管理： 企业通过数据库收集顾客数据以建立更强的营销计划。

Sky Pearl club of China Southern Airlines provides its loyal customers with services such as frequent flyer, mileage award, mileage accrual ,mileage redemption, award ticket redemption, etc.

9.7.4 Dissatisfaction responses

After evaluating the purchased product, consumers could be either satisfied or dissatisfied. A passive consumer might take no action and forget about it. But in more cases, they will not purchase the product again or recommend the product to others. It is essential for marketers to identify their unsatisfied consumers, since they will not only stop patronizing, but also proceed with more serious actions. Generally, there are two probable actions taken by consumers if they are unhappy with the products: public response and private response.

In terms of public response, there are several ways a consumer might go for solving problems. If you are unhappy about the smart TV you purchased a week ago, the most direct way is complaining to the merchant and claim for compensation. Or in some cases you will realize that taking legal actions can be quite effective, for instance, complaining to the consumers' association.

Private response indicates that you take private actions to show your dissatisfaction, or boycott the product privately. The general approaches are very familiar. For example, you stop buying anything from the store or the brand as a result of the unpleasant experience you had with previous purchases, or you warn all of your friends and families to not patronize it anymore, which can be regarded as **negative word-of-mouth**. While a consumer's expectations are not met, it is likely for him/her to spread negative information about the product. The negative information could be spread in face-to-face communication, or on such social media platforms like Weibo, WeChat, Douyin, online communities, and so on. Unlike positive word-of-mouth, negative comments cause extensive damage to brand image, urging marketers to work on solutions.

负面口碑：当消费者的期望没有得到满足时，该消费者很可能会传播关于该产品的负面信息。

Actions taken by dissatisfied consumers are summarized in Figure 9-7.

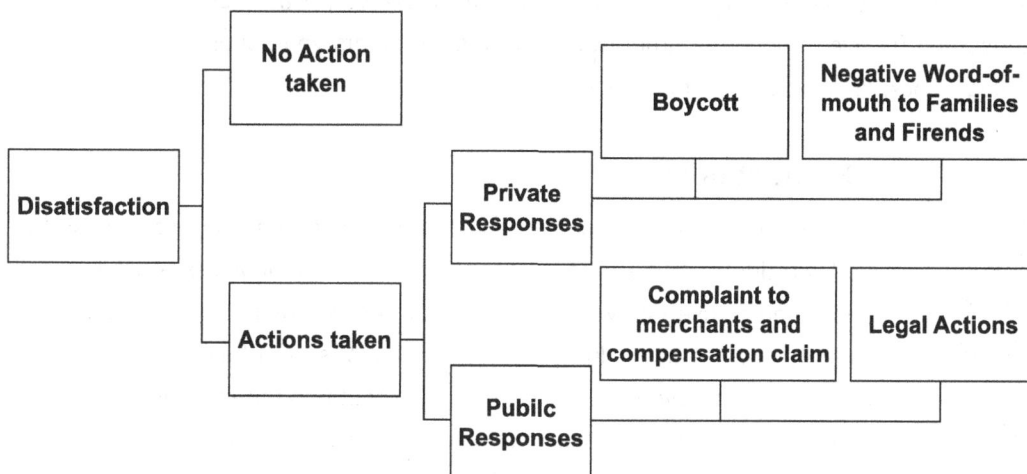

Figure 9-7 Actions taken by dissatisfied consumers

The extent to which the various actions are exercised varies with the nature of the product and how important it is to the consumer. If the product is crucially important to the consumer, he/she will be more likely to take public actions rather than private ones, whereas an unpleasant experience of less important products will always be ignored by consumers. Even though both public responses and private responses require marketers to make efforts, consumers are still encouraged to give feedbacks and complaints, in which way marketers could find defects and improve their products and services, rather than losing customers to their competitors without paying attention to them. That is one of the reasons for marketers to collect consumers' advices and complaints online and offline. Suppose you are not satisfied with the Huawei smart TV you have bought, you are encouraged to contact the customer service via telephone, email, and online customer service.

You will be able to contact Huawei customer service by visiting consumer/Huawei.

9.7.5 Product disposal

In some cases, consumers completely consume a purchased product within a short time, such as consuming a piece of cheese cake. However, if a product is not used or consumed for over a period of time, like a pair of snow boots you bought in summer, or a vintage clock, disposition might be involved.

1. Product nonuse

> **产品闲置：** 指消费者主动购买了某产品却搁置不用，或相对其潜在用途仅作有限的使用。

You will not be surprised to find that not all purchased products will be used. Product nonuse means a consumer actively acquires a product that is not used or used only thriftily relative to its potential use. Sometimes the products are not used due to objective reasons: you have bought a video game console for weekends, but you just cannot find time to play games on it. There are also subjective reasons leading to product nonuse: you spent one-month salary on a gym membership, but you are just loath to walk in the gym because of your laziness. If products are not used by consumers, they will be stored, ignored or forgotten. Storage of products leads to less purchase. Encouraging consumers to use their products in advertisements are practices to address the problem. For example, Wolong, a Chinese food brand, releases its core product — daily nuts, and suggests that each small pack of the nuts contains nutrients needed each day. The company reminds customers to consume one pack daily in their advertisement.

Wolong releases daily nuts and encourages customers to consume one pack daily to acquire essential nutrients.

2. Product recycling

Recycling could also be one of the alternatives of product disposal. Instead of throwing away the purchased products, consumers are encouraged to recycle the products and the packages. On the one hand, recycling of current products, in the form of trade-in policies in many companies, helps to decrease consumers' financial burden of purchasing an upgraded version of the focal product or a substitute. For instance, Xiaomi launched "Mi Recycle" to value and recycle consumers' existing smartphones, based on the physical conditions, hardware quality and market price. On the other hand, recycling behaviors are advocated for the purpose of environmental protection. Being an essential part of green marketing, which is defined as the process of promoting products or services based on their environmental benefits, recycling existing product contributes to reducing the amount of waste, conserving natural resources, preventing pollution and so forth. Today, a number of companies are engaging in formulating practical policies to facilitate product recycling actions. H&M is one of the participants, which launched a global garment collecting program in all of its stores since 2013. It has set a goal of having all clothing sold in its stores be made from recycled or sustainably sourced materials by 2030. In this way, consumers can just drop off any H&M clothes, shoes or accessories in its stores if they don't want them anymore. This approach could help reduce the globally rising volume of clothing waste due to the fast fashion development, and spread awareness about saving resources and adopting a more environment-friendly lifestyle.

Consumers are able to recycle their existing Mi smartphones on Xiaomi site and apps.

3. Product resale

Reselling the existing products could be considered likewise. Traditional approaches like flea markets, garage sales and at present, online secondary trading platforms make reselling possible. Most of the resales are C2C sales, referring to the transactions of used products that one consumer make directly to another consumer. Alibaba's Taobao Marketplace jumped on the trend of resale, by launching its online used-goods marketplace, a smartphone app called Xianyu, which bears a resemblance to a digital flea market, offering opportunities for consumers to sell and/or buy second-hand goods. Buyers can look for used goods and sellers can easily upload photos, audios and videos to promote their products. Furthermore, the marketplace is more than just an online second-hand product marketplace. It is also an online community to gather people with similar hobbies to share a particular interest and sell stuff to each other.

Summary

The consumer decision process model represents the steps that consumers go through before, during and after making a purchase. The five steps are: need recognition, information search, evaluation of alternatives, purchase and post purchase behavior. Based on the level of effort consumers make, the decision-making process can be classified into three types: extensive problem solving, limited problem solving and routine response behavior.

Need recognition is the first step of the consumer decision-making process, which reveals the difference between our current state of affairs and the ideal state we desire. Information search is the second step, including external and internal search, by which we search appropriate information from our long-term memory or/and the environment, to make reasonable decisions. A lot of consumers make decisions based on the combination of internal search and external search.

Evaluation of alternatives means using specific criteria to judge among a selected set of options to decide which one is suitable for the consumer. Evaluative criteria consist of a set of prominent or significant attributes, or a combination of facts and values, to aid consumers in order to judge the worth of a particular product. Consumer decision rules are the procedures used by consumers to facilitate alternative selection, including compensatory decision rules and non-compensatory decision rules. Non-compensatory decision rules can be summarized in four types.

After evaluating all the alternatives in the evoked set, consumers move on to performing the actual purchase behavior. There are three types of purchase behavior: trial purchase, repeat purchase and long-term commitment purchase. The conversion rate is used to measure how well marketers convert the intended purchase into an actual purchase, in other words, how well they convert visitors into paying customers.

During and after the processes of purchase and usage, the product will be evaluated by the consumer, which could either be satisfied or unsatisfied. Satisfaction contributes to repeat purchase, increase usage and recommendation to others, and enhance loyalty; whereas dissatisfaction leads to complaints, negative word of mouth and other adverse consequences. Post-purchase cognitive dissonance is a mentally uncomfortable state generated by an inconsistency between beliefs and behaviors after a purchased behavior engaged, resulting in the buyer's remorse.

After purchasing and using a certain product, a consumer would form overall feelings towards this product, which are referred to as postpurchase satisfaction/dissatisfaction, which has to do with whether the product performance lives up to the consumer's expectations. The expectancy disconfirmation model (EDM) refers to that disconfirmation (the distinction between expectations and perceived performance) affects consumers' satisfaction.

Lastly, in the end of the consumer decision-making process, there are different ways of product disposal, namely, product nonuse, product recycling, and product resale.

Exercises

(1) Interview five of your classmates about a recent purchase or consideration of a purchase. Specifically, questions could be but not limited to what factors led them to problem recognition, and any gap between the desirable state and the current state.

(2) What sources of information are useful to you when making a decision on purchasing (a) a laptop, (b) a pet (a dog/a cat), (c) destination for summer holiday, and (d) formal costumes for parties?

(3) List the criteria that you considered when you choose universities. How do you evaluate the alternative universities by whether compensatory or noncompensatory decision rules?

(4) Develop a survey to measure the satisfaction of your classmates' most recent purchase. Ask them the actions they take if they feel dissatisfied with a certain product to solve the dissatisfaction, and what are the results of their efforts?

(5) Conduct a research on companies' efforts on recycling and trade–in policies. Describe their contribution to consumers, companies and public service.

Case Analysis

Read the news item below. Suppose you are going to buy a car, what are the factors you need to consider? Give details about your decision-making process. Compare this process with the content below and summarize why Wuling EV has achieved satisfying sales results.

Creative Approach Gives Wuling Edge over Tesla

A mini-sized model from the Chinese brand Wuling, the Hong Guang Mini EV, toppled Tesla's Model 3 as the world's best-selling electric car in January, with deliveries exceeding 36,000 in the month, more than those of the Model 3 and Model Y combined. "The number will be even greater in February," said Zhou Xing, a senior executive of Wuling, a brand hailing from Liuzhou, a city in South China's Guangxi Zhuang

autonomous region.

Zhou did not expect such sales a year ago. "I thought it would be around 3,000 a month," he recalled last week. Even more pessimistic were auto reporters. Scores of them were invited to share their views in March 2020, four months before the debut of the model priced from just 28,800 yuan ($4,427.68) and which has a range of 170 kilometers on one charge. They argued that it would not sell in big cities where people prefer international brands and the chance would be slim in small towns as well, where people tend to choose gasoline vehicles.

These views were soon proved wrong. Within 200 days, 200,000 Hong Guang electric cars were sold, and the demand continues to soar, not only in China. "Businesspeople from over 150 counties and regions are asking us when we will sell cars there," Zhou said. Statistics show that the majority of buyers are in smaller cities and towns, and 72 percent of the buyers are those born in the 1990s, and 60 percent of them are female. If Tesla started its journey as a toy of the rich in California, Wuling's two-seaters (four-seaters are also available) can be regarded as the companions of young women in China's small towns.

The selling points are obvious: they are easier to park and maneuver for new drivers; the driving range, though short compared with others, it is more than enough for them to commute; they can be charged at home; they are cute and affordable.

With most owners being female, Wuling is adding a bit of fashion into its models. "We don't sell them like cars, but more like designer clothes," Zhou said. Last week, the carmaker unveiled Macaron variants, which are available in three colors and released in cooperation with Pantone, the global authority on color and design. "It is like a collection for different seasons. In the auto industry, it will take three years or so for a new vehicle to come out. So one of the few things we can do quickly is on color, and they like it," Zhou said. Wuling is not stopping there. Many of its plans include unveiling co-branded vehicles with the entertainment company Disney, and joining hands with other big names like sportswear brand Nike.

"So you see? It is about how you consider the electric car segment. Many followed suit by launching coupe-style sedans and SUVs resembling those of Tesla's. We did a different thing by focusing on the last miles of mobility," Zhou said. He said the company is also going to launch e-bikes or scooters, adding that Wuling does not see itself as a car manufacturer anymore. It aspires to become a creative, popular and boundary-free lifestyle brand.

CHAPTER TEN

Circumstantial Factors Influencing Consumers' Decision-Making Process

Learning objectives

After learning this chapter, you will be able to:

- identify elements of physical surroundings;
- describe other situational factors impacting the consumer decision-making process;
- understand factors related to retail outlets affecting consumers' buying;
- articulate how e-commerce makes a difference on consumer behavior;
- analyze and summarize effects of marketing efforts on consumer behavior.

Lead-in Case

MINISO: Creating a Fantastic Retail Experience that Keeps Bringing Customers Back for More

Bring new and trendy products to shelves frequently to let consumers keep "treasure-hunting". This is Miniso's "7 - 11" philosophy— "Every 7 days, we carefully select from a large library of 10,000 product ideas to launch about 100 new SKUs, so that consumers have new products to shop for every time they visit the store." said the Vice President of Marketing Robin Liu.

Miniso is a lifestyle product retailer, offering high quality household goods, cosmetics, food, and toys at affordable prices. Since its first store opened in Guangzhou in 2013, Miniso has opened more than 4,587 stores in over 90 countries and regions. With a focus on sleek design and fun trends, its mission is to assure through its

products that "a better life has nothing to do with the price". More than 95% of Miniso's products retail for under RMB50 (US$7.08) in China and under 10 USD in overseas markets, but the products are still high-quality and well-designed. This means that Miniso offers high-quality, value-for-money, good-looking, functional and localized products that hit consumers' different needs.

This mission drives the brand to deliver well-made and highly-designed goods for value- and quality-conscious consumers worldwide. There are over 200 experienced buyers to learn about consumer trends, whose input into what Miniso has to offer fits today's consumer demands and trends very well. It's part of the reasons why it's one of the retailers who was able to expand during the pandemic.

The reason why Miniso can deliver those valuable yet stylish products is largely attributed to its supply chain management capability. It has a wide range of 800 suppliers that can offer quality, affordable products with minimal lead time. This allows Miniso to execute its product strategy that is called the "three highs and three lows". "Three highs" stand for high appeal, high quality, and high efficiency, while "three lows" refer to low cost, low markup, and low price.

It also allows Miniso to update shelves very frequently, bringing fresh and fashionable products to shelves frequently to let consumers keep "treasure-hunting". With the famous "7 – 11 strategy" mentioned above, customers can always find something new and exciting down the aisle, so they will come back more often too.

For a company that based most of its business on physical stores, Miniso is convinced that great customer service and great customer experiences are critical for its success in general and for retail in particular. At its core, great customer service builds consumers' trust and fosters brand loyalty. Subsequently a great customer experience can create positive word of mouth bringing customers back for more, and all of those impacts can collectively lead to business growth. Altogether, these two aspects enhance brand image as well.

Customer experience is even more important for physical retailers as the on-site, inter-person experience is the key advantage compared to online stores. Consumers can actually see and touch the product, interact with the in-store staff, and that's irreplaceable. Miniso takes in-store experience very seriously, as one can see that the in-store layout and decoration are frequently changed to create an ever-fresh, relaxing and immersive experience. The shop assistants will also minimize interruptions to customers to give them more freedom and privacy while they are wandering around the store, offering help only when consumers need it. Miniso intentionally keeps more than 50% of the store's floor space for non-sales purposes such as interactive installations and Instagrammable decorations and setups so that customers can have more fun in the store.

What's more, a combination of online and offline channels gives people the option to acquire products in the most convenient way. Miniso is one of the Direct-To-Consumers brands, and as such, its strategy is to diversify sales channels, expand beyond physical stores, but also not to rely too heavily on online channels.

It is believed that brand image building is very important for retailers. At the end of the day, you want your brand name to be top-of-mind for customers when they buy or search for a certain product, not the sales channel. Increasing independence from a sales channel goes hand-in-hand with the hard task of brand image building, a project that collectively results from product quality, design, marketing activities, customer service, etc.

Introduction

One can never explain why young consumers just keep dwelling in the shops of Miniso with no particular shopping plans in mind. The refreshing color combination, the eye-catching decoration and the abundant product collections of the stores just keep drawing their attention and make them linger in the shops to discover more. Basically selling affordable and trendy commodities for daily use, the business of Miniso is thriving despite of the difficult situations most physical stores encounter under the context of e-commerce development. There are a number of factors influencing consumer behavior when they are making purchase decisions in the store, including the physical displays in outlets, promotional approaches, the moment when consumers make purchase, etc., all of which will be explored in this chapter.

10.1 Situational factors

情境因素：并非来
自个人内部，而是
发生在其他地方，
如环境和他人的、
会对消费者当前行
为产生影响的因素。

A consumer's decision-making process involves several steps, which is influenced by a lot of factors. Both the amount of information the consumer can search and the alternatives available impact the exact type of product this consumer will purchase, the time and the way the consumer purchases it. In addition, a consumer's psychological factors like the individual's motives, attitudes, perception and learning process make differences. As mentioned in previous chapters, other social factors like reference groups, culture, a consumer's demographic characteristics, and others all impose influences. The product, its packaging and promotions also play significant roles. Nevertheless, sometimes, some other factors specific to the situation, affect how purchase decisions and consumption processes occur. Figure 10-1 illustrates the factors affecting consumers' decision-making process.

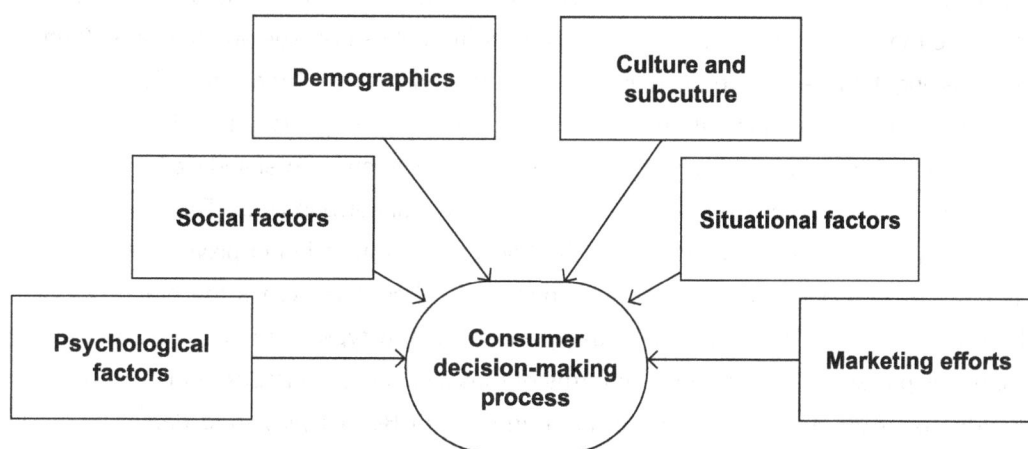

Figure 10-1 Factors affecting consumers' decision-making process

Situational factors are those that do not occur from within the individual but from elsewhere like the environment and others around the consumer, which will make impacts on his/her current behaviors. It has been proved that consumers will respond to the situational factors. For example, compared to an empty restaurant, a crowded one seems to be more attractive to you. Or, upbeat music played in stores might keep you excited and enable you to shop energetically.

Generally speaking, there are five key dimensions of situational factors that should be considered: *physical surroundings, social surroundings, temporal factors, goal direction* and *state of mind*.

10.1.1 Physical surroundings

As soon as a consumer enters a store with the intention of purchase, he/she will observe many things in the store, including location of the store, sound, aromas, lighting, décor, display of merchandise, proximity to other objects and other materials surrounding the stimulus, all of which are known as physical surroundings. These physical aspects are noticeable and the most obvious part of the purchase atmosphere. At present, retailers widely apply multiple elements of physical surroundings in their stores. There are several aspects of physical surroundings influencing consumers' decision-making process, which will be examined as follows.

Décor refers to decoration, i.e. the layout and interior furnishings of a store. Consumers' purchases are facilitated and enforced by the décor of a store, owing to the specific feeling that the décor of a store could generate to a buyer. For instance, as the "heart and soul of Apple stores", the simple, clean and bright décor of Apple Genius Bar delivers a professional image to its consumers, to support the use of its products and services. *Color* is also quite functional in motivating a consumer to take the next step. A study reveals that while people typically generate their first impression about a product in fewer than 90 seconds, 62% to 90% of the judgment is based on color alone. Let us take red for example. Not surprisingly, you might have noticed that the color of red is particularly arousing, and could actually elicit strong reactions and stimulate consumers to try the foods in a restaurant. McDonalds', KFC, and Chinese fast food brand Kung Fu Restaurant all use red as the primary color in their stores, aiming to draw attention and encourage visitors to consume more food. On the contrary, cool and softer colors like blue and gray are effective in increasing the level of expertise and consumers' satisfaction. Therefore, it is not difficult to find that a lot of brands with relatively high standards for specialty take blue or gray as their dominant tone in logo design and store decoration, such as Intel and Dell.

Sound cannot be ignored when it comes to physical surroundings. The main element of sound in a physical store should be the background music being played. Music has a unique effect on our brain, and activates many neural centers across the brain, including the emotional ones. For marketers, being aware of the type of music that their target audiences prefer is very important. In terms of music volume, a number of fashion garment brands, like Abercrombie and Fitch, Zara and Urban Revivo play loud dance music in their stores catering for the needs of their main target audience—the young generation. Likewise, the background music being played in a restaurant changes consumer behavior. A study developed by American National Restaurant Association indicates that customers chew food 30% faster when they listen to fast-paced music. Therefore, high-energy songs that get people excited would be the best choice for fast food chain restaurants, to increase table turnover by encouraging them to eat faster.

Odor is believed to be the most powerful atmospheric element linked to emotion, with over 75% of our feelings being generated by odors. You might realize that when you are about to have a bite of a croissant, smelling it can trigger a happy emotion in a faster way than touching it or even biting it. Nike found that flower scents in retail stores increased the intent to purchase by 80%. Pleasant scent stimulates consumers to generate more positive feelings and stay longer in the stores. **Aroma marketing** is the practice of providing a delightful smell to increase a company's brand image, improve customer experience and increase sales, which is widely used in luxury hotels. For example, Shangri-La provides a signature and unmistakable scent to evoke serenity and calm feelings in consumers, with bottom notes of vanilla, sandalwood and musk and delicate top notes of light bergamot and tea spiced with ginger. Every time you walk into a hotel of Shangri-La, you are telling yourself: Yes, this is it. The smell of Shangri-La. Precisely because of such uniqueness, a product that consumers can buy in the hotels and its online store is developed based on this aroma, called Shangri-La Essence.

> **气味营销：**通过提供令人愉悦的香味来提升公司品牌形象、改善客户体验和增加销售额。

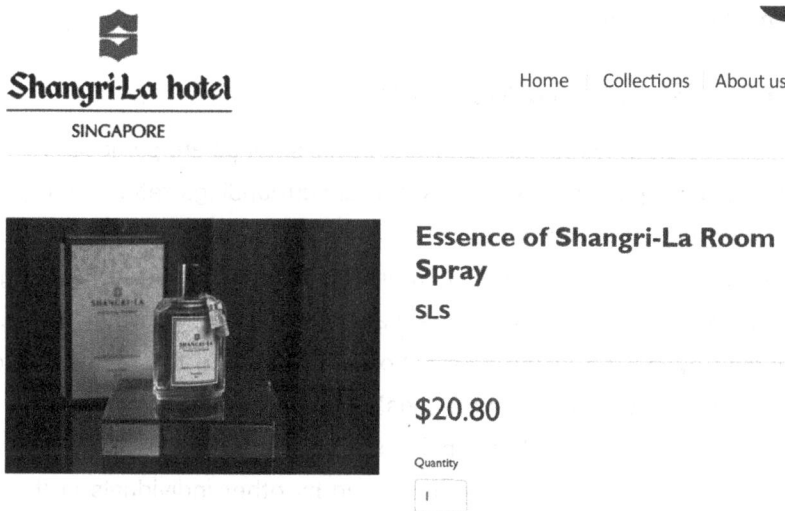

"Shangri-La Essence" is sold on Lobby shop at Shangri-La.

Proximity to other consumers is regarded as one of the essential components of physical surroundings. If you found limited space between you and other consumers in the store, in other words, the store is very crowded, it surely will change your consumer behavior. In most cases, crowdedness creates negative impacts on consumers. A store that is too crowded might negatively influence consumer's shopping experience and reduce satisfaction. But marketers find it difficult to control store crowdedness, since consumers tend to visit their stores at a specific time, like weekends, shopping festivals, etc. Correspondingly, marketers should decrease the level of crowdedness when designing the layout of stores, or explore other approaches to enhance consumers' shopping experience. Even though it is generally accepted that crowding poses negative impacts on consumers and retailers, under particular circumstances, crowding to a certain extent is conducive to stimulating purchase behavior. It explains the phenomenon that crowded restaurants always seem to be more appealing than desolate ones. For instance, Super Wenheyou in Hisense Plaza, a local restaurant in Changsha, attracts up to 20,000 customers daily sitting outside of the premises, waiting for a single table inside.

A large number of consumers are waiting outside of Super Wenheyou, Changsha.
Source: Super Wenheyou

10.1.2 Social surroundings

社会环境：指其他成员在特定场合的存在。

Apart from physical surroundings, social settings are particularly influential on consumer purchase behaviors. Social surroundings refer to the presence of other members in a particular occasion. Let's take a look at the scenario: you are shopping with three of your friends in a high-street clothing store, where you have an eye on the new arrival of clothes. You try it on and enjoy yourself by looking in the mirror. You are hesitating to buy it until you find embarrassment on all of your friends' faces. "Have to give it up, even though I like it", you told yourself. Shopping is a social experience, and a consumer's consumption process will be influenced by other individuals in the stores, including their acquaintance—friends in the above-mentioned case—and buyers they don't even know. Studies show that consumers shopping with their friends tend to visit more stores, spend more time in the stores and make many unplanned purchases. Psychologically, a lot of individuals are more likely to take their friends' advices, since they believe those objective views are superior to their own judgments.

共同消费者：在商店里购物的其他人被称为共同消费者。

Other people in a store when purchases are made are called **co-consumers**. The presence or absence of co-consumers, their opinions and choices, the number of them and the types of them can also influence a consumer's decision-making process, which can be either positive or negative. Assume you are indecisive about the entrée in a French restaurant and it is not surprising that the dishes on the table next to you might inspire you. A high level of density of a store, leading to in-store crowdedness, which has been discussed in the previous part, mainly delivers negative shopping experience to consumers since it will create an intense feeling. Similarly, the type of other patrons in a store can affect consumers' evaluations on the store. In most cases, consumers tend to visit a store with other consumers who are like themselves. You might expect other customers to wear formal clothes in a fancy restaurant if you are told to do so. Otherwise, negative impressions of the restaurant might arise.

10.1.3 Temporal factors

Temporal states show how time influences consumers' purchases decisions. Time mentioned here could be the time of a day, the time of a year, and the time consumers could spend on buying or the other forms of time. At what time a consumer visit a store might impact his/her purchase. For instance, a morning shopping tends to be exhausting and unappealing to a night owl—a person who likes to stay up late at night. Shopping in the afternoon seems to be a better choice to some particular consumers since they are more likely to obtain attentions from the salespeople, because there are fewer customers in stores generally. Also, some consumers only patronize certain stores at weekends because they could not make time for shopping on weekdays.

> **时间状态：**表示时间对消费者购买决定的影响。

Furthermore, the time available for us to make purchase decisions has an effect on consumer behaviors. If we don't have enough time, we are more likely to make terrible decisions, and regret performing the purchase behavior, which might decrease the perceived quality and satisfaction of the product. Suppose it only took you 5 minutes to buy a quite expensive pair of running shoes. You can easily be regretful since you didn't collect enough information about it and think it through.

It is evident that the time of purchase also varies from product to product, from individuals to individuals. Higher involvement of products like cars and/or apartments requires more time to make decisions. A housewife might spend more time in purchasing a bottle of laundry detergent than a busy marketing director.

Generally speaking, a problem we have to face is that there is less time for us to shop than before. Time pressure urges us compare a less number of alternatives and make quicker decisions. Consequently, a lot of the consumers cling to well-known national brands on the account of reliability of them. In order to address it, more and more brands serve in longer opening hours. For instance, many of the HaiDiLao, a chain of hot pot restaurants, open 24 hours, catering to consumers who want to have hot pot any time of the day.

HaiDiLao, a Chinese hot pot restaurant chain, opens for 24/7 in some cities.

Time pressure also contributes to the development of e-commerce. Across all the online shopping platforms, consumers can purchase products according to their own personal schedule but not the regular business hours of stores. It is also feasible for consumers to spend more time comparing products without the pressure from salespeople and the urgency of checking out. From another perspective, online shopping changes consumers' purchase time. At present, in order to encourage consumers to purchase more frequently and in larger quantities, various online shopping festivals emerged. As Chinese consumers' favorite e-commerce festival, Double 11 can be a significantly typical example. A substantial amount of consumers are more willing to spend on this special day than other time of a year, which creates the exponential consumption growth during Double 11. This digital shopping festival has already become the benchmark of e-commerce consumption in China. In 2020, Taobao's gross merchandise value (GMV) peaked at RMB 498 billion in 24 hours.

10.1.4 Goal direction

目标导向： 表示消费者的购买意图或动机。

Goal direction refers to the purchase intention or motive, which also plays an important part in decision-making. On some occasions, we purchase a product for personal use. For instance, we get a cup of coffee in Starbucks every morning to refresh ourselves. Purchase can be done for gift giving for some special occasions in some other cases. The purchase of a gift for your parents' 30-year wedding anniversary should be decided seriously and taken longer time to make. Instead, buying a pair of blue jeans for yourself might be an impulsive purchase, which takes less than 5 seconds to make the decision. The selection of gifts will be decided according to the occasions and your expectations of the responses from the recipients of the gifts. You might choose a pink dress for your best girlfriend, even if pink is the last color you will choose for yourself. The price of the gift you purchase for others is also determined by the goal direction. A wedding gift for your sister might be more expensive than a birthday gift for your colleague.

The nature of products defines the use of the product. Some of them are mainly positioned as a gift in advertising, for the reason that they are frequently purchased for gift giving. Flowers and chocolates in Valentine's Day, diamond rings in a proposal, and bottles of champagne for housewarming are examples. Marketers find it essential to understand how consumers perceive the purpose of buying the product, so that they can develop more effective marketing campaigns to appeal to their target audiences. Naobaijin (a form of melatonin product), a Chinese health supplement brand, has been sold as a gift for the elderly since 2000s, after Yuzhu Shi, the chairman and founder of Giant Network Group conducted a survey among old people. The survey displayed that those elderly interviewees expected to receive health supplement products as gifts from their offspring since they are too thrifty to purchase them personally. In the following years, various versions of Naobaijin commercials are featured by an animated elderly couple dressed in different kinds of costumes such as ballet dresses, Hawaii hula skirts, football suits, etc., with the slogan "People do not take gifts during the Spring Festival, except for Naobaijin".

Naobaijin positions its products as a gift in commercials.

10.1.5 State of mind

The state of mind is another factor influencing consumers' purchase decisions, which is defined as one individual's mood or mental state at a particular time. Various dimensions are employed to identify consumers' state of mind, including pleasantness, excitation, anxiety, etc. Consumers' state of mind is interactive with their consumption process. If a consumer realizes it is particularly urgent to replenish his/her medicine stock, and the retailer selection or price would be less important, the consumer will make purchase decisions with little hesitation. Conversely, the consumption process also has an impact on one's mind state. A nice store image, proper background music, and attentive service provided by the staff contribute to the positive mood of a consumer.

In order to explore how consumer's state of mind affects decision making, two dimensions of mood, *pleasure* and *arousal* are developed to measure our response to consumption environment, both positively and negatively (See Figure 10-2). Pleasure reflects the degree of the well-being of the person, or various feelings such as happiness, contentment or satisfaction. Arousal signifies the level of awakening and activation, which is used to measure the degree of excitement an individual feels in the environment. A specific mood of a consumer is a combination of pleasure and arousal. Different combinations of the two dimensions result in different moods of the consumer. For instance, if a consumer feels aroused and pleasant when he/she is in a musical festival, the mood of this person can be described as excited. On the contrary, a combination of unpleasantness and sleep—the opposite of being aroused—makes the consumer gloomy. A long and tedious speech might be an example.

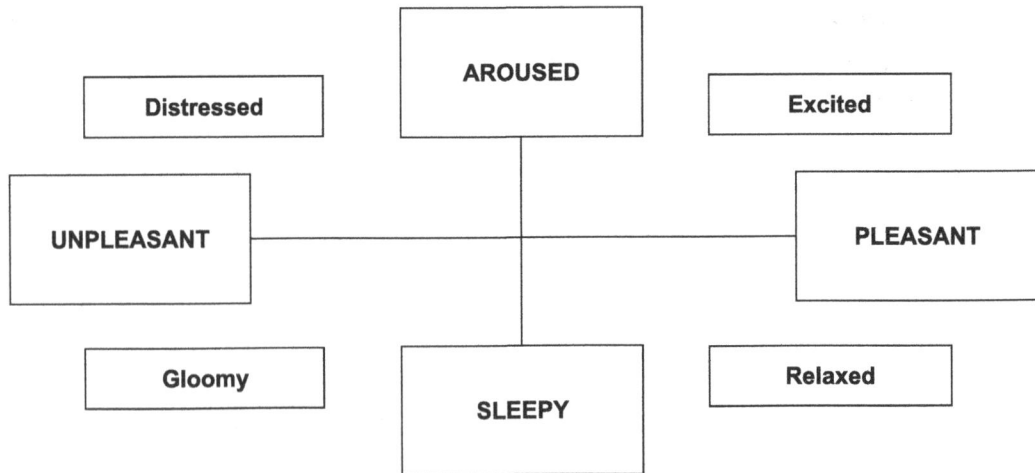

Figure 10-2 Pleasure-Arousal dimension

Marketers should be conscious of the power of consumers' emotional responses. It is believed that positive emotional responses are more likely to keep consumers staying longer in the stores and perform impulsive buying. Arousal and pleasantness also show a significant effect on consumer satisfaction and word-of-mouth. Therefore, designing proper marketing activities to activate consumers' positive mood is vital. A cozy shopping environment, intelligible layout designs, efficient customer services and a lot of other tactics can be reasonable ways to improve consumers' positive mood level. A special form of catering emerged in the Chinese market in recent years. Hutaoli, a brand that combines restaurant, bar, music and art, commits to delivering positive emotions to customers with the use of immersive store decoration and live music show every night.

Hutaoli, a suave restaurant for Chinese eats, cocktails, and live music, aims to engage customers by activating their positive mood.

10.2 Marketing efforts

It is understood that marketing efforts impact the consumers' decision-making process. The elements of marketing mix have been discussed in previous chapters, including product, price, place and promotion. In terms of each marketing mix element, marketers work hard on appealing to their target markets. Let's explore the influence of some of the marketing efforts on consumers respectively.

10.2.1 Packaging

Packaging is a very important element of brands, including the packages' color, images, typography, brand name, etc. Marketers spend a large amount of money designing and updating packages of their products, in order to draw consumers' attention and encourage potential buyers to purchase the product. Particularly when it comes to less expensive and lower-risk products, consumers have lower involvement with the products. In this case, the only motivating factor might be the packages. For example, when you are selecting a pack of napkins in a supermarket, have you ever been influenced by the packages? Appealing packages also help a product stand out from its competitors. Psychologically, packages can evoke feelings of excitement and happiness. Some of the product packaging arouses urgent purchase desires, which might drive hedonic consumption. It is not surprising for you to find that in a book store, an exquisitely designed cover of the book is like asking you to "buy it!", as if there were magic to prompt you to make the decision in a short period of time.

10.2.2 Retail outlet

Retailers are businesses selling goods to ultimate consumers for personal or household consumption. For consumers, their decision-making process is influenced by many aspects of retailing.

1. Retailer brands

It is supposed that retail outlets are like brands. From consumers' perspectives, established retailers attract more consumers to patronize, since the brands of the retailers can be an evaluation criterion equivalent to product quality. Also, a lot of consumers believe that well-known retailer brands provide various sales promotional activities. Nowadays, some retailers have developed their own brands of products, also known as **private label brands**, competing with major famous brands — the brands owned by manufacturers. Traditionally, private label brands are regarded as lower-cost alternatives of major brands, like the low-priced brands of Vanguard supermarket, Runzhijia (润之家) and Simple Combination (简约组合). However, there are premium brands with high quality and high price that emerged in markets in recent years. Presidents' Choice of Loblaws, a Canadian retailer introduces high quality and relatively higher price products.

> **自有品牌：** 由零售商开发的品牌。

2. Store image

The retail store image has been shown to play an essential role in store visits and purchases. Store image refers to the overall perception that consumers have of a particular store and of the shopping experience there. In a store, the atmosphere of it, including the color, sound, scents, store layout and other elements, influences the way consumers buy products, and the kinds of products they will buy. Details of atmospherics have been discussed previously.

> **商店形象：** 指消费者对某一特定商店及其购物体验的整体感知。

Studies show that consumers tend to spend more money and time in a store if they enjoy being in this store. Sometimes, in order to enhance consumers' participation in a store, store activities might be launched. Game participation and temporary exhibitions are typical examples of enhancing store image by store activities. Some other retailers find that offering convenience to consumers is also a way to enhance store image. For example, IKEA Småland is a special play area for children. By providing this area, IKEA optimizes the shopping experience of the customers who come with their children.

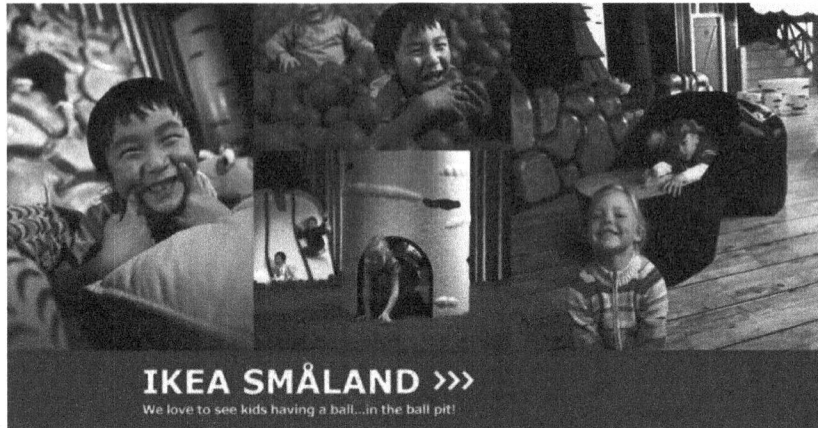

IKEA Småland makes it more convenient for customers with children.

3. Point-of-purchase displays

Point-of-purchase displays, also known as P-O-P displays, are significantly useful for a retailer's merchandising. In the retailing business, P-O-P displays can be one of the most effective ways to catch eyes of consumers and encourage them to purchase products. An elaborative design of P-O-P display could especially stimulate an impulse purchase. P-O-P displays take various forms, which range from product displays, free samples to interactive installations, as long as they are engaging consumers with the merchandise. A small sign next to the new arrivals, a stand-alone standing in the aisle, products placed at the checkout area, and free samples of freshly baked cakes are all common applications of P-O-P displays in retailer outlets.

Bottles of beer and beverage are displayed as a football field in a local supermarket in Zhejiang Province, during South Africa World Cup in 2014.

10.2.3 Online retailing

Online retailing, also called electronic retailing, is the sale of goods and services through the Internet. At present, e-commerce has developed rapidly in recent years. As a new retailing medium, it impacts consumer behaviors remarkably. Therefore, it is not difficult to find that online consumer behaviors are distinctive from traditional consumer behaviors. According to a survey of consumers' online shopping behavior trends 2021, consumers spend an average of 5 hours a week shopping online and 92% of consumers said they shop online at least once a year. Online retailing makes it possible to reach consumers all over the world without contacting them physically—even when they are 5,000km away from the company—and provides an efficient way to cut intermediaries, which could effectively lower the price to end consumers. On the other hand, to consumers, online retailing simplifies the search process, alternative evaluation and the purchasing process. If you want to buy a pair of running shoes, the only thing you need to do is typing in keywords in the search bar, including brand, color, style, etc., and click on "enter". Results will be displayed, and you can filter them in a further step. So there is no need for you to visit dozens of stores, put all of them on, and compare them physically anymore.

> **线上零售：** 指通过互联网对消费者进行商品和服务的销售。

However, surveys showed that 51% of respondents believed the biggest drawback of online shopping is not able to touch, feel, or try a product. Indeed, it is still a defect up to now. Some solutions have been implemented to address that. For instance, the 7-day unconditioned return policy is carried out in many e-commerce companies, allowing consumers to try them on and return their products if they are not satisfied. Some other companies provide high-tech services to deliver convenience. Uniqlo introduced virtual Fitting Room service, to make well-fitting and functional clothing accessible to everyone. By releasing the app and the web page of an augmented reality fitting room, it allows users to try on anything currently in the store by using their mobile app. This approach effectively leads the way for retail innovation and increases online sales.

Uniqlo released its virtual fitting room, allowing consumer to try clothes on without visiting their retail outlets.

Mobile shopping apps on consumers' smartphones provide alternatives to purchase online. According to the 46th China Statistical Report on Internet Development by CNNIC, the mobile phones are the top platform used for online shopping at 49%, followed by PCs at 43%, and tablets at 8%. And 27% of consumers said they used their smartphone to make monthly purchases worldwide. In China, 79.7% of online users participated in online shopping and 80.1% purchased online via mobile phones in 2020. Mobile phone shopping allows consumers to purchase anytime, anywhere, and makes it more likely to carry out **personalized marketing**. Nowadays, companies are able to deliver individualized content to recipients through data collection, analysis, and the use of automation technology, which is an ultimate form of targeted marketing, creating messages for individual consumers, and satisfying their specific needs. You might not be surprised to find that every time when you log into your Taobao account on your mobile phone, products recommended on the homepage are exactly the ones you might be interest in.

> **个性化营销：** 公司通过数据收集、分析和自动化技术，向消费者提供个性化的内容及服务。

10.2.4 Advertising

There is no doubt that advertisements are especially impactful in creating an image of a product in the minds of consumers. Advertising is designed to deliver messages, which is an effective way to raise brand awareness and initiate buying behavior. For instance, without an advertisement of the latest Huawei mobile phone, a lot of consumers might not be aware of it, let alone buy it. Recently, with the assistance of new technology, some other types of cutting-edge advertising become possible. **Precision targeting** is a marketing tool directed at existing customers to encourage brand loyalty and buying behavior. Precision marketing relies less on creating persuasive ads, but more on creating deals, offers, and gimmicks that will appeal to existing customers. For example, a musical ticket agency can narrow down consumers who tend to show their interest in musicals, and precisely deliver interesting and targeted advertisements on their WeChat Moment.

> **精准定位：** 一种针对现有客户的营销工具，旨在鼓励品牌忠诚度以及购买行为。

In some cases, marketers use price advertising to communicate sales prices, price reduction and other sales promotional messages to their target audiences. Undoubtedly, price advertising is very effective in driving consumers to visit the outlets. In stores, price advertising can be essential for motivating patrons to close a deal. A reference price is one of the tactics to persuade consumers to buy the product. **Reference price** is the price at which a manufacturer or a store owner sells a particular product, giving a certain discount compared to its previously advertised price. A sticker on the shelf saying: "original price — ￥100, present price — ￥70" could be very appealing, especially to price-conscious consumers.

> **参考价格：** 制造商或商店老板在出售特定产品时，与之前的广告价格相比给予了一定折扣而定出的价格。

10.2.5 Online community

Today, the Internet makes chatting and communicating with people far away from you a reality. Virtual groups and online communities emerged, gathering a group of people to interact, share, and work toward a common goal. Opinion leaders and reference groups have been discussed in previous chapters, and online communities just provide a platform for consumers to be influenced by them. Brand communities are communities formed on the basis of attachment to a brand, and established to increase consumer participation and brand loyalty. For instance, Huawei fan club (花粉俱乐部) is built, which is an online community for users of Huawei electronic products for communication and interaction. It is an effective approach to aggregate its fan groups.

> **线上社区：** 在互联网上将一群人聚集在一起，使他们互动、分享，并为一个共同的目标而努力。

Huawei fan club provides a way for Huawei users to get to know each other and share product experience.

10.2.6 Salesperson

Even though self-service in online and offline stores has become a trend, as you can find self-checkout and online self-service purchase are very widespread, salespeople are still very important in the consumer purchasing process, especially when it comes to high-involvement decision making. There are various functions that salespeople serve. Being knowledgeable and helpful is critical for a salesperson to achieve great sales records. By providing beneficial information of the products that consumers are interested in, salespeople can simplify the purchasing process for consumers by convincing them to make the right final decision. For example, a salesperson in a 4S store of a car brand is indispensable in helping potential customers make up their mind to buy the first car. Less time and effort will be spent in searching information of the car by receiving advices from the salesperson. Salespeople can also boost consumers' trust in their choice by reducing dissonance in the consumers' minds. Cognitive dissonance can easily happen when the product presented for purchase is new or expensive to consumers. By emphasizing the positive features of the product and the brand, salespeople can consolidate the confidence the customer has in the product and therefore reduce cognitive dissonance. Furthermore, a competent salesperson is more likely to establish a more reliable relationship with customers, and enhance their shopping experience. You must have gone through a pleasant or terrible shopping experience owing to various types of salespeople.

With the development of e-commerce, online salespeople become a key to consumers' online purchase decision making. Online salespeople are expected to provide prompt and efficient services, who contribute to building up consumers' benign attitudes towards the brand and increasing their possibility of buying.

10.2.7 Sales promotion

价格促销：一种以鼓励试用或购买的短期营销刺激。

Sales promotion is a short-term incentive to trigger trial or purchase. As one of the most significant component of the promotional mix, sales promotion takes different forms: coupons, discounts, free samples, free gifts, rebates, buy one get one free, etc. It is proved that sales promotions can be the determinant factor in consumers' purchase decision-making process, which aids to sustain competitive advantages, stimulate consumers to place an order and increase sales.

Sales promotions stimulate consumers to increase purchase volume and even stockpile products. During the "Double-11" online shopping festival in China, stores on T-mall and Taobao provide special offers when a certain amount of money spent has been achieved. For instance, with each deal of RMB 400 across all stores, customers can get a RMB 50 rebate. This approach facilitates consumers to spend more money on the platform, in order to get a more favorable discount. Sometimes, even though they don't need that many products, they just want to reach the amount of RMB400 so that they can get the price reduction.

Sales promotion can also help shift consumers to a promotional product. A consumer who is a frequent user of Dior eye shadow might shift to purchase ColorStudio in Sephora only for the discount and the free gifts it offers.

Price reduction, free gift and samples ColorStudio offers on Sephora.com.

Nevertheless, regular purchasers of certain products, like housewives engaging in routine purchase, might be more attracted by the EDLP pricing strategy. **EDLP**, also known as everyday low price, is a pricing strategy in which a company charges a consistently low price over a long-time period. The EDLP pricing strategy simplifies consumers' decision making and lower their search costs. Wal-Mart is a company carrying out the strategy for years, which promises the lowest price they can offer every time consumers make a purchase.

| **每日低价定价策略:** |
| 指公司在很长一段时间内保持低价。 |

Everyday Low Price Strategy taken by Wal-Mart, making shopping time efficient.

Summary

There are a number of factors influencing consumer behavior when they are making purchase decisions, including the physical displays in outlets, promotional approaches, and the moment when consumers make purchase, etc.

Situational factors are those that do not occur from within the individual but from elsewhere like the environment and others around the consumer, which will make impacts on his/her current behaviors. Generally speaking, there are five key dimensions of situational factors that should be considered: *physical surroundings*, *social surroundings*, *temporal factors*, *goal direction* and *the state of mind*.

Marketing efforts impact the consumer decision-making process. In terms of each marketing mix element, product, price, place and promotion, marketers work hard on appealing to their target markets. Various types of marketing practices like packaging, retail outlet, point-of-purchase displays, online retailing and online community, advertising, salesperson and sales promotions all have an impact on consumer behavior.

Exercises

(1) Let 3–5 students form a group and visit three small local clothing stores and observe their physical surroundings. What differences can you find between the three outlets? Would you recommend any physical surroundings change based on observation? Summarize your findings in a report and give a presentation to the class.

(2) Visit two local grocery stores and observe their use of P-O-P displays and explain the differences. Which one is more effective to you? Analyze both cases and share your findings in class.

(3) Go to www.taobao.com. Select an online shop and examine its online sales promotional strategies and activities. Analyze the influence of those activities on consumers' purchase decisions.

(4) Interview five of your friends about how their mood affects their purchases. Present your findings.

Case Analysis

Study the introduction to blind box marketing, and list the reasons why they are so popular, drawing upon your own experience and the knowledge learned in this chapter.

The Art of Marketing Blind Boxes with Eyes Wide Open

Blind boxes, in terms of how they reach the consumers, are an innovation. Digging deeper into the issue, you will learn the very nature of marketing blind boxes is called probabilistic selling. That is to say, even after making the payment for a blind box, the buyer still has no idea what the contents inside will be. Suspense. A sense of thrill amid an air of expectation ensues. The sheer anticipation of a surprise can be intoxicating even as it can keep the consumer on tenterhooks, in a nice sort of way.

Such marketing has been used for a while now, in the form of grab bags on Amazon, the global online marketplace. For shoppers, uncertainty about the box content equals excitement and surprise combined, a potential neural hit in the brain typically experienced by gamblers and thrill-seekers. The experience could hook the consumers and more purchases might follow.

Blind boxes are not exactly an addiction, but represent a harmless, or manageable rush of adrenaline for some consumers, especially Generation Z, a consumer group defined in popular online reference material as "a demographic cohort succeeding Millennials and preceding Generation Alpha", born in the period from mid-to late-1990s to early 2010s.

Why are blind boxes so popular among Gen Z? Well, they are consumers raised in a relatively good or happy period characterized by abundant supplies, when demand for food and clothing was easily met. Satisfaction or gratification derived from daily consumption tends to be transient or short-lived for Gen Z, but that's the way they seem to prefer it, say marketing gurus.

Therefore, the pursuit of consumption that can also pack in surprise and joy leads them to products and concepts like blind boxes. Gen Z are willing to pay for such experiences as evidenced from Pop Mart blind boxes' runaway success in the marketplace.

But Gen Z have been displaying a tendency to become segmented in terms of shopping behavior or preferences. Some consumers pursue novelty, excitement and risk, and are more likely to be attracted by the surprise brought by uncertainties. Others tend to be risk-averse who prefer careful planning before they make their purchases. There will certainly be more risk-happy consumers in Gen Z, but companies should not completely ignore risk-averse consumers either, say experts.

Companies should study the characteristics of target consumers, risks of utilizing such a mode, and then determine whether or not to use blind boxes to market their products in order to boost sales. There is a bit of a scientific approach developing to determine where blind boxes can be introduced.

This marketing model can be applied to different scenarios. The food industry, for example, can use such mode to popularize certain food products. More and more snack makers are launching their products in blind boxes. After consumers register for a blind box service, they will receive a box of snacks each month, like potato chips, nuts, dry fruits, without having any idea what they might receive in the box.

Similarly, travel agencies can put forward blind box arrangements for group travelers; air carriers can launch blind boxes for seats in different classes; even cinemas can sell tickets in blind boxes, where moviegoers will only know the name of the flick they are about to watch only after they are seated in front of the screen.

Marketing mavens vouch that blind boxes offer many advantages. In addition to the surprises, consumers can sometimes receive a "lucky shot", a high-value product at a price much lower than its actual value—a jackpot as it were. For enterprises, blind box marketing can help them navigate the market and discover its contours and characteristics.

Probabilistic selling can be used as a tool to clearly identify target consumers and their needs. It seemed that Pop Mart's popularity was an overnight success, but its first store opened in Beijing in 2010. Ever since, it has been exploring and upgrading the products through blind box marketing, finding the most popular items, to figure out product packages that suit the company's sales strategies and make the company more and more welcomed by the market.

Second, blind boxes can help companies better plan production and manage inventory. For example, clothing companies usually launch new series by quarters, but they are not sure which one will be a hit, and which one will make it difficult to arrange production and may lead to backlog of inventory. However, gathering feedback from blind box sales can give companies insights into styles that are more popular, and can function as a compass in adjusting production plans.

While trying to stimulate consumption demand with such marketing, companies should be aware of the hidden risks. First, blind box sellers should not hold the surprise tricks as a way to fool consumers, nor indiscriminately include products in blind boxes. Consumers may not return for repeat purchases if they feel cheated once. It's still the value of the products in the blind boxes that will define the price. Also, the knowledge of how to plan blind box combinations and how to sell them is critical.

Blind box is just a marketing method, and cannot become a symbol of the brand, because it is easy to be duplicated. The products and services provided behind the blind boxes are the key. Take Pop Mart as an example. The company has its own intellectual property rights and has cooperation agreements with many big names among designer groups. Pop Mart's flagship product "Molly", a little girl designed with pursed lips and big blue eyes, is very popular among consumers. Supported by such fancy designer product, and the blind box marketing strategy, the company is able to reap juicy awards. Without solid products that deliver value, no company can go far. Once the wave of blind boxes subsides, a company without good products may never be able to catch the next wave.

GLOSSARY

Consumer behavior refers to a series of consumption activities of choosing, buying, using, evaluating and disposing of the products and services to fulfill the needs of individuals or organizations.

消费者行为： 指的是个体或组织为满足需求而进行的一系列挑选、购买、使用、评价和处置产品或服务的消费活动。

Market segmentation is the practice to divide the market into groups of consumers possessing common needs or features.

市场细分： 将消费者分成具备共同需求或特征的组别的行为。

Demographics are the measurable and descriptive characteristics of a population, including age, gender, income, and educational level etc.

人口统计特征： 可测量及可描述的人口特征，包括年龄、性别、收入和教育程度等。

Psychographics is the way to classify people according to their lifestyle, personality and attitudes.

心理统计特征： 根据生活方式、个性和态度对人进行分类的方法。

A reference group is any individual or group in reality or imagination perceived as having significant relevance upon a person's evaluations, aspirations, or behavior.

参照群体： 在现实生活或虚构想象中，被认为对事物的评价、志向或行为有显著关联的个体或群体。

Group norms refer to the code of conducts that is established among group members and followed by each one of them.

群体规范： 群体所确立的、每个成员必须遵守的行为准则。

Brand community consists of a group of consumers whose social relationships are based on the usage of or interest in a brand or a product.

品牌社区： 由一群消费者组成，他们的社会关系基于对某品牌或产品的使用或兴趣。

Opinion leader is a person who gives advice and information regarding a certain product or service, and can frequently influence others' attitudes and behavior in informal communications.

意见领袖： 能够就某一特定的产品或服务提供建议与信息，并能在非正式沟通中经常影响他人的态度和行为的人。

Word-of-mouth (WOM) is information about products and services created and delivered by individuals to others.

口碑： 由个体产生并向他人传播关于产品或服务的信息。

Family can be defined as a group of individuals living together who are related by marriage, blood, or adoption.

家庭： 因为婚姻、血缘或收养关系而共同居住的一个群体。

Household refers to one person living by himself/herself, or a group of individuals living together in a common dwelling, whether they are related or not.

户： 单独居住的个人；或者在同一屋檐下生活的一群人，不管其是否有亲属关系。

Culture is the sum total of learned beliefs, values, and customs that serve to direct the consumer behavior of members of a particular society.

文化： 引导某一特定社会成员的消费行为的已习得信念、价值观和风俗的总和。

Values help people to determine what actions are best to do or what way is best to live, or to assess the significance of different actions.

价值观： 帮助人们确定最好的行为、最好的生活方式，或评估不同行为的意义。

Sensation is a mental process (such as seeing, hearing, or smelling) resulting from the immediate external stimulation of a sense organ, which is often distinct from conscious awareness of the sensory process.

感觉： 外部即时刺激作用于感觉器官引发的精神过程（如看见、听见或闻到），通常有别于感官过程的有意识感知。

External senses are seeing, hearing, smelling, tasting and touching.

外部感觉： 即视觉、听觉、嗅觉、味觉和触觉。

The internal senses are common sense, memory (storage and retrieval of information), imagination and evaluation.

内部感觉： 即常识、记忆（信息的存储和回溯）、想象力和评价。

The absolute threshold is the lowest level of stimulus that an individual can perceive using their senses such as sight, taste, hearing, touch, and smell.

绝对阈限： 个体通过视觉、味觉、听觉、触觉和嗅觉等感官所能感知到的最低刺激量。

The differential threshold is the smallest change in stimulation that a person can detect, also known as the just noticeable difference (JND).

差别阈限： 个体能察觉到的最小刺激变化，也称为最小可觉差。

Perception is the process by which an individual selectively absorbs or assimilates the stimuli in the environment, cognitively organizes the perceived information in a specific fashion and then interprets the information to make an assessment about what is going on in one's environment.

知觉： 个体选择性地吸收环境中的刺激物，从认知上对所感知的信息以特定方式进行梳理，并进行解读的过程。

Perceiver refers to a person whose awareness is focused on the stimulus, and thus begins to perceive it.

感知者： 将意识集中在刺激物上，从而开始感知该刺激物的人。

Target is the object of perception.

目标： 感知的对象。

The situation includes the environmental factors, timing, and degree of stimulation.

情形： 包括环境的因素、时间、刺激的程度。

Consumer learning is the process by which individuals acquire the purchase and consumption knowledge and experience that they apply to future related behavior.

消费者的学习： 个体获取有关购物和消费的知识及其体验，并在将来将其应用于相关行为的过程。

Motivation refers to the processes that lead people to behave as they do.

驱动力： 引导人们行为的过程。

Cue is a stimulus that suggests a specific way to satisfy a silent motive.

提示： 一种刺激，它提出了满足隐性动机的特定方式。

Response means how individuals react to a drive or cue or how they behave.

响应： 个体对驱动力或提示的反应，或者他们的行为方式。

Reinforcement is a positive or negative outcome that influences the likelihood that a specific behavior will be repeated in the future in response to a particular cue or stimulus.

强化： 是一种积极或消极的结果，它影响着某一具体行为是否会重复发生以响应某一特定提示或刺激。

Conditioning means a kind of "knee-jerk" or automatic response to a situation built up through repeated exposure.

调节：对通过反复暴露而构建的情形产生"下意识的"或自动的响应。

Classical conditioning refers to learning that associates an unconditioned stimulus that already results in a response (such as a reflex) with a new, conditioned stimulus.

经典条件反射：将已经引发反应（如反射）的无条件刺激物与新的条件刺激物联系起来的学习。

Stimulus generalisation occurs when an organism responds to a stimulus in the same way that it responds to a similar stimulus.

刺激泛化：与条件刺激相似的刺激会引起类似条件反射的现象。

Product line extension is the strategy of introducing variants of the same product.

产品线延伸：引入同一产品的变化的策略。

Family branding is a marketing strategy that involves selling several related products under one brand name.

家族品牌：在同一品牌名称下销售多种相关产品的营销策略。

Licensing: Allowing a well-known brand name to be affixed to products of another manufacturer.

品牌授权：知名品牌允许其他制造商的产品贴上该品牌的营销策略。

Stimulus discrimination is a reaction to differences among similar stimuli.

刺激分化：对相似刺激物的差异作出的反应。

Instrumental conditioning (also known as operant conditioning) is a behavioral theory of learning based on a trial-and-error process, with habits forced as the result of positive experiences (reinforcement) resulting from certain responses or behaviors.

工具性条件反射（也称作操作性条件反射）：消费者基于试错过程的学习行为理论，在此过程中，由于某些反应或行为导致的积极体验（强化）而被迫养成了习惯。

Reinforcement is a term used in operant conditioning to refer to anything that increases the likelihood that a response will occur.

强化：操作性条件反射中的一个常用术语，指的是任何提高反应发生可能性的事物。

Positive reinforcement consists of events that strengthen the likelihood of a specific response.

积极强化：增强某一特定反应发生可能性的事件。

Negative reinforcement is an unpleasant or negative outcome that also serves to encourage a specific behavior.

消极强化：鼓励某一特定行为发生的负面结果。

Punishment is designed to discourage behavior.

惩罚：行为发生后导致的有害或负面事件，降低同一行为在将来发生的可能性。

Cognitive learning theory explains how internal and external factors influence an individual's mental processes to supplement learning.

认知学习理论：个体对整个问题情景进行感知和理解，领悟其中各种条件之间以及条件和问题之间的关系，并在此基础上产生新的行为的过程。

Observational learning occurs when people change their own attitudes or behaviours simply by watching the actions of others.

观察学习：通过观察他人及他人的行为结果而改变自身态度或行为的过程。

Modeling is the process of imitating the behaviour of others.

树立榜样：模仿其他人的行为的过程。

Memory refers to the process of retention of information about past events or ideas.

记忆：保留关于过去事件和想法的信息的过程。

Encoding is the process by which we select a word or visual image to represent a perceived object.

编码：选择文字或视觉映像以代表被感知的物件的过程。

Memory storage is the process of information coming into the memory system (from sensory input), then changed into a form that the system can cope with and store.

记忆储存：信息以感觉输入的形式进入记忆系统，转变成大脑系统能处理的方式从而得到保存的过程。

Retrieval refers to the process in which individuals getting information out of storage.

记忆检索：个体从记忆储存中调取信息的过程。

Motivation is the driving force within individuals that impels them to action.

动机：推动个体行动的内在驱动力。

Need is a basic biological motive.

需要：一种基本的生物动机。

Goals: The sought-after results of motivated behavior.

目标：驱动行为所追求的结果。

Attitude is an acquired predisposition to behave in a constantly favorable or unfavorable way concerning a given object and is an evaluation of an object with some degree of positivity or negativity, which lasts for a long time.

态度：一种后天形成的倾向，对某一客体以有利或不利的方式行事，形成对该事物正面或负面的评价，并会持续很长一段时间。

An attitude object is anything to which one holds an attitude and can be either a physical object or an abstract idea.

态度对象：人们对其持有态度的客体，可以是客观物体，也可以是抽象概念。

Affect means how a consumer feels about an attitude object.

情感成分：消费者对态度对象的感觉。

Behavior is what the consumer intends to do, that is, the consumer's actions concerning an attitude object.

行为成分：与态度对象有关的行为或行为倾向。

Cognition is what the consumer believes to be true about the attitude object.

认知成分：消费者对态度对象的认识、理解和评价。

Personality: the internal psychological features that define and embody the ways a person reacts to the surrounding environment.

个性：决定和体现每个人对环境的反应的内在心理特点。

Consumer ethnocentrism embodies how different individuals can be in terms of their tendency to hold prejudice against the behavior of buying foreign products.

消费者民族主义：体现个体对于购买国外产品持有偏见的倾向程度。

Brand personality refers to the varied personality-like features consumers associate with a brand.

品牌个性：消费者与品牌相关的各种类似个性的特征。

The consumer decision process model represents the steps that consumers go through before, during and after making a purchase.

消费者决策过程：消费者在购买前、过程中和购买后经历的各个阶段。

When consumers have no or few information/ experience about the products, they usually go for **extensive problem solving** when a completely new need is discovered which requires significant efforts to be satisfied.

扩展式问题解决：当消费者没有或只有很少产品相关的信息和经验，需要付出较大努力去解决问题时，他们便会寻求扩展式问题解决方案。

Limited problem solving: consumers have had some previous experience and information about the products, but have not fully established their strong preference to select from the alternatives.

有限型问题解决： 当消费者已经有了关于某产品的信息和经验，但尚未完全建立强烈的品牌偏好。

Routine response behavior involves the regular purchase of low cost products that requires little decision making effort.

例行性反应行为： 表示仅需很少决策投入的定期购买低成本产品的行为。

Need recognition is the first step of consumer decision-making process, which reveals the difference between our current state of affairs and the ideal state we desire.

问题识别： 消费者意识到当前状态与所期望的理想状态之间的差异。

Information search is the second step in the consumer decision-making process, by which we search appropriate information from our long-term memory or/and the environment, to make reasonable decisions.

信息搜索： 消费者从长期记忆、和／或外部环境中搜索信息，从而做出购买决策。

Internal information search: Information collection from past experience, or rather, from the storage in consumers' long-term memory.

内部信息搜索： 从消费者的既有经验，即长期记忆中搜索信息的过程。

External information search: the consumer will search information from the external environment to make the purchase decision.

外部信息搜索： 消费者从外部环境中搜索信息的过程。

Evaluation of alternatives means using specific criteria to judge among a selected set of options to decide which one is suitable for the consumer.

选项评价： 对一组选定的选项使用特定的评判标准，以决定哪个选项更适合消费者。

All possible choices for a product category are categorized in **universal sets**.

普遍阈： 包含某一产品品类所有可能的品牌选项合集。

Retrieval sets refer to the brands that the consumer can readily bring forth from memory.

回溯阈： 消费者能随时从回忆中调取的某些品牌的选项合集。

An evoked set includes all the brands that a consumer is aware of, and thinks well of, when considering a purchase.

激活阈：包含消费者为了解决某一特定问题将要评价及考虑的所有品牌。

Evaluative criteria consist of a set of prominent or significant attributes, or a combination of facts and values, to aid consumers in order to judge the worth of a particular product.

评价标准：由一系列显著或重要的属性，或某些事实与价值的结合组成，消费者依靠评价标准来判断某一特定产品的价值。

Consumer decision rules are the procedures used by consumers to facilitate alternative selection.

消费者决策规则：消费者为更方便进行备选方案选择而使用的程序。

Compensatory decision rules: a consumer arrives at a choice by considering all of the appropriate attributes of a product and by mentally trading off the alternative's perceived disadvantages on one or more attributes with its perceived advantages on other attributes.

补偿式决策规则：消费者将选择在有关评价标准的判断上总体表现最好的品牌，即考虑所有合适的评价标准，并认为好的属性可以抵消不好的属性。

Non-compensatory decision rules: consumers find positive performance on one evaluative criterion does not offset or compensate for negative performance on another evaluative criterion of the brand.

非补偿式决策规则：消费者选择一个品牌是基于某些特定属性，而不考虑其他属性。

The conjunctive rules suggest that consumers establish a minimum, separate acceptable level for each considered criterion and accept an alternative only if it equals or exceeds the minimum cutoff level all the criteria.

连接式决策规则：消费者对每一评价标准设置最低的可接受水平，选择所有等于或超过每个标准的最低可接受水平的备选方案。

The disjunctive rule is the mirror image of the conjunctive rule, referring to a consumer establishes a separate minimally acceptable cutoff point for each attribute (in most cases a relatively higher level than by the conjunctive rule).

析取式决策规则：消费者对每一评价标准设置最低的可接受水平（通常比较高），任一品牌只要有一个属性超过了该水平都会被接受。

The elimination-by-aspects rules: When a consumer is exposed to several alternatives, he/she first identifies the most important attribute of brands when evaluating alternatives.

排除式决策规则：消费者根据重要程度对评价标准进行排序，并对每一评价标准设置临界点，按顺序依次排除没有超过临界点的备选方案。

The lexicographic rules: an alternative is better than another alternative if and only if it is better than the other alternative in the most significant attribute on which the two alternatives differ.

编纂式决策规则： 消费者根据重要程度对评价标准进行排序，选择最重要属性中表现最好的品牌。

Comparative advertising: brands are compared to one another in such ads.

比较广告： 直接将自有产品与竞争对手产品进行比较的广告。

Trial purchase refers to the purchase behavior that a consumer purchases the product for the first time, usually buying a smaller amount of the product as a "trial".

试购： 消费者第一次购买某产品，通常购买少量的产品作为"尝试"的购买行为。

Repeat purchase: If a consumer has been satisfied with a brand and has established clear brand preference, he/she will purchase the same brand to replace the previous purchased products.

重复购买： 如果消费者对某一品牌有较高满意度，并建立了明确的品牌偏好，该消费者就会再次购买同一品牌。

Long-term commitment purchase: If a consumer is satisfied with a certain brand, he/she will agree to purchase the products over a period of time.

长期购买： 消费者对某一品牌有较高满意度并在一段时间内持续购买该产品。

The conversion rate: how well marketers convert the intended purchase into an actual purchase.

转换率： 将访问者转换成实际购买者的比率。

Post-purchase cognitive dissonance is a mentally uncomfortable state generated by an inconsistency between beliefs and behaviors after a purchased behavior engaged, resulting in buyer's remorse.

购后认知失调： 消费者在购买行为发生后，因信念和行为之间的不一致产生的一种心理上的不适感。

Post-purchase satisfaction/ dissatisfaction: After purchasing and using a certain product, a consumer would form overall feelings towards this product.

购后满意度： 消费者在购买和使用某一产品后，会形成对该产品的整体感受，即购后满意 / 不满意。

The expectancy disconfirmation model (EDM) refers to that disconfirmation (the distinction between expectations and perceived performance) affects consumers' satisfaction.

期望不一致模型： 显示不一致（期望和感知性能之间的区别）对消费者满意度的影响。

A loyal customer doesn't only purchase a certain brand, and he /she excludes other brands in his/her evoked set.

顾客忠诚度： 忠诚顾客不仅会只购买特定品牌，并且会在其激活阈中排除其他品牌。

80/20 rule: 80 percent of a specific company's profits derive from 20 percent of its customers.

80/20 法则： 一个公司 80% 的利润来自其 20% 的顾客。

CRM (customer relationship management) programs are launched, showing how companies use databases to collect data on customers to build stronger marketing programs.

客户关系管理： 企业通过数据库收集顾客数据以建立更有力的营销计划。

Negative word-of-mouth: While a consumer's expectations are not met, it is likely for him/her to spread negative information about the product.

负面口碑： 当消费者的期望没有得到满足时，该消费者很可能会传播关于该产品的负面信息。

Product nonuse means a consumer actively acquires a product that is not used or used only thriftily relative to its potential use.

产品闲置： 消费者主动购买了某产品却搁置不用，或相对其潜在用途仅作有限的使用。

Situational factors are those that do not occur from within the individual but from elsewhere like the environment and others around the consumer, which will make impacts on his/her current behaviors.

情境因素： 并非来自个人内部，而是发生在其他地方的因素，如环境和他人会对消费者当前行为产生影响。

Aroma marketing is the practice of providing a delightful smell to increase a company's brand image, improve customer experience and increase sales, which is widely used in luxury hotels.

气味营销： 通过提供令人愉悦的香味来提升公司品牌形象、改善客户体验和增加销售额。

Social surroundings refer to the presence of other members in a particular occasion.

社会环境： 其他成员在特定场合的存在。

Other people in a store when purchases are made are called **co-consumers**.

共同消费者：在商店里购物的其他人被称为共同消费者。

Temporal states show how time influence consumers' purchases decisions.

时间状态：表示时间对消费者购买决定的影响。

Goal direction refers to the purchase intention or motive.

目标导向：表示消费者的购买意图或动机。

Private label brands: brands of products developed by retailers.

自有品牌：由零售商开发的品牌。

Store image refers to the overall perception that consumers have of a particular store and of the shopping experience there.

商店形象：消费者对某一特定商店及其购物体验的整体感知。

Online retailing, also called electronic retailing, is the sale of goods and services through the Internet.

线上零售：通过互联网对消费者销售商品和服务。

Personalized marketing: companies are able to deliver individualized content to recipients through data collection, analysis, and the use of automation technology.

个性化营销：公司通过数据收集、分析和自动化技术，向消费者提供个性化的内容及服务。

Precision targeting is a marketing tool directed at existing customers to encourage brand loyalty and buying behavior.

精准定位：一种针对现有客户的营销工具，旨在鼓励品牌忠诚度以及购买行为。

Reference price is the price at which a manufacturer or a store owner sells a particular product, giving a certain discount compared to its previously advertised price.

参考价格：制造商或商店老板在出售特定产品时，与之前的广告价格相比给予了一定折扣而定出的价格。

Virtual groups: a group of people to interact, share, and work toward a common goal.

线上社区：在互联网上将一群人聚集在一起，使他们互动、分享，并为一个共同的目标而努力。

Sales promotion is a short-term incentive to trigger trial or purchase.

价格促销：是一种以鼓励试用或购买的短期营销刺激。

EDLP, also known as everyday low price, is a pricing strategy in which a company charges a consistently low price over a long-time period.

每日低价定价策略：指公司在很长一段时间内保持低价。

References

1. Abderrahmane Chenini, Sabrina Elbachir, 2016. The emotional states of the consumer in stores: the PA (Pleasure-Arousal) adapted to the Algerian context[J]. Expert Journal of Marketing, 4 (1):10–19.

2. Deji Ajibola, 2019. Sales promotion and consumers' purchase decision in the beverage industry in Nigeria[J]. Humanities, management, arts, education and the social science,7 (2):1–10.

3. Del. I. Hawkins, Roger J. Best, Kenneth A. Coney, 2002. Consumer behavior: building marketing strategy[M]. 8th ed. China: China Machine Press.

4. Del.I.Hawkins, Roger J.Best, Kenneth A. Coney, 2002. Consumer behavior: building marketing strategy[M]. 8th ed. China: China Machine Press.

5. Dhruv Grewal, Michael Levy, 2015. Consumer behavior: marketing[M]. 3rd ed. Beijing: China Renmin University Press.

6. Dhruv Grewal, Michael Levy, 2015. Consumer behavior: marketing[M]. 3rd ed. Beijing: China Renmin University Press.

7. Gopal Das, 2013. The effect of pleasure and arousal on satisfaciton and word-of-mouth: an empirical study of the Indian banking sector[J]. VIKALPA, 38 (2):95–103.

8. Leon G.Schiffman, Leslie Lazar Kanuk, 2015. Communication and consumer behavior[M]. 9th ed. Beijing: Tsinghua University Press.

9. Leon G.Schiffman, Leslie Lazar Kanuk, 2015. Consumer decision making and beyond: consumer behavior[M]. 9th ed. Beijing: Tsinghua University Press.

10. Mary Jo Bitner, 1992. Servicescapes: the impact of physical surroundings on customers and employees[J]. Journal of Marketing, 56 (2):57–71.

11. Mehrabian A., 1996. Pleasure-arousal-dominance: a general framework for describing and measuring individual differences in temperament[J]. Current Psychology, 14:261–292.

12. Mehrabian A., Russel J.A., 1974. An approach to environmental psychology[M]. Cambridge: M.I.T. Press.

13. Michael R. Solomon, 2018. Consumer behavior: buying, having and being[M]. 10th ed. Beijing: China Renmin University Press.

14. Michael R. Solomon, 2018. Consumer behavior: buying, having and being[M]. 10th ed. Beijing: China Renmin University Press.

15. Rainer Reisenzein, 1994. Pleasure–arousal theory and the intensity of emotions[J]. Journal of Personality and Social Psychology, 67 (3):525–539.

16. Robaka Shamsher, 2016. Overall perception that consumers have of a particular store and of the experience of shopping there[J]. ELK ASIA PACIFIC JOURNAL OF MARKETING AND RETAIL MANAGEMENT, 7 (2).

17. Russel W. Belk, 1974. Situational influences in consumer behavior[M]. Illinois: University of Illinois Urbna-Champaign.

18. Stephan Grimmelikhuijsen, Gregory A. Porumbescu, 2017. Reconsidering the expectancy disconfirmation model: three experimental replications[J]. Public Management Review, 19(9):1272–1292.

19. Thompson, K.E., Ling Chen, Y., 1998. Retail store image: a means-end approach[J]. Journal of Marketing Practice: Applied Marketing Science, 4(6):161–173.

KEYS TO EXERCISES

Chapter One

1. Consumers and the items they consume can take many forms. Give examples of three different types of consumers and examples of three different types of items they could consume, including products, services, and ideas.

Answer: Examples will vary. Consumers can include individuals of any age, groups, and organizations. Items consumed can include products such as toys, cars, food; services such as dentist appointments, haircuts, and massages; and ideas such as environmental protection.

2. List the three stages in the consumption process. Describe the issues that you considered in each of these stages when you made a recent important purchase. Identify questions that might be asked from the consumer's perspective and from the marketer's perspective in the prepurchase and purchase stages of the consumption process.

Answer: The three stages in the consumption process shown are: 1) prepurchase, 2) purchase, and 3) post purchase. The student selected should develop unique sets of issues related to each of these phases based on the different products and purchase situations.

Prepurchase phase:

Consumer's perspective—How does a consumer decide that he or she needs a product? What are the best sources of information to learn more about alternative choices?

Marketer's perspectives—How are attitudes toward products formed and/or changed? What cues do consumers use to infer which products are superior to others?

Purchase phase:

Consumer's perspective—Is acquiring a product a stressful or pleasant experience? What does the purchase say about the consumer?

Marketer's perspectives—How do situational factors, such as time pressure or store displays, affect the consumer's purchase decision?

3. Based on the knowledge learned in this chapter about research methods, could you design a project to explore an area or an aspect of college students' online purchase and/or consumption habits, using both QUAL and QUAN approaches? Present your ideas in the form of a research proposal, including the research topic, research objectives, sample sizes, sample criteria, research methods and detailed research design.

Answer: For the sake of concentrating limited resources on the most important issue, students should choose a specific area to focus on, rather than having a broad area as the research scope. For example, it could be a study of the online purchase habits of a certain segment of students for a specific product category. The research topic should be concise, accurate and reasonable. Then research objectives should be drafted correspondingly. Subsequently, research methods could be selected, sample sizes and sample criteria decided to the point that they could fulfill the research objectives.

4. Questionnaires and screeners are quite similar: both are presented to the respondent as a set of questions designed to elicit information in the research process, but what are the differences between the two? Based on the research topic selected for Question 3, draft a questionnaire according to your research objectives.

Answer: The function of a questionnaire in quantitative research is quite different from that of a screener for qualitative research. The former is meant to draw out meaningful information from a sizable audience; whereas the latter serves to select the right kind of people to participate in the discussion. As a result, a carefully drafted questionnaire is crucial to the quality of research data. When compiling questions, several principles should be followed: 1) No leading questions; 2) Don't ask two questions in one; 3) Ask clear questions; 4) Use consumers' language; 5) Respondents must be able and willing to answer the questions. A well–written questionnaire should have a reasonable structure with a logical flow.

ChapterTwo

1. Think about every one of your family members, friends, or acquaintances. Could you identify the people who act as opinion leaders, product innovators, and market mavens? Describe what each person does. Give a specific case when this person had some influence on other people's decision making. Share you observations with the class.

Answer: Check if the students can differentiate between opinion leaders (knowledgeable consumers who are frequently able to influence others' attitudes or behaviors), product innovators (consumers who actively seek out the latest and greatest in a product category and are willing to take risks), and market mavens (individuals with a general interest in the marketplace).

2. Think about some goods and services that you have purchased recently. Did word-of-mouth communication influence your purchases? To what extent?

Answer: It seems that advertising is less credible than word-of-mouth. In high involvement purchase categories, it's more likely that students rely on word-of-mouth and external search. They rely more on word-of-mouth due to the fact that they are more self-conscious and have more concerns about social risk, like whether they'd be accepted by their reference group. Negative word–of–mouth tends to be a larger consideration in purchase decisions than positive word-of-mouth.

3. Students in groups are assigned with the task of forming or joining a brand community. Decide upon a brand that none of the group members would actually use. Then, search information of the brand widely and post positive comments of the brand among group members. It can be achieved on a message board (贴吧), an online chat room or a Wechat group. After having done this for a set period,

group members can discuss how they feel about the brand. Have you purchased any product of the brand or not, do you feel more "loyal"? Have positive attitudes been developed among group members? Do they find themselves engaging in WOM outside the group? Present your findings to the class.

Answer: Students should select a product they use, have an interest in, and are passionate about, if possible. Figure 11.1 indicates how brand communities create collective value. Look for students to connect with the ideas in the figure (e.g. social networking, community engagement, impression management, and brand use).

4. Describe how opinion leaders can be formed and found on the Internet. Analyze and summarize the advantages and disadvantages of using opinion leaders on the Internet. How would this form of opinion leadership be different from any other form of opinion leadership (if at all)?

Answer: Opinion leaders can be formed via the Internet because of the availability of product information to be synthesized and the ability to connect with a large number of individuals. Opinion leaders might be found in top organic search results, by having a high circle of trust/positive feedback from other users, or having many followers. They may be less likely to be similar to the consumer in terms of values and beliefs.

Chapter Three

1. The debate on the status of TCM and Western medicine is getting more heated recently. Simultaneously, health awareness of Chinese people is on the increase. Which medicine will you adopt to maintain your health? Why? How, do you think, should the advertisers and marketers adjust their strategies to meet consumers' demands for better health conditions?

Answers vary.

2. Interview two or more people from two different foreign cultures. Ask them what major differences they see between the cultural values in their country and those in the Chinese culture. Ask the students to explain these to the class.

Answer: Chinese core values are: harmony, filial piety, face, collective spirit, etc. Core values from the other culture will vary.

3. Groups of students compare a list of rituals that will probably be performed (or that were performed) at their friends' or families' wedding ceremony and reception. What are the marketing implications of these rituals? Another important question might be asked: How are wedding plans affected when people from different subcultures get married?

Answer: It is interesting to point out the different rituals based on a religious, ethnic, or racial subculture and rituals that seem to be solely local. Students should do outside research on the rituals and the role of subculture in the rituals.

Chapter Four

1. What is the difference between sensation and perception?

Answer: Sensation is the immediate response of sensory receptors (such as the eyes, ears, nose, mouth, and fingers) to such basic stimuli as light, color, odor, texture, and sound. Anything that activates a receptor is called a stimulus. Perception is the process by which people select, organize, and interpret these sensations. The eventual interpretation of a stimulus allows it to be assigned meaning.

2. Outline and explain the parts of the perceptual process that would allow a shopper to recognize Nestlé coffee in a supermarket.

Answer: The sensory stimuli is the brand that is detected by the sensory receptors in the shopper's eyes. This exposure will result in a sensation. If the shopper pays attention to the sensation, her mind will organize and interpret these sensations through the process of perception.

3. Blind taste tests in the 1980s showed that most Coke drinkers preferred a cola that was sweeter than the current product. When Coca-Cola attempted to make its product sweeter, brand loyal customers revolted and demanded the old product be returned. Explain how Coca-Cola marketers could have used the principles of psychophysics to introduce the new coke without creating these problems.

Answer: If the sweetness of the cola was increased by less than a j.n.d. in stages over time, the final product would be much sweeter without most brand loyal customers recognizing the change.

4. At a business meeting, a consultant states that "perception is reality, because a customer never works with the actual product, but only with his or her perception of that product." In a university lab, researchers determine that when a rat is looking at a brightly colored rectangle, a close inspection of the rat's optic nerves (that connect the eyes to the cortex) show no visible change from when the rat is looking at a green circle; however, electrodes placed in the nerve show a different pattern of transmitted codes. How are these two events related, and what does this relationship tell us about perception?

Answer: The human mind never actually comes in contact with an outside stimulus such as a product. The mind only receives sensations created by the receptors, and then must interpret what those sensations are. This interpretation is a perception. The only thing the mind processes of the product is the perception created by that mind of that product, hence "perception is reality."

Chapter Five

1. Visit a grocery store or a supermarket or a hyper market in your neighborhood and silently observe the behavior of individual shoppers and groups of shoppers for an extended period. Record any behaviors that you witness that could be examples of the following concepts: incidental learning,

classical conditioning, and instrumental conditioning. Present your findings to the class or discuss them in groups.

Answer: Some of these learning examples may be challenging to observe directly. Students may need to draw on their own exposure to marketing communications and make inferences about why consumers are behaving as they are. Examples of incidental learning examples should reference the idea that the consumer learned about the product without necessarily having an interest in the product or product category. Examples of classical conditioning will probably be the easiest to observe because the applications of stimulus generalization and the repetition of likeable spokes-characters or endorsers as cues are likely to be present. Instrumental conditioning examples may include frequency rewards or gifts with purchase.

2. Locate a print/digital advertisement that is a clear example of a marketer employing the concept of stimulus generalization or stimulus discrimination. Present the ads to the class and explain how it works.

Answer: For stimulus generalization, students may select private label/generic brands that are packaged to look like the national counterpart, examples of companies that use family branding, product line extensions, or brands that license a brand name. For stimulus discrimination, students are likely to find examples where a national brand clarifies what distinguishes its brand from private label/generic competitors, and/or urges consumers not to settle for cheap imitations.

3. [In-class activity] Write down your favorite brand name, and then draw an associative network around the brand that includes three attributes/features, three benefits, three competitors, attributes, benefits for the competing brands, etc. You can add personal opinions and feelings about the brand to the network.

Answer: The exercise should help students visualize the web of connections between nodes that characterize the associative network theory of memory. The teacher can tie the exercise to further exploration of the concept of the evoked set (since they identify competitors). Since they start with brand identification, ask them to identify when the related nodes are brand-specific (claims), ad specific, product category specific, or related to evaluative reactions (positive or negative emotions).

4. Create a long list of brand slogans from the past 10 or more years. Divide the class into teams or simply in half. Read the brand slogans one at a time, omitting the brand name. Award points to the first team to correctly identify the brand associated with each slogan. Afterward, point out how memory was strong, even for older slogans (some may be able to identify slogans from when they were very young children). Discuss why this is the case according to the principles of memory in this chapter.

Answer: Students should recognize that they are retrieving brand information from long-term memory. They may note differences are cognitive, physiological and situational factors that helped them retrieve (or caused them to forget) the slogans. Depending on the brands selected, they also may recognize stronger memories for pioneering brands and the effects of the brand spacing out repeated messages.

Chapter Six

1. Briefly describe the motivation process based on needs, tension and goals.

Answer: Motivation refers to the processes that causes people to act according to their behavior. This happens when the consumer wants to satisfy a need. Once the need is activated, there will be a state of tension that drives the consumer to try to reduce or eliminate the need. Needs may be utilitarian or hedonic. In either case, there is a difference between the current state of the consumer and a certain ideal state. This gap creates a state of tension. There are many ways to satisfy needs, depending on the consumer's cultural background. Once the goal is achieved, the tension and motivation can be reduced and receded temporarily.

2. Marketers create advertisement appeals by portraying an individual who solves a particular frustration with the use of the advertised product. Find one or more ads which utilize one aspect of the defense mechanisms (e.g. aggression, rationalization, withdrawal, projection, daydreaming etc.) to help consumers address their psychological issues.

Answer: Open-ended. Individuals incline to develop their own ways to redefine frustrating situations to protect their self-esteem from the anxiety caused by failures in the attainment of their goals. Defense mechanisms include aggression, rationalization, withdrawal, projection, daydreaming etc.

3. Since a purchase decision may involve multiple motivations, consumers often find themselves in situations where positive and negative motivations conflict with each other. Identify and discuss the three general types of motivational conflict. In addition, please comment on how these conflicts help to produce satisfaction of needs. Provide an example of how marketers adjust their marketing communications to suit consumer needs in each situation.

Answer: The three types of motivational conflicts are:

- Approach-approach conflict—a choice between two desirable alternatives;
- Approach-avoidance conflict—involves a choice in which some aspects of the product are positive and others are negative;
- Avoidance–avoidance conflict—involves a choice between two negative alternatives.

Usually, every time a consumer is confronted with a choice, the dissonance that is created can potentially make the consumer unable to feel satisfied with his or her decision. In each case, marketers should provide other information that the consumers can use to rationalize the option he or she made:

- In approach-approach conflicts, marketing communications should accentuate "no lose" and "win either way" information.
- In approach-avoidance conflicts, information should focus on the positive aspects, downplay negative aspects or provide other counterbalancing information about the options.
- In avoidance-avoidance conflicts, information should give priority to the need for making an option and connect it with some other more alluring value that the consumer has.

4. List the primary needs demonstrated in Maslow's hierarchy of needs. Give an example of a

product that is suitable for each form of need

Answer: Physiological—Products: medicines, staple items, generics.

- Safety— Products: insurance, alarm systems, retirement, investments.
- Belongingness—Products: clothing, grooming products, clubs, drinks.
- Ego Needs—Products: cars, furniture, credit cards, stores, country clubs, liquors.
- Self-Actualization—Products: hobbies, travel, education.

Note to the instructor: Make sure to provide any specific guidance that you think is necessary for the sample portion of this question to ensure consistency in students' answers.

Chapter Seven

1. Describe the functional theory of attitudes and its elements (functions).

Answer:

The functional theory was first held out by Daniel Katz to explain how attitudes improve social action. Attitudes occur for the reason that they provide several functions for the individual; in other words, they are decided by a person's motivation. The following functions are the key ones identified by Katz:

Utilitarian function—this is relevant to the basic standard of award and punishment. Attitudes towards products or services are developed by consumers easily on the prejudice of whether they provide pleasure or pain to consumers. Advertisements emphasizing direct product profits appeal to this function.

Value-expressive function—attitudes referring to this function mainly stand for the consumer's self-concept or chief values. Advertisements that underline how making use of a product or service reflects him as a consumer himself appeal to this function.

Ego-defensive function—this function focuses on protecting a person from reality or imagination, interior or exterior, dangers to recognizable defence. Advertisements addressing how to use the product to avoid the threat (often not explicitly) appeal to this function.

Knowledge function—consumers form the attitude towards the product or the service to stress the person's demand for sequence, configuration, definition, and control over one's surroundings. Advertisements that stress the strength of product information, especially at which an ambiguous situation or a new product shows up and a consumer is faced with them, appeal to this function.

2. Attitude researchers have held out the concept of a hierarchy of effects to demonstrate methods to study attitudes and how they form. Introduce and simply describe all the three hierarchies which were delivered in this chapter. Be clear about your description.

Answer:

The three hierarchies are:

1) the standard learning hierarchy,

2) the low-involvement hierarchy,

3) the experiential hierarchy.

a. The standard learning hierarchy—in this hierarchy, a consumer deals with a product decision as a procedure which refers to solving the problem. The sequence of issues is beliefs, to feeling, then to behavior, eventually to an attitude, which is based on cognitive information processing. The standard learning hierarchy states that an individual is actively involved in making a decision about whether to buy the product or service. The consumer is inspired to seek out a large amount of information, carefully weigh substitutes, and summarize a thoughtful decision.

b. The low-involvement hierarchy—in this hierarchy, the individual does not have a strong preference among different kinds of brands at first, instead of acting on the preference of limited knowledge and creates an assess until the product is purchased or used. The attitude tends to take place through learning about the behavior; After purchasing the product or service, good or bad experiences reinforce the consumer's choice. The sequence is beliefs, to behavior, then to feelings, eventually to attitudes, which is based on behavioral learning processes.

c. The experiential hierarchy—this hierarchy underlines the concept that untouchable product attributes like packaging attitudes can largely affected the attitude. The sequence is feelings, to behavior, then to beliefs, eventually to attitude, which is based on hedonic consumption.

3. A consumer's level of involvement for the attitude object influences the range of attitude he behaves. Define the power of commitment relevant to the following aspects and present an example:
- Compliance
- Identification
- Internalization

Answer:

Compliance—compliance is at the lowest level of involvement. A consumer forms an attitude for the reason that it works in obtaining awards or getting rid of punishment coming from other people. The attitude is not deep. It tends to shift when the consumer's behavior is not supervised by other people any more or when another choice becomes available. (Example: An individual might choose Coca-Cola because the cafeteria sells this brand; besides, going elsewhere for Pepsi causes plenty of troubles.)

Identification—a procedure of identification takes place when consumers form the attitudes in order to get along with another individual or team. Advertisements that describe the social results of choosing several products rather than others are depending on the tendency of people to simulate the action of desirable models. (Example: when marketers choose Budweiser beer, it creates social acceptance at the nearby bars or hotels.)

Internalization—at a relatively high level of involvement, deep–rooted attitudes are created and become a segment of the individual's value system. It is quite difficult to change the attitudes. (Example: A lot of consumers behaved very badly when Coca-Cola tried to change the Coke formula. As for the company, the allegiance to Coke coming from the majority of people matters obviously more than those who preferred a new formula; the brand had to deal with their social crisis and protect its previous properties which come from those people with intense patriotism and nostalgia.)

4. Compare the usages of the emotional appeals of sex, humor, and fear in advertisements. What are the advantages and disadvantages of each appeal?

Answer:

a. Sex appeals— though the usage of sex seems to arouse attention to an advertisement, its usage might be contrary to the marketers. A provocative photo could be very effective, gaining so much attention that it prevents processing and recall of the advertisement's content. Female nudity in print ads creates negative feelings and strain among female consumers, while male's reactions appear more positive. Sexual appeals seem to be less effective when they are used merely as a "trick" to gain attention. However, they seem to work when the product itself is relevant to gender, such as perfume, or a product or service that is aimed to promote attraction among people.

b. Humorous appeals— this kind of appeals are often productive in enhancing recognition, but catchy. Humour seems to be quite subjective and culture–bound. What's more, it can interrupt the procedure of product attributes. Unclear humor is often better merged with product information.

c. Fear appeals— these appeals are efficient in certain situation and are relevant to perceived presentation risk for a product or service. Negative results might show up if the consumers don't feel like changing their behavior or attitude. Fear appeals are often used in advertising, however, they are more popular when faced with social context, where institutions encourage people to change their lifestyles.

5. What is the elaboration-likelihood model of persuasion? Depict and summarize its features. What are the implications of the ELM for marketing promotions?

Answer:

The source and the message, which is the two main elements of the communications model, have an influence on convincing consumers to change their attitudes, but which has more impact depends upon variations in consumer involvement. The elaboration likelihood model of persuasion (ELM) states that after an individual receives a message, he begins to take steps to deal with it. Relying on the personal relation of this information, quite different cognitive processes will be actuated when the message is given to the consumer; they will decide which parts of a communication are dealt with. The following is the two routes to persuasion, and one of them will be chosen in the end.

Under situations of high involvement, the individual chooses the central route to persuasion. Improvements should be formed on rational patterns, that is, supplying causes why the consumer is supposed to buy the product, product attributes, etc.

Under situations of low involvement, the individual tends to take a peripheral route instead. Improvements should be formed on emotional or non-attribute cues such as source attractiveness.

6. Why should marketers know about consumers' cognitive consistency and cognitive dissonance? How can dissonance be decreased? Make use of the post purchase behavior coming from a customer as an example.

Answer:

In terms of the rule of cognitive consistency, consumers tend to be harmonious among what they think, feel, and behave, and they are inspired to remain uniformity among these components. If necessary, consumers will shift their thoughts, feelings, or behaviors in order to make them consonant with other experiences.

Cognitive dissonance theory is one of the most influential methods to attitudes based upon the consistency rule. The theory concentrates on situations where two cognitive components are not consistent, forming such an uncomfortable feeling that the consumer is motivated to decrease by making things get along with each other. Dissonance could be reduced by deleting, increasing, or shifting components. The stress to decrease dissonance is more likely to be observed in high-involvement situations where the components are significant to the consumer.

Evaluations of a product is likely to become more positive after the product has been bought. Individuals find more reasons to be fond of something after it becomes their own things. An implication of this situation is that consumers actively turn to support for their purchase determinations; marketers are supposed to provide them with extra reinforcement to set up positive attitudes towards the brand.

Chapter Eight

1. Retell the concept of id, ego, and superego in your own words. Describe how they function according to Freudian theory.

Answer: The id is totally oriented toward immediate gratification—it is the "wild animal" of the mind. The superego is the counterbalance to the id. This system is particularly an individual's conscience. It internalizes the society's codes of condcut (especially as the ones our parents teach us and work to prevent the id from seeking selfish gratification. Lastly, the ego is the system that mediates between the id and the superego. It is in a way a referee in the conflict between desire and morality.

2. Establish a list of key words to describe brand personality for three different brands within the same product category. Ask a small number of consumers to give a score to each brand on ten different personality dimensions. What differences can you find? Do these "personalities" relate to the advertising and packaging strategies used to differentiate these products?

Answer: Initially, students will have to do to complete this task is to identify the ten personality dimensions. They are free to construct the list of words; however, the content in this chapter offers some suggestions. The differences will be the result of differences observed. It will be easier for the students if they choose products from a brand category with which they are familiar. (Quite frequently students will know more about the brand than what is shown in the advertisement.) Students need to demonstrate "the ways" personalities relate to the advertising and packaging used by the marketer to differentiate these products.

3. List three products that seem to have personalities, preferably the ones you are familiar with. Describe the perceived personalities. What types of people would buy these products? Is there a connection between the purchaser's personality and that of the brand or product?

Answer: Examples of personality dimensions include the old-fashioned, wholesome, traditional, and lively. Depending on the products, the personalities may match the consumer's or not. If not, remind students that a consumer may select a product with a different personality if she/he desires to have more of that personality trait.

4. Extreme sports. Shooting short videos and uploading them to Tik Tok. Playing video games. Veganism. Can you foresee and estimate what will be popular in the near future? Identify a lifestyle trend that is just emerging in your university. Describe this trend in detail and give reasons to your prediction. What specific styles and/or products are parts of this trend?

Answer: Depending on the time this exercise is assigned, the responses will vary significantly. Many trends tend not to last long. This will be particularly true of trends that have not actually become "hot" yet. Many students will likely identify an underground trend simply because they resonate with it. This is all acceptable. The aim of this exercise is to describe a trend according to lifestyle and to figure out styles and products that would be consistent with this description.

5. Collect a selection of recent advertisements that attempt to relate consumption of a product to a specific lifestyle. In class, give a presentation and demonstrate what you have found. Discuss how the

goal of linking product consumption to a lifestyle is usually achieved.

Answer: There are plenty of brands that use sports sponsorships (e.g. tennis, golf, X-games) to associate with a specific lifestyle. Well-known spokespeople can also be used to create a link.

6. Student groups should identify three examples of lifestyle marketing on the Internet. Members of the group would demonstrate these examples in class. Show how the social media platform uses lifestyles to the organization's advantage.

Answer: Students should choose websites that are attracted to people with common leisure activities and discretionary spending habits. Many sites are aimed at a specific lifestyle so they can attract a certain type of advertiser.

Chapter Nine

1. Interview five of your classmates about a recent purchase or consideration of a purchase. Specifically, questions could be but not limited to what factors led them to problem recognition, and any gap between desirable state and current state.

Answer: Students should ask for specific stimuli that led to problem recognition and note if the problem was recognized because of a difference from the ideal state or deterioration of the actual state.

2. What sources of information are useful to you when making a decision on purchasing (a) a laptop, (b) a pet (a dog/a cat), (c) destination for summer holiday, and (d) formal costumes for parties? Explain.

Answer: Student responses may vary. Look for students to explain why they rely on those sources of information.

3. List the criteria that you considered when you choose universities. How do you evaluate the alternative universities by whether compensatory or noncompensatory decision rules?

Answer: the responses could be various. Make sure students weight the criteria by compensatory decision rules, and utilize four types of non-compensatory decision rules in the right way.

4. Develop a survey to measure the satisfaction of your classmates' most recent purchase. Ask them the actions they take if they find dissatisfied with a certain product to solve the dissatisfaction, and what are the results of their efforts?

Answer: Students could explain it by the expectancy disconfirmation model. If students are dissatisfied and attempted to take actions, both public responses and private responses should be considered.

5. Conduct a research on companies' efforts on recycling and trade-in policies. Describe the contribution of them to consumers, companies and public service.

Answers: Look for students to focus on the positive dimension of existing efforts as well as the areas for improvement and to tie their recommendations back to what they learned in consumer behavior about product disposal.

Chapter Ten

1. 3—5 students form a group and visit three small local clothing stores and observe their physical surroundings. What differences can you find among the three outlets? Would you recommend any physical surroundings change based on observation? Summarize your findings in a report and give a presentation to the class.

Answer: Look for students to select specific aspects of the store environment to improve and to tie their recommendations to the store's overall positioning.

2. Visit two local grocery stores and observe their use of P-O-P displays and explain the differences. Which one is more effective to you? Analyze both cases and share your findings in class.

Answer: Answers might be varying. Students should define P-O-P displays precisely and explain its influence to consumer behavior.

3. Go to www.taobao.com. Select an online shop and examine its online sales promotional strategies and activities. Analyze the influence of those activities on consumers' purchase decisions.

Answer: Sales promotions take different forms. Students should identify the form of sales promotion accurately and evaluate the relationship between those approaches and consumer behavior.

4. Interview five of your friends and ask them how their mood will affect their purchases. Present your findings.

Answer: Answers can be varying. The pleasure-arousal dimension can be used to explain it.